Edinburgh Textbooks in Applied Lin
Series Editors: Alan Davies and Keit

Language and Politics

John E. Joseph

LIS LIBRARY

Date

Order No

246S218

University of Chester

WITHDRAWN

Edinburgh University Press

© John E. Joseph, 2006

Edinburgh University Press Ltd
22 George Square, Edinburgh

Reprinted 2011

Typeset in Garamond
by Norman Tilley Graphics, Northampton,
and printed and bound in Great Britain
by the MPG Books Group, Bodmin & King's Lynn

A CIP record for this book is available from
the British Library

ISBN-10 0 7486 2452 X (hardback)
ISBN-13 978 0 7486 2452 2 (hardback)
ISBN-10 0 7486 2453 8 (paperback)
ISBN-13 978 0 7486 2453 9 (paperback)

The right of John E. Joseph
to be identified as author of this work
has been asserted in accordance with
the Copyright, Designs and Patents Act 1988.

Accession no.
36206907
WITHDRAWN

Language and Politics

Edinburgh Textbooks in Applied Linguistics

Contents

Series Editors' Preface

This series of single-author volumes published by Edinburgh University Press takes a contemporary view of applied linguistics. The intention is to make provision for the wide range of interests in contemporary applied linguistics which are provided for at Master's level.

The expansion of Master's postgraduate courses in recent years has had two effects:

1. What began almost half a century ago as a wholly cross-disciplinary subject has found a measure of coherence so that now most training courses in Applied Linguistics have similar core content.
2. At the same time the range of specialisms has grown, as in any developing discipline. Training courses (and professional needs) vary in the extent to which these specialisms are included and taught.

Some volumes in the series will address the first development noted above, while the others will explore the second. It is hoped that the series as a whole will provide students beginning postgraduate courses in Applied Linguistics, as well as language teachers and other professionals wishing to become acquainted with the subject, with a sufficient introduction for them to develop their own thinking in applied linguistics and to build further into specialist areas of their own choosing.

The view taken of applied linguistics in the Edinburgh Textbooks in Applied Linguistics Series is that of a theorising approach to practical experience in the language professions, notably, but not exclusively, those concerned with language learning and teaching. It is concerned with the problems, the processes, the mechanisms and the purposes of language in use.

Like any other applied discipline, applied linguistics draws on theories from related disciplines with which it explores the professional experience of its practitioners and which in turn are themselves illuminated by that experience. This two-way relationship between theory and practice is what we mean by a theorising discipline.

The volumes in the series are all premised on this view of Applied Linguistics as a theorising discipline which is developing its own coherence. At the same time, in order to present as complete a contemporary view of applied linguistics as possible, other approaches will occasionally be expressed.

Each volume presents its author's own view of the state of the art in his or her topic. Volumes will be similar in length and in format, and, as is usual in a textbook series, each will contain exercise material for use in class or in private study.

Alan Davies
W. Keith Mitchell

Foreword

In the last two decades, applied linguistics has abandoned the structuralist view of language as a self-contained, neutral system, in favour of a conception of language as *political* from top to bottom, in its structure as well as its use. This book examines the consequences of that conceptual shift, as it draws together key topics including language choice, linguistic correctness, (self-)censorship and hate speech, the performance of ethnic and national identity in language, gender politics and 'powerful' language, rhetoric and propaganda, and changing conceptions of written language, driven in part by technological advances.

In teaching language and politics to undergraduate and postgraduate students, I have felt my efforts hampered by the lack of a book that unites these topics and shows how they relate to the more structural aspects of language analysis as well as to the core concerns of applied linguistics. Nor did it appear that anyone was going to be rash enough to attempt such a book, given the breadth of areas that 'language and politics' potentially covers, and the fact that people working in some of these areas believe the rubric applies exclusively to what they do. A book like this one is bound to meet with a certain amount of adverse criticism from those who find that what they consider to be the core of language and politics is under-represented. Although breadth of coverage has been my aim, the exigencies of coherence, the need to demonstrate how a sampling of apposite questions might be probed in at least moderate depth, and the publisher's rather strict length parameters have forced me to omit or skim over topics that certainly deserve fuller treatment. I have tried at least to guide readers to a further range of relevant topics through bibliographic references and suggestions for further reading, which will in turn lead to a still more ample literature.

I am grateful to Alan Davies and Keith Mitchell for the invitation to contribute this volume to their series, and to Sarah Edwards of Edinburgh University Press for guiding it safely through what is never an easy process. Thanks are due again to Alan, along with Catherine Elder, for including my chapter on 'Language and politics' in their *Handbook of Applied Linguistics* (Blackwell, 2004). That chapter, which benefited from John Cleary's bibliographic assistance, became the template for this book – but getting from there to here required a sabbatical leave, generously granted by the School of Philosophy, Psychology and Language Sciences of the University of Edinburgh.

Among the many others to whom I am indebted I must single out Talbot J. Taylor, as it has been mainly through long years of discussion with him that the general understanding of language contained herein arose. Although I read from time to time that I was his fellow student at Oxford in the 1970s, it isn't true, and the fact that we have been able to understand each other at all is due above all to his remarkable gifts as a communicator, as well as an originator, of ideas. It has also helped that, while he was in England, I was in Ann Arbor, under the tutelage of Ernst Pulgram (1915–2005), whose own approach to language had been social and political since long before it was fashionable to be either. Ernst died when this book was in its last stages, and I offer it to his memory.

Chapter 1

Overview: How politics permeates language (and vice versa)

1.1 WHAT DOES IT MEAN TO SAY THAT LANGUAGE IS POLITICAL?

Over the last decade, some highly regarded and influential scholars of the origins of language have been putting forward the view that it began for fundamentally political reasons. Dunbar (1996) believes that language evolved as an ultra-efficient means of distinguishing allies from enemies and of grooming allies and potential allies. Dessalles (2000) locates its origins in the need to form 'coalitions' of a critical size, representing the initial form of social and political organisation:

> We humans speak because a fortuitous change profoundly modified the social organisation of our ancestors. In order to survive and procreate they found themselves needing to form coalitions of a considerable size. Language then appeared as a means for individuals to display their value as members of a coalition. (Dessalles 2000: 331–2, my transl.)

While this is an area of scholarship in which nothing can ever be definitively proven or disproven, it is significant that a political take on language origins should coincide with the rise of a political approach within applied linguistics and sociolinguistics. Thirty years ago one would have had a much harder time finding anyone prepared to take seriously the idea that language might be political in its very essence. Yet it is an idea with a venerable heritage:

> Hence it is evident that the state is a creation of nature, and that man is by nature a political animal ... Now, that man is more of a political animal than bees or any other gregarious animals is evident. Nature, as we often say, makes nothing in vain, and man is the only animal whom she has endowed with the gift of speech. (Aristotle, *Politics* I, 2, Jowett transl. [1885])

All animals are political, but some are more political than others, and one in particular is the most political of all, the reason being language. So wrote the Philosopher some 2,350 years ago, and who today would disagree?

Any number of people might, actually. And necessarily so, if Aristotle's claim is right, because disagreement is the necessary condition for politics. Man is first of all the animal who disagrees, and then the animal who tries to get his own way. Disagreement is as natural to human beings as speaking is.

But there are those who would disagree even with that. Proponents of consensus politics see disagreement as a social ill, a destructive force, a primitive, maybe specifically male instinct. After all, Aristotle's translators tell us that *man* is a political animal, not woman.[1] Few aspects of language have provoked such heated disagreement as the use of the masculine to denote any person regardless of sex. But did he mean that *man and woman* are political animals? Some would argue – or would form a consensus – that women's ways of discoursing and interacting are less confrontational, less overtly political than men's.

Another bone of contention is the extent to which 'the gift of speech' is bound up with politics. Every sentient species forms social bonds and groups, which are created and maintained through grooming, display and other ritual practices that manifest hierarchies within groups and territorial boundaries between them. What then puts human politics on a different plane from animal politics? Is it just the greater efficiency that language affords? Or the fact that language enables us to *think* politically?[2] Or does language itself have a deeply political dimension, one that runs to the very core of its functioning?

This book is based on the premise that language does have such a political dimension. This premise is shared by people working in various branches of applied linguistics, sociolinguistics, linguistic anthropology and related fields. It is however denied by most theoretical linguists, for whom the real function of language stands above its interpersonal uses, having instead to do with cognition. Such linguists see the politics of language as at best an after-effect, a sideshow, a trivial epiphenomenon, neither worthy of nor susceptible to serious study. But then, the internal politics of linguistics are notoriously fraught – it is sometimes said to be the most disputatious of academic fields – and bound up with vested interests in keeping a narrow range of activities defined as the 'mainstream'. This is not to contend that those who would exclude the politics of language from linguistic study are necessarily acting in a self-interested and intellectually dishonest way, but rather that all of us, whatever our convictions, would do well to examine the rhetoric with which we define what can and cannot be a legitimate object of study, to ensure that we are not simply perpetuating outdated prejudices in the name of a methodological rigour that is in fact *rigor mortis* for any full understanding of language.

One more thing is in dispute: namely, what we mean by 'politics'. In everyday usage it signifies what politicians do, affairs of the *state*, just as Aristotle assumed and as the etymology of the word *politics* (from Greek *polis* 'city, state') suggests. On the other hand, 'office politics', 'sexual politics' and the like have become perfectly common vernacular phrases, so it is not just in academic parlance that we find a broader application of the political to any situation in which there is an unequal distribution of power, and where individuals' behaviour reflects the play of power, or is guided (or maybe even determined) by it. But, as we shall see, few words are as contentious as *power*. Though its meaning is surprisingly hard to pin down, the very act of using the word has political overtones.

This book is about politics in both the narrow and the broad sense. It takes the study of language and politics to be aimed at understanding the roles played by speech and writing in human interaction. It is concerned with how we use language to organise our social existence, at any level from the family up to that of the state, and also with how this activity shapes the way we conceive of the language itself. This study does not take language to be something given in advance, existing independently of the uses to which it is put. Rather, it takes seriously the massive body of evidence that

- languages themselves are constructed out of the practices of speech and writing, and the beliefs (or 'ideologies') of those doing the speaking and writing;
- my language is shaped by who it is that I am speaking to, and by how my relationship with them will be affected by what I say;
- the politics of identity shapes how we interpret what people say to us, so much so as to be a prime factor in our deciding on the truth value of their utterances.

This first chapter will introduce real examples of the problems and tensions that make language and politics a central concern of applied linguistics. It will not delve deeply into the mechanics of their analysis, or cite large numbers of publications that have treated such problems – this will happen in later chapters, where some of the situations introduced here will be revisited, and further examples supplied.

1.2 THE POLITICS OF DIFFERENT WAYS OF SPEAKING

One morning my son Crispin, then aged three years four months, showed me a toy that needed mending. 'Bring it me', said I, to which he replied disdainfully, 'Dada, bring it *to* me'. My smile of interest at this early attempt to enforce a linguistic norm no doubt encouraged his incipient pedantry – unwise on my part, since similar corrections made to his schoolmates might have produced not pleasure but teasing or a thumping. If they saw the correction as Crispin's attempt to show himself superior to them, their instinctive reaction would have been to bring him down a peg. Happily, in the years since he has survived bloodied but unbowed, and although I overheard him at six years, six months say 'Give it me' to his older brother Julian, his use of markedly standard forms continues to be noticeable – he is less likely than Julian is, for example, to tell a story using 'X was like' to introduce quotations (see below §4.6). The research literature suggests that, if he does get thumped for correcting a classmate's English, his use of standard forms will make him the more persuasive speaker when it comes to convincing the teacher that he didn't start the fight.

The 'Bring it to me' correction is of a usage over which native speakers disagree, both across and within dialects. 'Bring me it' is acceptable to many but not all speakers; 'Bring it me' is likewise semi-acceptable, but only in some parts of Britain. 'Bring them them' is fine for me in spoken usage, though not in writing, and most native speakers seem to reject it in either mode. What matters for present purposes is that any given speaker you might ask is unlikely to respond that all these forms are perfectly fine. They will normally be quite certain that one is right, another possible but bad, a third simply meaningless. This is true even of people who might be quite non-judgemental on non-linguistic matters.

This singular capacity of language to be a locus of disagreement over what is correct is at the centre of its social functioning. Issues of linguistic correctness go far deeper than the particular grammatical or lexical quibble at hand. They are interpreted as reflecting the speaker's intelligence, industry, social worthiness, level of exposure to the elders of the tribe. In modern societies, exposure to tribal elders has been institutionalised into systems of 'education', but the fundamental principle remains unchanged from the earliest human groups and existing primate groups.

Interpreting language use in this way is a political act. It determines who stands where in the social hierarchy, who can be entrusted with power and responsibility. There is a further linguistic–political dimension in how those in power, or desiring power, deploy language in order to achieve their aims. This is traditionally the domain of rhetoric, defined by Aristotle as the art of persuasion. In modern times, particularly in the climate of twentieth-century ideas about the unconscious mind and the possibility of thought control, it has come to be classified under the still more loaded rubric of 'propaganda'. Applied linguistics, as the study of language in use, can be thought of as the approach to language that takes its political dimension directly into consideration, whereas theoretical linguistics attempts to abstract it away. Language teaching and learning, which occupy a privileged place within applied linguistics, are political in the sense that they normally involve two languages with differing cultural prestige in the world at large and in the particular situation in which they are being learned. These differences are reproduced in the relationship of teacher and learner, and in the discourses they generate in the classroom.

The kind of linguistic authority that runs counter to ordinary usage is a powerful social force, as every educated person knows. Consider a language standard such as the use of the subject pronoun when the subject is conjoined. As a child I would always spontaneously say sentences of the type *Can me and Bobby go to the movies?*, only to have an adult reply, *You mean Bobby and I*, followed by an explanation of the rudeness of putting oneself first and, depending on the adult, the solecism of the *me* in subject position. Eventually, my usage did change, and as an adult I am sure I have only ever uttered sentences of the *Bobby and I* type.

Still, my son Julian was twelve before I heard him produce such a sentence spontaneously; he normally said *Can me and Thomas go to the movies?*, and I was the one saying *You mean Thomas and I*, followed by the familiar explanations – except that I do this not because I think the *me* is illogical, as my teachers did. I know that in the Romance languages, for example, only the stressed object pronoun is possible in this position, and the very strength of the tendency to use it in English suggests to me that this is a 'natural' feature of English grammar if ever there was one.[3] But that is precisely why this feature functions so powerfully as a shibboleth separating the educated from the less educated. As a father, I want to do what I can to help my children not to be perceived as uneducated. I have no desire to stop English grammar from changing, which would be a forlorn hope. So long as this shibboleth functions, however, I do not want my children to suffer exclusion on its account. Still, it is an open question whether, from the child's point of view, the motive behind the correction makes any difference.

1.3 THE POLITICS OF TALKING TO OTHERS

It would not be true to say that all language is social in the sense that it is always conceived and performed with others present. For me it is so, since even when I am alone, thinking, writing, praying or talking to 'myself', there is an 'other' present in my mind to whom my utterances are addressed. But a significant number of people in all societies at all times do not talk to others in the way you and I do, and the consequences for them have been severe – they have been classified as mad, or intellectually sub-human, and usually removed from a society that feels their anti-social presence as an offence or a threat. (I say 'they', but it could be you or I in the Alzheimer's ward one day.) Language of the socially sanctioned sort is central to the definition of what it is to be rational and even human.

In discussing my interchange with Crispin over 'Bring it me' I have already touched upon the personal politics of talking to others. Correcting what someone else has said to you is liable to be interpreted as an attempt to criticise and manipulate that person, and to manifest your superior knowledge, regardless of whether you were aware of any such intentions on your part. But it isn't necessary to correct people to prompt such political interpretations – interrupting them can have the same effect. So can addressing them by their first name if they expect you to call them by title and surname (or vice versa), and indeed a wide range of far subtler stimuli. The person mainly credited for introducing awareness of the ubiquity and power of such political factors in linguistic exchange is the sociologist Erving Goffman (1922–82), who described them in terms of *face*, as in 'losing face' and 'saving face', a concept traditionally associated with East Asian cultures. Goffman's analysis will be discussed in more detail in §4.2, but by way of introducing the basic concept, here is an example from a conversation in which I, as one of the two participants (indicated as J), inadvertently threatened the face of my interlocutor (T) on two separate occasions within the thirty-six seconds in which this excerpt unfolded.

J_1: Did you do a lot of shopping when you were in Edinburgh? Clothes shopping?

T_1: Uh, no. I bought a lot of jeans that are not available in Singapore –

J_2: Uh-huh.

T_2: – and a few t-shirts, but not … jackets, or things like that. Because when the waist fitted, the sleeve lengths were too long –

J_3: Oh.

T_3: – and the … lengths … didn't fit.

J_4: 'sit the same when you shop in Australia? Or is it better –

T_4: Australian clothes are better.

J_5: Uh-huh.

T₅: The price is also … closer to Singapore prices.
J₆: Yeah, Edinburgh's expensive –
T₆: Yes … it is.
J₇: – UK's expensive.
T₇: The British pound … is, I think a little bit more expensive than the Australian dollar.

Only after months of studying this conversation did I realise why T was in mild distress, as is apparent from her tone of voice and the pauses that occur in most of her turns. She had spent some time in Edinburgh as my guest, a few weeks before I recorded this conversation with her in Singapore. The fact that she always dresses elegantly is what prompted me to ask whether she had done much clothes shopping during her stay. In the exchanges that ensue, what she is struggling *not* to say is that clothing in Edinburgh is outrageously overpriced, and that she doesn't have the figure of the average Scottish woman, at least not the upper-middle-class woman who wears the elegant sort of clothes T prefers. If the waist fits, but the lengths are too long, it is because the person trying the item on has a big waist.

I realised at the time that this was what she was saying, and tried at J₄ to steer the conversation in a face-saving direction. I thought perhaps she wouldn't have so much of a problem in Australia, where she also spends a good deal of time, and where elegant women of Dame Edna-like proportions are less rare. T seized on the opening I provided, but differently than I had intended. She used it to achieve a rather abrupt switch of topic to the *quality* of clothes in Australia (T₄), and of value for money relative to Edinburgh (T₅). But by the time she has said 'The price is also …' (T₅), something has restrained her from continuing with simply 'better' or 'lower'. In retrospect, I believe that she had now become concerned about the threat to *my* face, as a resident of Edinburgh, if she were to assert baldly that the Australians, unlike *us*, don't charge a fortune for shoddy clothes. 'Closer to Singapore prices' seems more neutral, implying that even Australian clothes are a bit overpriced to a Singaporean, and making it a question of what she is used to rather than some objective standard of what prices should be.

At the time I was oblivious to this, however, and simply agreed with her that 'Edinburgh's expensive' (J₆), then corrected this to say that actually it isn't just Edinburgh but the whole UK. By doing so I really created a conundrum for her. To agree with me would give me face by virtue of acknowledging that I have spoken the truth, but the truth in question threatens my face by admitting something bad (in her eyes) about the country I live in. She finds a rather brilliant way to turn this round and make it into a *compliment* about the UK: 'The British pound … is, I think a little bit more expensive than the Australian dollar' (T₇). This shifts the focus to a *strength* of Britain, the solidity of the pound. If clothes cost less in Australia, it is not because the British are greedy cheats, but because the Aussies have a weak currency. Face has been saved for everyone but Australians, who don't matter in this context since none were present.

One further aspect of this brief conversation merits discussion: who talks when.

I interrupt her on two occasions (J_2, J_3), and she interrupts me twice as well (T_4, T_6). My first interruption is 'back-channelling', an 'Uh-huh' of agreement to signal our mutual engagement in the conversation. The second, when I say 'Oh', is slightly different; my intention was to show that I understood her somewhat intricate statement about the proportions of the clothes, but in retrospect I believe she interpreted it as an expression of surprise (which 'Oh' usually is), and perhaps of offence taken on my part at her rejection of Edinburgh clothing. The disjointedness of her response (T_3) suggests that she has become uncomfortable with where the conversation is going. As noted above, my question about it being better in Australia (J_4) offers the opportunity to change direction, and it is now that she interrupts me to assert that 'Australian clothes are better' (T_4).

Her second interruption occurs when I state flatly what she has been avoiding saying, 'Edinburgh's expensive' (J_5), and her 'Yes ... it is' steps upon my follow-up 'UK's expensive' (J_6), which I uttered continuously with J_5. The pragmatic ambiguity of her 'Yes' (T_6), giving me face while also threatening my face, paints her into a corner, from which she escapes by turning her criticism of British prices into a remark on the strength of the pound.

Interruptions are more heavily charged with political implications in proportion as the conversation is more overtly antagonistic. Indeed, for many analysts what I have called 'interruptions' in the conversation above would not even qualify, because they are not attempts to take over the floor. On the other hand, any time one interlocutor speaks when the other is already in full flow, a central conversational maxim has potentially been violated, and it is up to the first speaker to interpret the interruption as supportive or challenging, a one-off interjection or an attempt to usurp the floor. Such interpretation isn't always easy – after all, only a slight change of intonation would make my 'Uh-huh' sound sarcastic. All this verbal jousting takes place on the same field on which we are establishing and assessing our social status relative to one another.

1.4 THE POLITICS OF WHAT 'THE LANGUAGE' IS

Speakers of English generally take it for granted that we know what the English language is, in the sense that we can identify countries where English is spoken, identify certain books as authoritative guides to the English lexicon and grammar, and say with confidence whether a particular word or utterance is or isn't English. We tend to speak of the English language as though it were a thing, one that has existed for a bit over a thousand years, during which it has undergone a great deal of change, and that still retains an essential unity despite all the variation in how people use it. A linguist will (or, at any rate, should) point out that some of these views aren't historically tenable. A language isn't a thing, and it makes little sense to imagine one English language evolving over many centuries, rather than different English languages existing at different stages.

Moreover, it isn't the case that an original unity gave way over time to diversity. The diversity was always there. English has its origins in a variety of different

Germanic dialects that partially converged – but only partially – when their speakers migrated to Britain starting in the fifth century. There is continuity from those primordial dialect differences to today's regional differences in the English of the British Isles, and even to the Englishes of other parts of the world where English, Irish, Scottish and Welsh people settled. What had to be created, and enforced, over time was linguistic *unity*.

In various stages from the sixteenth through to the early twentieth century the concept and form of a 'Standard English' was developed for various purposes that will be explored in Chapters 2 and 3. Standard forms of other major European languages were developed over roughly the same period. The use of these standard languages was extremely limited at first, but would spread as education spread, starting with the Industrial Revolution and culminating with the instituting of universal education in the last four decades of the nineteenth century.

Today, although everywhere in the English-speaking world the concept of Standard English is recognised, and taught (or at least aimed at) in schools, it is far from being the case that everyone, even the educated, uses English in a standard way, especially in speaking. Indeed, as English continues its long-term spread as an international auxiliary language, variation in English is on the increase, and speakers of English in many places, including European countries, do not necessarily recognise the authority of a British or American standard over their particular English, but are claiming to have an English of their own, with the right to follow a standard of their own.

The nation in which I live, Scotland, happens to be rather ambivalent about what its 'native' language is. There is a primal split between the Celtic and Germanic candidates, with some seeing Gaelic as the one true language of Scotland, while others are no less fervently committed to the authenticity of Scots, that Germanic cousin of English. Scots runs along a continuum such that certain forms of it are quite comprehensible to English speakers from outside Scotland, while others are largely impenetrable. Scottish people whose language is not markedly distant from standard English have complex attitudes toward their countrymen whose speech tends toward the other end of the continuum. Depending on the context, they may feel national pride in its perceived authenticity, or embarrassment, cultural cringe, at the lack of education and refinement they perceive it to convey.

One aspect of this ambivalence is on display in a very successful book published in Glasgow called *A Study of Standard English*, by Barclay, Knox and Ballantyne. It first appeared in 1938, and my copy of it, published in 1960, is the twenty-first impression, which indicates how widely it was used in Scottish secondary schools in the middle decades of the twentieth century.[4] In its chapter on 'Errors in grammar', under the heading 'Laws of style' and the sub-heading 'selection' of words, it lists the six leading forms of *Barbarism*:

1. The use of **Archaic** or **Obsolete** words:– as *yclad, hight*.
2. The use of **Colloquial, Slang** or **Vulgar Terms**:– as *get even, awfully, rotten, that ugly, step on the gas, doss, boss*.

3. The unnecessary use of **Scientific, Legal** or **Technical Terms**:– as *leitmotif, a complex, epidermis.*
4. The use of foreign words or phrases :– as *café, kudos.*
5. The use of **New Words, Coinages** or **Neologisms** :– as *burglarize, enthuse, merger, pelmanize.*

It is awfully surprising, enough to give one a complex, that café should have been considered foreign and barbaric, or leitmotif so technical (rather than foreign) that its use should constitute an error in grammar. But then comes the last item on the list – and remember that this is from a book published in Glasgow:

6. The use of **Scotticisms** :– as *gigot, sort* (repair), *the cold, canny.*

To be sure, it is *only* in Scotland that 'Scotticisms' would occur often enough for anyone to consider including them in a list of 'barbarisms' in English. But it amounts to the authors of the book telling its readers that, insofar as their language reflects who they are, insofar as it *belongs* to them, it is barbaric, and that if they do not want to be perceived as barbarians, they must do away with these features.

Ambivalence toward Scots language among Scots is long-standing. It was said of the great eighteenth-century philosopher David Hume that he died confessing, not his sins, but his Scotticisms. Yet it is striking how deeply the politics of language in Britain has changed in the last forty years, such that a book classifying Scotticisms as barbarisms would be unprintable today, except as a historical relic. It would open author, publisher and printer to a charge of racism. Any readers who think such a charge would amount to political correctness run amuck had better brace themselves for the even more extreme examples in Chapter 5.

The matter of who has 'authority' over English is a political linguistic issue *par excellence*, centring as it does on the question of who English belongs to, and what exactly are the 'boundaries' of a language. That question is an eternal one, because it is unanswerable. As noted above, a language is not a thing, but a practice always characterised by diversity, into which attempts at imposing unity are introduced. These attempts are what we normally mean by linguistic authority, but they inevitably bump up against the sort of authority represented by *usage*, the earlier practice, which has behind it the force of custom and a certain social authenticity. These may lead to the earlier practice being thought of as 'natural' – though the analyst needs to tread with caution here, because authenticity and naturalness are always suspect concepts in the context of a cultural practice such as language (see further note 3).

Ever since being institutionalised as the 'scientific' study of language in the nineteenth century, linguistics has taken the position that any imposed authority in language is ultimately impotent in the face of the one authority that matters, namely, usage – what the people as a whole implicitly decides will be the course of their language. Just how usage functions is a complete mystery, which nevertheless does not prevent scientific linguistics from analysing the (standard) language as though it were an apolitical, 'natural' phenomenon, and distrusting any attempt to look specifically into its mechanisms.

1.5 THE POLITICS OF WHICH LANGUAGE TO SPEAK

In most of the world, the linguistic condition is one of stable bilingualism or multilingualism, or the not-quite-bilingualism known as diglossia, in which two quite divergent linguistic systems co-exist in a community that recognises them as forms of 'the same language', but with one of them reserved for use in especially prestigious functions. In all these types of non-monolingualism, the choice of which language to use in a particular circumstance is a political matter, in two senses. First, because it simultaneously depends upon and determines the relationships among the speakers, and secondly, because sanctions of some sort are likely to follow from a wrong choice. In officially bilingual Belgium, for instance, the choice of French or Flemish is a sensitive one, with the wrong choice likely to offend one's interlocutor, and the right choice difficult to determine for anyone who has not been fully acculturated into the linguistic politics of any particular Belgian community. In a diglossic situation like that of the Tamil Nadu in southeast India, the use of 'low' Tamil in a 'high' prestige context – an official ceremony, for example – would be received as wholly inappropriate, and whoever committed the offence would find himself or herself suspected of subversive motives at least, and possibly of madness.

In post-colonial contexts, the choice between the former colonial or imperial language and an 'indigenous' language is almost always politically charged, though in different ways in different places. In Joseph (2004a) I have discussed how the use of English functions as a social-class marker in Hong Kong (Chapter 6), and how the use of French in Lebanon has functioned somewhat similarly as a religious marker (Chapter 8), with its significance evolving fairly rapidly in recent years. Indeed, studies from various parts of the world (e.g. Breitborde 1998) have been suggesting that the economy of use among small local languages,[5] medium-sized regional languages and big world languages has been shifting in the younger generations in such a way that the bigger languages no longer signify class aspiration so strongly as they once did. Rather, the private versus public sphere dichotomy has changed – perhaps through the influence of the mass media – in such a way that private space, though still defined by the local language, is more permeated than previously by larger languages. Resistance to larger languages is now what is politically 'marked' among the younger generation. The politically neutral choice is to go with the larger language on account of the educational and economic opportunities it offers; but this is not to deny that significant numbers of younger people will still resist such a choice, and will interpret those who opt for it as cultural traitors.

The politics of language choice become particularly difficult when *institutional* choices have to be made – in what language or languages the government will conduct its business and communicate with its citizens, and, above all, what the language or languages of *education* will be. The institutional issues are all the more sensitive when – as is the case in most of the world – the institutions were set up by a colonial power, and the ex-colonial language continues to be used in some institutional functions. A case of this kind is unfolding at present in some of the countries that were formerly under the control of the USSR, including Estonia,

Latvia and the Ukraine (see further Hogan-Brun 2005, Järve 2003, Priedīte 2005). Latvia, which joined the European Union in May 2004, began enforcing legislation the following September restricting the use in schools of the ex-colonial language, Russian. The term 'ex-colonial' is particularly justified in this case because large numbers of Russians moved to Latvia in the years of Russian control (from the Second World War to 1991) and occupied prestigious positions from which native Latvians were excluded. Their policy of making Russian the unique language of secondary and university education was understandably resented by Latvians, who had successfully developed a standard language of their own in the late nineteenth and early twentieth centuries, and who experienced this period of Russian ascendancy as an oppression. The effect of the language-in-education policy was that, still today, some 95 per cent of ethnic Latvians are able to read Russian and converse fluently in it. Among the 29 per cent of the population of Latvia who are ethnic Russians, on the other hand, only some 40 per cent speak Latvian fluently, and this figure includes the younger generations who were themselves born in Latvia. Both ethnic groups are keenly aware of a fact that is also readily observable to the outsider: even in an informal setting, if a large group of ethnic Latvians are joined by just one ethnic Russian, the language of the conversation switches to Russian.

While attesting to the natural politeness and hospitality of Latvians, this situation has also provoked resentment that has simmered beneath the surface over the decades. This has led to the present situation in which Latvians feel compelled to 'save' their language, and to that end have decreed that all school subjects must be taught exclusively in Latvian in years 10 to 12, with at least 60 per cent of the curriculum in Latvian in years 1 to 9. The European Union, which generally takes the side of linguistic minorities and their right to education in their mother tongue, has attempted to intervene on behalf of the ethnic Russian minority in Latvia (which however constitutes a small majority in some of Latvia's cities). But ethnic Latvians see themselves as the besieged group whose language rights were denied for the fifty years of Russian occupation and continue to be limited by the residual status retained by the ethnic Russian population, who have a powerful protector in their motherland to the east.

Chapter 3 will discuss Billig's (1995) idea of *banal nationalism*, those ways in which we experience and perform national belonging without necessarily being aware of it, such as when we use coins and currency imprinted with national symbols, or pass under the flag when entering the post office. For most people in most circumstances, speaking and writing too involve a banal form of the performance of their identity, whether national, regional, ethnic or something else. In a post-colonial situation like that of Latvia, the 'banality' is rather less banal, as people are aware of the politics of their language use, indeed are constantly talking about its implications and the need to change it. In the way they dress and in other aspects of how they behave, Latvians can be neutral about signalling their ethnic origins if they so choose. But not when they speak, at least not in ethnically mixed company, where every syllable is a political act of a not altogether banal sort.

1.6 THE POLITICS OF POLICING THE LANGUAGE

The impulse to police the *form* of the language in terms of standardness of accent, vocabulary and lexicon, is culturally inseparable from the impulse to police the *borders* of the language – what is and isn't English – and blends unsettlingly into the impulse to police *thought* as expressed in language. People want to feel that the language is somehow under control. It contributes to a sense of social order, as well as furnishing the basis for much of education.

It is also behind the feeling of satisfaction that we get from word games, such as crossword puzzles. Completing a puzzle is like bringing light to scatter darkness. The completed puzzle represents knowledge and order, replacing the emptiness and ignorance of its blank matrix. The popular board game Scrabble, manufactured in twenty-nine different languages, looks superficially like being modelled on the crossword puzzle but puts the player in something more like the position of a puzzle writer than a puzzle solver. Particularly in advanced play, attention often centres on the question of what is or isn't a word in the particular language in which the game is being played. Victory can depend on finding a word that meets the requirements of the game (non-capitalised, without apostrophes or hyphens, not designated as foreign) yet is not generally known to speakers of the language. For English, words using the rare letters x, j and q have an especially high value in the economy of the game.

In early tournaments, a particular dictionary (specific to each country) would be identified as the official one for determining whether a particular string of letters was or wasn't an English word. Before long, however, this practice bumped up against the fact that no dictionary can capture the whole of the language. Even a dictionary that attempts to include all the words of today's special technical vocabulary, new borrowings from other languages, and slang (in all its local variations), will not have the words invented tomorrow. Even online dictionaries cannot take immediate cognisance of new creations – and then there is the time lag between the creation of a new word and the nebulous process of acceptance whereby it enters 'the language'.

So lists of official Scrabble words were issued, and in time these came to be the recognised authority over what constituted the English language for the purpose of playing Scrabble in a particular country. The questions that had to be decided were of the order of whether the past participle of the archaic verb CLEEK should be spelt CLAUCHT or CLAUGHT; whether the plural of MOJO should be written MOJOS or MOJOES; whether the third person singular of HONDLE should be HONDLES or HONDLIES; and whether the adjective HOOTY should be admitted, along with its comparative and superlative forms HOOTIER and HOOTIEST. (The forms currently accepted are CLAUCHT, MOJOES and HONDLES, and HOOTY and its derivatives are allowed.)

But in 1995, caught up in a wave of political correctness, the US National Scrabble Association decided to endorse an Expurgated Scrabble Players' Dictionary, from which some 167 words plus their derivatives had been eliminated on the grounds of being 'offensive', in some cases to specific groups of people, in others because of vulgarity. Among the words were ARSE, ASSHOLE, BAZOOMS, BOCHE, BULLSHIT, DAGO, DICKED, DYKEY, FAGGOTY, FART, FATSO, FRIG, FUCK, GOY, GRINGO, JESUIT, JEW, JISM, LEZZIE, LIBBER, MERDE, MICK, NANCY, NIGGER, NOOKY, PAPIST, PEEING, POMMIE, POOFS, POPERY, POPISHLY, REDNECK, REDSKIN, SHKOTZIM, SHIKSA, SHITHEAD, SPIC, SQUAW, TURD, TWAT, WETBACK, WOG, WOP and YID. This led to some rather anomalous situations, in which for example a Jesuit priest or a Jewish person taking part in a Scrabble tournament would not be allowed to play the words JESUIT or JEW, because they are offensive.[6]

By 1998 Scrabble tournament play had reverted to the unexpurgated lexicon, making all the words above licit again – evidence that, although people desire the existence and exercise of an authority over language, such authority has its limits, and that while the limits are nebulous, they lie somewhere between the proscription against CLAUGHT and the ones against JESUIT and BAZOOMS. Issues arising from this example – the nature of linguistic norms, the limits of authority, the question of whether 'offensive' words are fully part of the language – will be examined in several of the chapters that follow.

1.7 LANGUAGE, THOUGHT AND POLITICIANS

Man is by nature a political animal, but some take it to extremes and become politicians. The qualities that make a successful politician include the ability to lead others by articulating a clear and inspiring vision of a better future. The prototypes of great leaders are also great orators, such as Churchill, or Roosevelt ... or Hitler. For the inspiring orator can also lead a people, or rather mislead them, into believing that the narrow self-interests of the governing party are actually the interests of the people as a whole, when in fact they work directly against the people. It is also the case that a notably inarticulate individual can be a powerful leader – Caesar was no Cicero, Stalin was no Lenin. George W. Bush is not even a George H. W. Bush, let alone a Reagan or a Clinton, yet his legendary inarticulateness actually gains him the trust of a considerable portion of the American electorate, who have come to associate slick rhetoric with a lack of forthrightness, indeed a desire to manipulate people's perceptions of a reality that could be depicted more truly through straight talk.

The great political 'propaganda' issue of the first half of the present decade has been the arguments made by the USA-led coalition of governments in support of the invasion of Iraq in 2003. In January 2005 the White House, without fanfare, released the news that the search for the weapons of mass destruction in Iraq had been abandoned. The leaders of the invading countries had been maintaining that the weapons would eventually be found, though over the preceding months they had also been progressively shifting the emphasis of the discussion away from WMDs, and toward the toppling of Saddam Hussein and the flawed intelligence with which they had been provided. To charges that they misled their citizens, the coalition leaders consistently replied that they were acting truthfully based on the reports they were given.

The central document at issue is the CIA's October 2002 report on 'Iraq's weapons of mass destruction programs'. It is so ambiguously drafted that one could find justification in it for any position on the invasion, rather like the Bible demanding an eye for an eye in the Old Testament and turning the other cheek in the New. But the ambiguity in the CIA Report is not haphazard. It is structured in a powerful way which, for anyone trained in the American rhetorical tradition, makes one particular reading difficult to resist, even though it is not the reading that the bulk of the document supports.

The Report opens with a section called 'Key Judgments', seven short paragraphs, the last five followed by some bullet points. The first two paragraphs are bald assertions of fact:

> **Iraq has continued its weapons of mass destruction (WMD) programs in defiance of UN resolutions and restrictions. Baghdad has chemical and biological weapons as well as missiles with ranges in excess of UN restrictions; if left unchecked, it probably will have a nuclear weapon during this decade.**
>
> **Baghdad hides large portions of Iraq's WMD efforts.** Revelations after the Gulf war starkly demonstrate the extensive efforts undertaken by Iraq to deny information.

These strong assertions are placed at the head of the report for maximum impact. The lack of limiting or qualifying words is striking. In the first paragraph, there is just one: *probably*, which still tilts the balance in favour of Iraq having a nuclear weapon within the decade. But this hint of caution is dispelled in the fourth paragraph:

> **How quickly Iraq will obtain its first nuclear weapon depends on when it acquires sufficient weapons-grade fissile material.**

Will obtain, *when* it acquires – not *could* obtain *if* it acquires, the appropriate wording given even the slight attenuation of the earlier *probably*. Indeed, in the immediately following bullet point the conditional appears:

• If Baghdad acquires sufficient weapons-grade fissile material from abroad, it could make a nuclear weapon within a year.

But this is not in boldface, unlike the paragraph to which it is subordinated. The second bullet point is even more heavily conditional:

• Without such material from abroad, Iraq probably would not be able to make a weapon until the last half of the decade.

Read in isolation, this would seem to offer an argument against invasion. But as an appendix to the bald-faced, boldface statement that *Iraq will obtain its first nuclear weapon*, it reads rather differently, as a best-case scenario that means an invasion will still be required sooner or later.

The way the qualifiers proliferate in the bullet points is as striking as their absence from the opening paragraphs. In the following selection, BW stands for biological weapons and UAV for unmanned aerial vehicles (e.g., missiles), and the italics are mine:

- *If* Baghdad acquires material, it *could* produce a nuclear weapon.
- Iraq has *some* lethal BW agents for delivery *potentially* against the US Homeland.
- Iraq maintains a *small* missile force, and is developing a UAV that *most* analysts believe *probably* is intended to deliver BW agents.
- Baghdad's UAVs *could* threaten Iraq's neighbours, and the United States *if brought close to, or into*, the US Homeland.

Regardless of whether, as appears likely, the opening paragraph was imposed by someone other than the drafters of all that follows, the CIA Report is trying to have its cake and eat it. Anyone determined to believe that Iraq must be invaded finds a clear case made right at the start, while sceptics have the rest of the report to back up their questions.

But the believers have an ace up their sleeve – the way American students are taught to structure arguments. In writing an essay or report, you begin by stating your main conclusions up front. Everything that follows will be the justification for those conclusions. Even at the level of the paragraph, you begin with a 'topic sentence', which the rest of the paragraph goes on to develop. Essayinfo.com offers this advice to students:

Introductory Paragraph

Introductory paragraph consists of general points or attention grabbing details leading to the main idea … The main idea is often written at the end of this paragraph in a thesis statement, which may also contain three or more reasons (written very succinctly) for supporting this main idea. Each of these reasons should be elaborated on in the body paragraphs that follow. Note: A thesis statement does not always come at the end of the introductory paragraph – some essays have the very first sentence as the thesis statement.

On www.write-an-essay.com all that differs is the wording:

Writing an essay Introduction

This introduces the main idea of your essay and draws the reader into the subject. A good introduction … should:
- Look at the issues raised by the question.
- Outline the main issues you intend presenting.
- Summarize the essay.
- Answer the question set.

This advice is in line with what is found in all manuals of essay writing put out by American publishers. It is very different from the way in which students have traditionally been taught to write in Continental European countries, where the aim is to build up an argument piece by piece toward a final conclusion. To state the conclusion at the outset would make it appear as something the writer decided in advance, rather than something arrived at through complex reasoning. Readers are far less likely to be convinced – indeed they have little motivation to read through the whole argument, devoid as it is of any suspense.

I am not suggesting that we can explain the unwillingness of France or Germany to invade Iraq, and the eagerness of the USA to do so, based on different national protocols for reading texts such as the CIA Report. Among other things, it would fail to account for why Spain joined the coalition, or Italy, or Poland or indeed the UK, where the rhetorical tradition falls somewhere between the American and Continental extremes. Rather, I am proposing that the CIA Report was drafted following a particular protocol for writing and reading that would lead many Americans to assume automatically that whatever followed the opening paragraph was proof of what was so baldly stated there, licensing them to interpret all the later verbal qualifiers not as challenges to the solidity of the 'thesis statement', but as indications that its veracity was so evident as to outweigh any apparent causes for doubt.

If we look back to what the Report's second paragraph says – 'Baghdad hides large portions of Iraq's WMD efforts' – it is clear from hindsight that it should have given rise to a serious question about how the CIA claimed to know what is in the first paragraph. But the force of that opening 'thesis statement' that 'answers the question set' suggests another interpretation: although *large portions* may be hidden, the bulk has been observed and verified by the CIA.

Whether these were acts of propaganda deliberately intended to deceive remains a matter of interpretation. But three points need to be made:

1. There is nothing intrinsically wrong with the rhetorical structure long popular in American education, where conclusions are stated up front and justified later. But more effort is needed to make everyone aware of the fact that what is stated up front might not in fact accord with what follows, in which case the 'thesis statement' is unjustified.
2. The leaders of the coalition countries and many of their key advisors are trained lawyers, hence experts in rhetoric. They know how to read ambiguous documents. For them to contend that they were simply acting in a straight-forward way on the intelligence that was provided to them is disingenuous at best.
3. Obviously, no intelligence agency should draw strong conclusions from shaky premises. But to issue a report structured in a way that ordinary readers, given how they have been trained to write, will be compelled to take the strong conclusion as fact, is dangerously irresponsible.

I very much hope that in the longer term the well-being of the people of Iraq will end up having been improved by the invasion and occupation. Even that good outcome, however, will not eliminate severe disquiet about what, by even the most charitable interpretation, was a gross lack of forthrightness on the part of the democratic governments of the invading powers, and an insult to the intelligence of their electorates.

More to the point, I hope to have indicated how an analysis of language and discourse structure can help to inform interpretation, and how issues of language and politics can have a global resonance.

1.8 LANGUAGE AND CHOICE

A central question runs through the whole of this book. Who has the ability to make *choices* where language is concerned? Power and politics are fundamentally about whose will, whose choices, will prevail. Who has the power to determine what is good and bad English, or what is grammatically right or wrong in any language? Who should decide on the language or languages of education in a multilingual setting? Who determines what is acceptable or offensive in a given language at a given time, and how? When I believe I am making choices in language, are they actually being forced upon me by some kind of hegemonic social structure? Or by the language itself? Are my interpretations of what I read and hear really mine, or are they too forced upon me by corporate and governmental interests seeking to control the way I perceive and think?

These are not questions that can be answered in a straightforward way, for the simple reason that whatever answer we might give will itself be subject to these very same questions. If I believe that my linguistic choices are free choices, what if this belief has *itself* been imposed on me by some hegemonic force? To avoid circularity, as well as to avoid toeing any simplistic political line, we need to probe the questions, to look into what they take for granted, and to learn from what others before us have found in trying to grapple with them. The chapters that follow will each do this, in relatively subtle ways, focusing more on actual cases than on the exposition of theoretical accounts. The final chapter will assess where things stand on the question of language and choice, with the goal being less to convince readers of my own answer than to leave them well enough informed to choose their own.

1.9 CONCLUSION: LANGUAGE IS POLITICAL FROM TOP TO BOTTOM

Come on, I hear you saying, surely it is an exaggeration to claim that all language is political. The shopping list on the wall of your kitchen? The early utterances of an infant? Your computer's instruction manual? Two people chatting in a pub? Shakespeare's sonnets? Verb conjugations?

I sense that you are disagreeing with me, reader, and as I said at the outset, disagreement is the mother of politics, so, first of all, thank you for substantiating my point by using language politically yourself. Now then, am I indeed maintaining that all language is political, including the examples you have cited, where a political interpretation would seem manifestly absurd? Reader, I am, with just this proviso: that every act of language is *potentially* political, in that, even if I do not have conscious political motivations in making a given utterance, it is still capable of positioning me in a particular way vis-à-vis my hearer or reader, who may infer that

I had motivations I didn't know I had. They may even be right. The point, though, is that I cannot control the way other people react to me, infer my motivations or construct an identity for me in relation to their own.

The shopping list. Very political in my house. It's my wife's list. If I add something to it, she is liable to perceive it as a criticism of her for letting us run out of something, or to resent it if it's an item I myself might easily have replaced. The precise language I use in writing any notes on the list ('We're out of X' versus 'Would it be any trouble for you to pick up X, darling?') will have a direct impact on our marital politics.

The early utterances of an infant – well, we interpret them as commands, mainly, that is, as a verbal means of getting someone else to do one's bidding. It doesn't get more political than that.

The computer instruction manual. This seems like the hardest case for a political interpretation – until I open it, when the first thing I see is: '© 2003', followed further on by 'No part of this document may be photocopied, reproduced, or translated to another language without prior written consent'. This is to establish legal ownership of the text of the manual, and to make clear to me that I do not have the right to do anything with it but read it and comment on it. 'The information contained herein is subject to change without notice' – perhaps this ought to be stated on the copyright page of every book, starting with this one. The intent is to protect the manufacturer from lawsuits arising from any error or ambiguity in the instructions, but it gives so much latitude that in fact it would absolve the manufacturer of any responsibility whatever (not that this would necessarily hold up in court). Finally, just to be safe:

> The only warranties for products and services are set forth in the express warranty statements accompanying such products and services. Nothing herein should be construed as constituting an additional warranty.

Drafted by the manufacturer's lawyers, these statements spell out exactly what their and my rights and responsibilities are in our implicit contractual relationship. The language is strikingly different from that of the rest of the manual, which uses the fewest words possible to tell how to plug in the monitor, relying instead on a hard-to-interpret graphic. In the legal part, everything is fully spelled out, and constructed so as to reserve the maximum leeway for the manufacturer while constricting my rights so that I don't try to get them to repair the thing if I break it, or give me a refund after I've had it for a few months and am ready for a newer model.

Two people chatting in a pub. Why do we like chatting in pubs at all? It's about bonding – the linguistic performance of a relationship. See p. 5 under 'The politics of talking to others'.

Shakespeare's sonnets. Give me a break. We are incapable of reading them without discovering subtexts that are political either on the grand scale – the politics of recusant Roman Catholicism in Elizabethan England – or the intimate one – the poet's relationships with his noble benefactor, with the young man and the dark lady

– and toward the end, propaganda for the city of Bath. All this is entirely constructed out of language, squiggles on a page, words and how they are put together.

Verb conjugations. As a generally sympathetic reader (henceforth GSR) put it to me by way of objecting to the title of this section, 'Does this mean that, for example, verb conjugations are political? If so, this pushes the bounds of "political" so far that it ceases to mean anything. If everything is political, then somehow nothing is'. GSR was prepared to accept that all language *in use* is potentially political, but not language structure, the forms that constitute a speaker's linguistic competence and are the objects of what GSR calls 'abstract analysis'. Yet as someone who grew up in a community where almost everyone says *it don't* despite having been taught that *it doesn't* is 'correct', and where access to higher education and white-collar employment demands the use of *it doesn't*, I cannot conceive of verb conjugations as anything other than very highly politicised indeed.

My disagreement with GSR closely recapitulates Voloshinov's critique of Saussure, to be discussed in §4.1. Without wishing to anticipate all the points that will be made there, I should state clearly that nothing prevents anyone from setting out to make an abstract, apolitical analysis of anything linguistic, whether it pertains to structure or use. Nothing forces anyone to interpret a form or an utterance politically, yet neither does anything prevent anyone from doing so, unless it occurs in solitude or 'inner speech'.[7] To ignore the manifold and sweeping ways in which language functions to position people relative to one another is to have a partial and distorted conception of what language is about. Language always does many things at once, and I do not claim that the political somehow outweighs its other functions (something we have no way of measuring), nor would I deny that, every day, countless acts of language occur without any political consequences ensuing. Still, if we take 'political' to embrace all the positioning that speakers, hearers, writers and readers engage in relative to one another, and if the claim is that acts of language are potentially subject to political interpretation, then only a tiny fringe of language would appear to be immune. This does not however bleach 'political' of meaning, any more than structural analysis would be meaningless just because the analyst maintained that all language is structured.

Moreover, although the common-sense distinction between language structure and use is a helpful one to be able to make, there is a danger of inferring from it that these are two essentially distinct realms, with structure the one that comes first and is most 'real', while use is secondary in every sense. In fact the opposite is true. Language 'use' is real and primary – it's what everyone does, it's the activity out of which children derive that 'knowledge' of language that grammarians subsequently organise into 'structure'. Grammarians don't 'discover' verb conjugations; neither do they invent them out of whole cloth; we don't actually have a word for what they do. No grammarian has ever simply recorded the whole range of variation in how speakers of a particular inflectional language inflect their verbs. Rather, they determine a paradigm, a logical, right way of inflecting verbs that captures how a particular segment of the population does it – generally an elite, educated, conservative segment. Already at this point, verb conjugations are political. Thereafter, the paradigm as determined by the grammarian is likely to be imposed upon other segments of the population through the education system, making verb conjugations political in the fullest sense.

One last point I want to make before proceeding. The politics of theoretical and applied linguistics sometimes make it difficult for people studying and working in those areas to see that they have common ground. In taking a strong view of the fundamentally political nature of language, it is not my intention to widen such divisions as already exist. It should be possible for someone committed to a strongly cognitivist, even nativist view of language to read and profit from this book, even if, by their lights, all the phenomena described are epiphenomena and incapable of a 'scientific' account. I do not agree that such is the case, and shall be laying out a vision of language as having no existence separate from the way in which we conceive of it and talk about it. Language itself, in other words, is a political–linguistic–rhetorical construct. What is more, the various theories of language which linguists have developed are likewise political–linguistic–rhetorical constructs, and quite as subject to the sort of analysis put forward in this book as are the acts of language they attempt to explain.

But whether you agree with me that language and languages are constructs that emerge from our activity as talking–writing–signing and, above all, interpreting beings – or whether you believe that they have some kind of existence that does not depend on us, and are systems we 'use' – so long as you accept that language and languages are bound up in significant ways with the lives of the people who use them, you are ultimately committed to the view that language is political. For man is by nature a political animal.

NOTES

1. Classical Greek *anthropos*, the word used in this passage, generally means a human being regardless of sex, while *andros* means a man as opposed to a woman (*gyne*). That this distinction is more easily made in the classical European languages than in their modern counterparts is the sort of fact that lends itself readily to interpretation about the societies that spoke or speak these languages. The limits of such interpretation will be discussed in Chapter 4 below.

2. This question raises issues of the politics of 'speciesism' that I shall pass over for the moment, along with the matter of whether the complex signalling systems possessed by bees and certain other animals ought to have counted as 'gifts of speech' in Aristotle's reckoning.

3. In fact I am wary of any attempt to construct natural versus unnatural dichotomies in the analysis of language, and have surveyed the history of such attempts in Joseph (2000a).

4. John Mitchell of Hodder and Stoughton, which bought out the publisher Gordon in 1998, kindly confirmed to me in an email message of 22 Feb. 2005 that the book was in 'almost endemic use throughout schools in Scotland'.

5. The 'size' of a language here is shorthand for the size of the community who speak it – a common but risky metaphor, particularly since the whole metaphorical space surrounding language is such a rich breeding ground for misunderstandings.

6. In the case of JESUIT, when applied to a Roman Catholic who is not a Jesuit, and in the case of JEW, particularly when it is used as a verb.

7. This is a real dimension of language, even a significant one for the linguistic function of representation, though not for the other main functions of communication and the phatic and performative uses of language. This means that apolitical language is of limited importance for an applied linguist.

Chapter 2

Language and nation

2.1 THEM AND US

The Book of Genesis says that after the Flood the descendants of Noah spread out over the earth, 'every one after his tongue, after their families, in their nations' (Gen. 10: 5).[1] The Judaeo-Christian-Muslim tradition is far from being the only one that makes such a strong link between 'tongue' and 'nation', or that gives a particular language a special, quasi-divine status as the repository of meaning and of cultural memory. But the Bible is the most direct source of the modern (post-Renaissance) conception of the nation as a people linked by birth, language and culture and belonging to a particular place.

This had not been the European way of thinking prior to the Renaissance, when religious belonging provided a first division among peoples, and dynastic rule a second. Feudal organisation was tighter and more all-encompassing than any of the systems of social relationships that have replaced it. Individuals were personally responsible to their feudal superiors, and for their inferiors. With such a high level of social investment, the loci of *symbolic* belonging mattered less than they would in later times, as this order gradually loosened its grip. 'Language' meant Latin, pan-European and largely insulated from the vernacular dialects spoken by most people going about their daily lives. These vernaculars were not thought of as 'language', or as having any importance beyond the practical needs of communication, whereas Latin was the sacred vehicle of divine rites and divine knowledge.

What changed in the Renaissance was partly that, in some places at least, people were reading and hearing the Bible. It had previously been reserved for the learned few, whose interpretations of it were alone deemed safe for ordinary people to encounter. As the sense of nation and of the nation–language nexus spread, we find greater concern expressed with the need to raise up the vernacular to the status of the language, to make it 'eloquent', able to fulfil some of the functions previously reserved for Latin. This would come to be perceived as a duty to the nation, though it also had the practical effect of increasing book sales to people who hadn't been educated in Latin or simply preferred to read in their own language.[2]

The Biblical-*cum*-modern conception of nation and language remains powerful today, despite having been weakened by various attempts to overthrow it. Among these, Marxism, with its internationalist aims, was the most potent. But nationalism made a quick comeback after the fall of Eastern European communism starting in

1989, and it took only five more years to get a reminder of why it is such a dangerous concept, when overzealous restorers of the Serbian nation undertook acts of genocide in order to achieve 'ethnic cleansing' of their land. Further to the east, in the Levant, dangerous tensions continued to grow between Israel and neighbouring states – Israel having come into existence as the realisation of the Hebrew nation's Biblically-grounded right to possess its own land after centuries of exile and diaspora. The textual authority of Genesis was such as to outweigh the rights of any other nation that might have been living there in the meanwhile, with decades of tragic consequences for Israelis and Palestinians alike, as well as for neighbouring countries and the world as a whole.

Not surprisingly, Israel sought legitimation of its new nationhood in the Biblical link of nation and language. Hebrew had been maintained as the language of Judaism in all its central textual and ritual manifestations, and since the late nineteenth century, in anticipation of the founding of a Zionist state, small communities of European Jews had begun reviving it for use in writing and speaking about contemporary subjects. Nevertheless, a fervent debate raged from this period down to the founding of Israel as to whether the interests of the Israeli people wouldn't be better served by adopting an international language such as English or Arabic, or at least a language widely spoken among immigrants such as Yiddish (closely related to German) or Judaeo-Spanish (see Myhill 2004). But the ideological and symbolic importance of Hebrew carried the day over any such practical considerations, and few could question the success of this decision in helping to establish a strong sense of Israeli nationhood.

At what point, though, does a 'strong sense of nationhood' cease to be a good thing? The answer, surely, is when it starts to make members of the nation hostile to those they perceive as non-members. It is necessary to specify 'perceive', because quite a range of factors can be brought into play when it comes to denying someone's national identity, to the point that virtually no one's status as belonging to the nation is 100 per cent secure. German Jews were officially declared non-German during the Nazi regime even if they and their ancestors had lived in Germany since time immemorial (see Hutton 1999). Native-born Americans of German ancestry were persecuted as anti-American during WWI for speaking German,[3] and Japanese-Americans were imprisoned during WWII even if they were fervently loyal to the USA. By the 1950s, no member of the Communist Party was a 'real American', and when I was growing up in Michigan in the 1960s, a commonly-seen bumper sticker read *Be an American – Get a haircut*.

Today, all the world's wealthier countries are experiencing a certain amount of hostility toward recent and would-be immigrants from poorer lands, and again, even those who have been here for several generations are liable to feel the effects. Sometimes the older immigrants themselves resent more recent arrivals. In France, at the time of this writing, the government is reviewing legislation that would require mothers to speak French with their children in their own home. It is aimed particularly at mothers for reasons attributed to language acquisition research, which has consistently shown that the mother primarily determines what the children speak, and that use in the home is the best way for children to develop a strong sense that the language is their own. The aim is to reduce the alienation felt by the children of immigrants, especially from North Africa, and to prevent them from developing their own sub-identities, bolstered by the use of their home languages, which the government fears will lead to a fragmentation of French culture.

The French legislation is probably unworkable, since enforcing it in people's homes would require installing CCTV and monitoring it à la *Nineteen Eighty-Four*. The popularity of the TV 'reality' programme *Big Brother* perhaps makes this less unthinkable than it might have been a few years ago. But the point I wish to make is that it is easy for well-meaning people to cross the line and begin trampling on the rights of others whom, in their own minds, they want to help. In the French case, no doubt those who drafted the legislation are sincerely concerned for the well-being of the minority families, and want to protect them by doing all they can to integrate them into French society. It remains truer in France than in any other European country that someone who speaks the national language is accepted as part of the nation, regardless of their origins. The French government does not see the matter in the way it appears to many people outside France, and some within: that by denying residents the right to choose their language, and to evolve their own sub-cultures that can provide new and rich ways of 'being French', they are monopolising control of Frenchness and revoking some basic human rights – this in the country which gave birth to the *droits de l'homme* in the eighteenth century.

The fundamental problem stems from the way nationalism itself operates. According to the Social Identity Theory developed by Henri Tajfel (1919–82) and his collaborators in the 1970s and early 1980s, national and other identities are 'that *part* of an individual's self-concept which derives from his knowledge of his membership of a social group (or groups) together with the value and emotional significance attached to that membership' (Tajfel 1978: 63, italics in original). The social group we perceive ourselves as belonging to is our 'in-group'; anyone we don't perceive as a member gets classified into an 'out-group' which can come to represent not just the Other, but the Threat, the Enemy. While all reasonable people, by definition, are opposed to prejudice against and oppression of minority Others, one has to remember that such prejudice is engendered through the same process that produces national identity.

Taken to extremes, national identity always becomes oppressive, but kept within bounds it is generally reckoned to be a positive force, helping to give people a sense of who they are, anchoring their lives and helping them avoid feelings of alienation. Since language and nation are conceptually so closely bound together, it is not surprising that the politics of language choice (discussed in the next chapter) rarely depend on purely 'functional' criteria, such as what language will be most widely understood. The symbolic and emotional dimensions of national identity are crucial, and language policies that ignore them prove dysfunctional in the long run.

2.2 WHAT IS OR ISN'T 'A LANGUAGE'

A German scholar and Nazi Party member named Heinz Kloss (1904–87) undertook detailed studies of the English-speaking world, especially the USA, as part of the Hitler regime's planning for the eventual takeover of these countries. After the war, Kloss reworked some of this research into the first large-scale study of modern Germanic *Kultursprachen*, 'culture languages', what are normally known in English as literary or standard languages. The model which Kloss put forward in 1952 (and revised in 1967 and 1978) would find wide acceptance. According to it, for a particular dialect to attain recognition as a language in its own right, two criteria must be met.

The first of these Kloss called *Abstand*, 'distance', the idea being that the dialect must be sufficiently distinct in linguistic terms from whatever recognised language it might otherwise be considered a dialect of. If the structural difference isn't great enough, the dialect will not be recognised as a separate language. In addition, however, the dialect must undergo the process which constitutes Kloss's second criterion, *Ausbau*, 'building out', by which he meant that a certain amount of literary production has to be carried out in the dialect, with the attendant elaborating effects that such production has, including the borrowing of learned words (and sometimes of syntactic devices) and at least a certain amount of standardisation of spelling and grammar.

Neither linguistic distance nor literary production on its own is enough to gain 'language' status for a dialect – both must be present, though there is no clear threshold to be met. The Chinese 'dialects' are a perfect example of the insufficiency of linguistic distance on its own. The structural differences among them are comparable to those distinguishing members of the Germanic language family (English, German, Danish, Swedish etc.), yet by virtue of *Ausbau* the Germanic family contains more than a dozen recognised languages, whereas the Chinese 'family' is recognised as a single language. The structural linguist doesn't see it that way, however. According to the Summer Institute of Linguistics' Ethnologue database (www.ethnologue.com), the Germanic family contains 53 languages (living or extinct), while Chinese subsumes 14 distinct languages. This is also the view of the venerable linguist John DeFrancis, who in his book *The Chinese Language: Fact and Fantasy* (1984) makes clear that the greatest fantasy of all, as far as he is concerned, is the illusion that there is one single Chinese family – an 'illusion' shared by the more than one billion mother-tongue speakers of the language.

What about *Ausbau* on its own, without *Abstand*? Here Kloss had to acknowledge that there actually are pure '*Ausbau* languages' which the linguist knows to be actually one single language, though the speech communities involved insist that they differ. A classic case is that of Serbian and Croatian, which are mutually comprehensible, differing on a level comparable with dialects of English rather than the Chinese dialects. But they have undergone literary development in a way designed to maximise the appearance of difference between them. Serbian, the language of a majority Orthodox Christian nation, is written in the Cyrillic alphabet, as Russian is. Croatian, the language of a majority Roman Catholic country, is written in the Latin alphabet, as English is. Linguists often prefer to speak of 'Serbo-Croatian' as a single language, on the grounds of the lack of linguistic distance, but this is not a concept one often encounters among Serbians or Croatians, for whom the religious and attendant cultural differences have remained strong enough to provoke war and 'ethnic cleansing' as recently as the 1990s.

There is a curious imbalance in Kloss's model. On the one hand, he insists that both *Abstand* and *Ausbau* are required for a dialect to achieve recognition as a language. On the other hand, he acknowledges the existence of '*Ausbau* languages' which have such recognition despite the absence of *Abstand* – but that reception is only partial because it comes just from people who lack training in linguistics. It is a sort of illusion which the linguist can see through, the mirror image of DeFrancis's treatment of the Chinese dialects. The *Ausbau* languages are truly languages, because the linguist says so, while the speakers maintain the contrary because they are are in thrall to a culturally and politically motivated illusion of unity.

For anyone coming at these questions from even a moderately anthropological direction, however, it is Kloss and DeFrancis who are in thrall to an illusion, that of the unique power of their own 'objective' linguistic analysis. I do not dispute that when what a people believes about their own language conflicts with the expert's analysis, the expert is right by definition, since expertise means being able to observe and understand in ways an ordinary person cannot. But when the 'expert' is an outsider to the culture under study, there is an important sense in which every insider to the culture is an expert in it, and the outsider is their student. The outsider may not see it that way – it would after all put him or her in the inferior position, and that isn't what expertise is traditionally about.

We are dealing here with the politics of knowledge, views on which have shifted massively over the course of the last century.[4] The modern anthropological view takes a culture's own shared traditions of belief about itself as the primary reality. It may be 'mythical' in the sense that it contradicts documented facts or invokes super-natural events and beings, but if the people treat it as truth and organise their lives, thought and identity around it, that alone makes it real in a more significant sense than the analysis that sees it as mythical. In the grand scheme of things, what does it matter if a few thousand linguists are convinced that Serbian and Croatian are the same language, or that Chinese is a family of distinct languages, when umpteen millions believe the opposite, and it's on their lives that the question has a direct impact?

Kloss drew the wrong conclusion from his own analysis, for in fact only *Ausbau* ultimately matters in his model. If linguistic distance is lacking, literary development can rectify that by increasing the apparent distance, as in the case of Serbian and Croatian and many others besides. Irish Gaelic and Scottish Gaelic are universally recognised as two distinct languages, and the Ethnologue database lists as well 'Hiberno-Scottish Gaelic', identifying it as an 'Archaic literary language based on 12th century Irish, formerly used by professional classes in Ireland until the 17th century and Scotland until the 18th century'. But people in the Gaelic-speaking areas of Scotland up until well into the seventeenth century recognised just one language, which they called Erse (Irish). Only around that time did the desire arise to have *their own* authentic Gaelic, and some of those who shared the desire brought it into existence by deliberately writing Gaelic in ways that broke with the norms of what today, in retrospect, is called 'Hiberno-Scottish Gaelic'. Ever since, the separateness of Irish and Scottish Gaelic has been more immediately apparent on the page than to the ear – an indication that they are primarily *Ausbau* rather than *Abstand* languages in Kloss's terms.[5]

Literary development always extends distance and sometimes creates it, not just from other related dialects, but even from the dialect base of the very language that is undergoing the building-out process. In the end, though, it isn't even *Ausbau* that determines what is or isn't a language. Literary development is a symptom rather than the root cause. So long as people *believe* that their way of speaking constitutes a language in its own right, there is a real sense in which it *is* a distinct language. They will probably find ways to 'perform' their distinctive linguistic identity for the benefit of others, but ultimately what matters is the 'imagined community' of their language, to borrow the term created by Anderson (1991) to describe the nation.

Putting it another way, the question of what is or isn't a language is always finally a *political* question.[6] The linguist cannot answer it objectively by measuring degrees of structural difference or mutual comprehensibility. The linguist can contribute to the answer by finding out what the community itself believes, and what surrounding communities believe, at various levels from the grass-roots to the elite, including relevant governmental and educational policies. It is possible too that the linguist's 'objective' analysis of the putative language may be used to help shape popular beliefs, though any impact the structural or theoretical linguist has on the issues tends to be indirect at best.

Applied linguists however can have a significant impact. They are the ones who contribute the dictionaries and grammars that mark a key point in the *Ausbau* of any emerging language. They influence the teaching of the language, and inform the government policies that determine to what extent it will be used in education (see Wright 2004 for an overview). This is true not only at the time of the initial emergence of the language but through its subsequent history, as language change and shift necessitate re-evaluation, followed by new ways of conceiving the language and talking about it, followed in turn by measures for resolving the new tensions. Such is the case at present with English, as 'World Englishes' create a tension between maintaining the standards of a unified language and opening up space for the recognition of new languages – in this case, new Englishes (see §2.6). It is no coincidence that the rise in awareness of this tension has come in tandem with an increase in the 'political turn' of applied linguistics over the last thirty years.

2.3 THE ROLE OF WRITING

Languages which lack any written tradition are often regarded, even by their own speakers, as having only a tenuous claim to being a 'language' at all. This can lead to language endangerment, which the creation of a written version of the language can help to forestall. But there is a political side to this as well, since writing represents a cultural borrowing which some will see as an invasion, a colonisation. Moreover, even when a community accepts writing for its language, there is rarely agreement on *how* the language should be written. This raises political issues of its own that may endure for decades or centuries, culturally fracturing the community of language users (though also giving them something to write about, passionately).

Much to the chagrin of modern linguistics, which treats only the spoken as real language and writing as a secondary indication of speech, the fact is that cultures generally recognise themselves as having 'the same language' so long as they share the same written language, regardless of how much variation there may be in how they speak. There are several ways in which this denial of linguistic difference through shared writing can be achieved. Even in countries with a long tradition of writing, if that tradition has been conservative – as it is in the nature of writing to be – then, over time, language change can lead to a situation in which a sort of diglossia (see below, §3.2) divides the written language from the spoken, even though the people themselves still conceive of them as one single language. 'French Canadians' and Frenchmen both speak 'French', to the frustration of the partisans of a distinctive Québécois, because their standard written norm is (or can be) nearly the same, despite the fact that the spoken languages differ greatly. The same is true of many countries across the Arabic-speaking world. Here the effect of writing is even stronger than in the English example given earlier, for two reasons. The first is that everyday Arabic is not normally written or printed with the vowels indicated, only the consonants (and long vowels). The second is that a very strong sense of an original and correct Arabic exists, represented for Muslims by the language of the Koran. The millions of Christians for whom Arabic is a mother tongue are hardly less committed to the status of the classical written language, even though the Koran does not have the same sacred authority for them.

More dramatic however is the effect of a non-alphabetic writing system, and particularly the Chinese system of character writing. Chinese characters are logographs, which is to say that each character represents a word. Some characters are basic and cannot be broken down, while others are composed of a basic character plus some other indicator, often part of another character used to indicate pronunciation. However, despite the inclusion of phonetic elements, the characters do not analyse each word into its component sounds the way alphabetic writing does. The result is that a character such as 然 corresponds to the spoken Mandarin word *ran*, the Cantonese *jin*, and the Wu *zø*, each pronounced with a different tone in addition to the consonant and vowel differences. Yet speakers of Mandarin, Cantonese and Wu, while fully aware of the divergences and of the fact that they cannot understand one another's speech, are entirely certain that there is one single Chinese word 然 that they are each saying in their particular dialectal way. When asked why they believe this, the proof they cite is usually the existence of the written character, which *is* the word as far as they are concerned.

Speakers of English and German, on the other hand, do not think of *yes* and *ja* as being the same word; rather, they will say that '*ja* is the German word for *yes*' and vice-versa. This is true even though, in colloquial usage, English speakers normally say, not *yes*, but *yeah* or even *yah* – phonetically identical to German *ja*. For the average English speaker, *yes* and *yeah/yah* are 'the same word', one being the formal way of saying it and the other informal; and the word itself, the real word, is *yes*.

Whether different writing systems caused the different ways of thinking about words, or vice versa, is a chicken-and-egg question. However it would be difficult to believe that the two are unconnected. Although Chinese writing is partially phonetic, and English writing partially non-phonetic, the Chinese system, by allowing so much more latitude in the visual-sound link, enables belief in a single Chinese language much more robustly than an alphabet does, even for a pair of languages as closely related as English and German. Yet neither *determines* the cultural beliefs in question. The fact that Taiwan has maintained a more traditional system of Chinese writing rather than adopting the simplified characters of the People's Republic of China represents a choice with clear political motivations and ramifications. If the future brings desire for greater unity with the mainland, undoubtedly the Taiwanese will make the switch; if not – and if the switch is not forced upon them – they won't. The maintenance of even a minimally distinctive writing system is a potent way of performing a distinct national identity.

2.4   CONSTRUCTING 'THE LANGUAGE' BY CONTROLLING VARIATION

The development of a written form of the language has, throughout history and across cultures, been closely bound up with the recognition of a *standard* form of the language. As the standard emerges, the myth arises that it is the one, true, original form of the language – the language proper. All the other dialects, formerly on a par with it, are now taken to be variants of the standard, regional ways of using it, or decadent misuses.

We can observe this conception of the standard developing in the first modern treatise on the subject, *De vulgari eloquentia* ('On the eloquence of the vernacular') by Dante Alighieri (1265–1321). It was written in around 1306, though not published until 1529 (see Dante Alighieri 1996). The vernacular in question is that of Italy, which is remarkable given that the modern nation of Italy did not come into existence until 1860–70. Before that it was a collection of small states, of which San Marino and the Vatican City remain today as isolated relics. Up to Dante's time, with a few exceptions restricted almost entirely to poetry, Latin was the language of writing. What people spoke were local dialects that varied greatly from one end of the peninsula to the other, and could be unintelligible even to speakers who lived just a few miles apart, especially if a mountain or river separated them. Dante began by asking himself what it is that binds these dialects together as 'Italian' – not just what they have in common with each other, but what they *do not* share with French, Spanish and other Romance idioms.

In determining the common Italian dialect, Dante was creating a myth of a time somewhere in the past when all Italians spoke the same way, and differently from all non-Italians. In truth, there never was such a time – inscriptions and other textual evidence uncovered since the eighteenth century have made that clear. Even before the rise of Rome, various Indo-European languages such as Oscan, Umbrian and Greek were spoken up and down the peninsula alongside Early Latin and unrelated languages like Etruscan. During the centuries of the Roman Empire, all this variety didn't disappear but did diminish, giving way to variation within the Latin language itself, where a wide gulf separated the classical usage of the Greek-educated patrician elite from the ordinary speech of the plebeian masses. The regional variation that would produce the Italian dialects as Dante knew them had always been there.

Perhaps Dante realised this but was intent on creating the myth of a unified Italian period all the same. It scarcely matters, because, in the event, he succeeded in his aim. The *volgare illustre* (illustrious, illuminated and illuminating vernacular) which he devised and used in his *Divina commedia* became not only the basis of Standard Italian, but the prototype of modern European standard languages generally. The fact that the supposedly supra-regional *volgare illustre* actually was very close to one particular dialect – Dante's native Tuscan – would also prove to be generally true with the standard languages that emerged over the fifteenth and sixteenth centuries. The French language is based upon the dialect of the region around Paris, the Île-de-France; that of Spain upon the dialect of Castile; that of Portugal upon the dialects extending from Lisbon to Coimbra; that of English on dialects of the southeast of the country; that of Germany on dialects of the central eastern region around Erfurt and Leipzig.

In each of these cases what those involved believed they were creating was not the 'standard dialect' – that is a modern linguistic concept – but *the language*. Up to the Renaissance, 'language' and 'grammar' meant a well-ordered written idiom, usually Latin, though Greek, Hebrew, Arabic, Syriac and a handful of others were recognised as qualifying, while the vernacular and speech of the masses did not. A 'French language' or 'English language' implied something conceptually on a par with Latin – and it would take a further century or more from the emergence of the modern languages before the perception arose that they might actually approach or even equal Latin in eloquence.

The most salient difference between Latin and the modern languages for which it served as model was that, unlike them, it was dead. That is, it did not exist as a vernacular with living communities of ordinary, uneducated people growing up using it as their mother tongue. It did have significant communities of speakers, in monasteries and universities, but for them it was a second, learned language. Exceptional individuals such as Michel de Montaigne (1533–92), who was raised with Latin as his mother tongue, are noteworthy precisely for their rarity (see Burke 1993: 56). People learned Latin from *grammars*. This did not mean that no variation existed in how Latin was spoken; on the contrary, variation abounded, traceable largely to interference from speakers' mother tongues and to deeper historical causes.

But with Latin there was no question as to *what the language was* – it was wholly contained in the grammar books, together with the texts that formed the classical and Biblical–patristic canon. With Italian there was a question, the *questione della lingua*, over who among modern Italians the Italian language 'belonged' to. With Latin, it belonged above all to Cicero and Augustine, Donatus and Priscian, in other words, to books. It was under total control.

This was the prototype that the pioneers, the cultural avant-garde, of the modern European languages would strive to recreate. In order to do this, they had to control variation by putting the modern language into a condition as much like that of Latin as possible, identifying *one correct form* for every word, every inflection, every syntactic construction. To a lesser extent, every pronunciation too – lesser because again, as with Latin, spoken language was perceived as secondary. To take the case of Castilian, the basis of modern standard Spanish, within that dialect alone significant variations persisted into the period when the standard language was formed. The more conservative Castilian of Cantabria retained features that had changed in the more innovative dialect of Burgos. Here are a few examples (drawn from Lapesa 1968: 133–4):

- where the Castilian of Cantabria still had the final vowel *-u* in words whose Latin etymons ended in *-um* (e.g., *buonu* 'good', from Latin *bonum*), these had changed to *-o* in Burgos (*bueno*);
- where Cantabria kept the *mn* in words such as *nomne* ('name', from Latin *nomine*), it had changed in Burgos to *nombre*;
- where Cantabria kept the sequence *mb* in words such as *ambos* ('both', Latin *ambo*), in Burgos it had simplified to *amos*;
- where Cantabria kept forms in which a preposition was merged with a following feminine definite article *la*, such as *enna* 'in the' and *conna* 'with the', in Burgos these were replaced with *en la* and *con la*.

The fact that Standard Castilian has the Burgos form in three of the four cases (*bueno, nombre, en la/con la*) and the Cantabrian form in one (*ambos*) indicates how complex the process was by which the standard language was formed.

It was an intensely political process – or rather, *is* so, because the process does not come to an end at some point when the language is 'complete'. Ongoing change in the vernacular dialect base, together with lexical growth and the impact of other languages, all mean that the standardisation process must go on. The politics have to do with issues of language and identity: each of the variants onto which a hierarchy of correctness is imposed *belongs* to some speakers and not others, and if your town's variant becomes the standard form, while mine gets stigmatised as sub-standard, the social and political consequences are obvious.

Alternatively, and quite exceptionally, a standard form can be created for 'logical' reasons, perhaps reflecting the structure of some prestigious model language, but not aligning with what is found in any of the vernacular dialects. A well-known case in English is the language standard ascribed to Lindley Murray's *English Grammar* (1795) that proscribes the 'split infinitive', *to boldly go*, on the grounds that infinitives like *to go* are a single word (à la Latin *īre* 'to go'), hence unsplittable. This became a powerful shibboleth of standard English usage, despite the fact – or more probably, *on account of the fact* – that all English dialects very readily accept, even demand the split infinitive. The 'naturalness' of the split infinitive construction, the ease with which native speakers use it, makes it all the more powerful as a shibboleth separating those prepared to master the wholly arbitrary rule proscribing it from those not so prepared, or unable to control their own 'natural' behaviour to this degree. The former are admitted to realms of social responsibility and prestige from which the latter are excluded.

Moreover, professions are created for those who do the separating, and who inculcate the standards on which the separation will be based – teachers, examiners, hiring committees and other 'gatekeepers'. They are not always native speakers, but they play a very direct role in determining 'what the language is', through the red strokes they make through non-standard variants, the marks they assign to written work, the choices they make when it comes to degree classification, whom to hire, what to publish. The last case is a bit different, in that it is possible to get something published even if it contains non-standard language, but the publisher is expected to employ editors to tidy it up, standardise it into proper language – which is to say, the language proper – before it appears in print.

2.5 LANGUAGE, KNOWLEDGE AND POWER

All the great religions are true to the etymology of *religion*, 'tying back', in that they bind the multiplicity of individual minds back to a unified teaching, itself held within a unified textual tradition. The monotheistic religions further tie the multiplicity of reality back to a single source and truth. With any religion, it is easy to see why a single, unified and unchanging language would seem to be implied: for the maintenance of the textual tradition, and in some cases, to satisfy the requirement for a language of truth itself.

Even in modern secular culture, when linguists and anthropologists have set out to re-envisage human origins, their imaginations have always harked back to something very like the Biblical picture – the unified and isolated tribe, an extended family, without writing and therefore without history, or rather frozen in history, leading a purely synchronic existence. In harmony with nature; enjoying long periods of peace punctuated occasionally by conflict with neighbouring tribes. Homogeneous in culture and language, and all of one mind, so that significant political differences are not part of the picture. Hence there is no need for democracy – monarchy (or oligarchy) perfectly serves the needs of the people and therefore is implicitly democratic.

It is an idyllic picture. It takes us back to our early childhood, when we were part of a small tribe of brothers and sisters headed by a benevolent joint monarchy. Or if such was not our childhood, it is the ideal one we imagine and regret, with some help from our surrounding cultural narratives (stories, films, television programmes). It is important to remember this when trying to understand why people get so violently upset when the reality around them threatens the picture – when large-scale immigration makes it impossible to suspend disbelief in our unified tribal character, as against those other tribes in opposition to whom we define ourselves; or when 'our' language is threatened, not only by immigrants, but by the enemy within, those who 'misuse' it. The misuse generally represents a more evolved form of the language than the one I use (or think I use) and certainly more evolved than the conservative form frozen in grammars and dictionaries.

Multilingualism, language change and non-standard usage all feel like threats to the very foundation of a culture, since the language itself is the principal text in which the culture's mental past and its present coherence are grounded. Linguists like to insist that language is constantly changing, and that therefore all linguistic 'prescriptivism' represents reactionary prejudice (in extreme cases, even racism) on the part of 'language mavens' (a term beloved of Stephen Pinker, for example) and is always bound to fail. The conclusion is valid in the sense that such intervention will never stop language from evolving, but it misses the crucial point that, nevertheless, the interventions support a differential rate of change among various groups within the population, such that some will emerge as more conservative than others. This difference then serves as the basis for the differential distribution of resources and responsibilities, such that those who control the more conservative, 'educated' forms, receive more than those who do not. Insofar as linguistics fails to take account of this massively important cultural force, linguists end up cutting themselves off from the issues involving language that matter to the bulk of the population because they and their children are directly affected by them.

The fact is that, throughout modern times, societies have operated with a very real economy based on language change. The distribution of resources and responsibilities must be based on something, after all. In earlier times heredity was the principal criterion, but as the modern world has been increasingly democratised, especially since the mid-nineteenth century, the role of heredity in determining one's place in the world has been gradually giving way to measures based upon linguistic performance, such as examinations and job interviews. In the world I inhabit, academe, one's rise through the ranks is obviously conditioned by one's ability to write the language in the standard way, and to speak it in a way that is not perceived as non-standard. In Britain I have twice had the experience of serving on appointment committees for lectureships and seeing well-qualified candidates with northern English accents be turned down with the remark made (after they had left the room) that they were obviously 'not as intelligent' as the other finalists, when those making the remark clearly had no other basis for such a judgement than the accent. Although I chastised my colleagues for their bigotry, I was forced at the same time to look into my own soul: for the fact is that in marking students' work I give a certain weight to the 'quality of the writing'. The criteria I apply are different depending on whether the student is a native or non-native speaker of English, and while it feels as though this is a distinct issue from judging intelligence based on accent, logically there is no sharp dividing line. I make a determined effort to read past mistakes in the English to the logical structure beneath – yet I do not believe it is wholly possible to separate the two, and at times I fear that I may be reading too charitably, imposing sense upon passages that don't necessarily have any.

Michel Foucault (1926–84) famously contended that knowledge is not something existing apart from us but is itself determined by power, as social forces make it possible for certain people rather than others to determine what knowledge will consist of in a particular place and time (see Foucault 1977: 27–8; 1980). Whether or not one accepts this view, whatever knowledge is, those institutionally warranted as possessing it have a certain kind of power – the power to grant or withhold the same institutional warrant from others, plus whatever resources such warrants can be 'cashed in' for.[7] They therefore have a great deal invested in the linguistic manifestations of power – the standards of correct usage of the language. My own early work (Joseph 1987a) is not unusual in seeing the value they place on these standards as representing pure self-interest.[8] Although that was not entirely wrong, it underestimated the importance of what people believe about language and knowledge, and particularly the religious belief that ties real knowledge to one original, correct form of the language. What has changed my mind is the realisation, confirmed by much experience, that, actually, no one has firmer faith in and commitment to the standard language as the one true measure of knowledge and social worth than do the people who have *not* mastered its norms. And the people who *do* display such mastery rarely show the signs of displeasure at the thought of everyone speaking the standard language that one would expect if it were really the sort of commodity that the educated and powerful wanted to keep selfishly to themselves.[9]

Most language snobs are actually democrats in the sense that their ideal would be for everyone to speak the language identically, by speaking it correctly. Honey (1997) is the classic modern exponent of this position, arguing that all class difference in English could be eradicated if every child were taught Standard English. That is profoundly different from the sort of democracy that says anything goes in language – that anybody's way of speaking is just as good as anybody else's – but it is also profoundly different from a view that a special, powerful form of the language should remain the unique purview of those in power and their hand-picked successors.

Our present-day way of thinking about these things has been inherited from a 2,000-year tradition of Christian doctrine in which the link between language and knowledge is fundamental. Knowledge consists ultimately of the true forms of things and concepts (a Platonic inheritance) and exists perfectly only in the mind of God. These forms are reflected, imperfectly, in the physical things around us, and in the minds of people who know them. They exist in us in a special kind of inner language that is distinct from any actual spoken human languages. The latter merely fulfil the human necessity for communication, which ranks far below the divine purposes of knowledge that the inner language serves (for more details see Joseph 2005). Officially in Christian doctrine language differences do not really matter – they are superficial – yet, even if people are born with some knowledge already implanted in their minds (particularly the idea of God), the great bulk of what they know comes to them through teaching. Here languages do enter in a significant way, because they are the vehicle for the human transmission of divine knowledge. To keep the human possession of knowledge 'tied back' (religion again), the safest way is to have a single, universal language. This maximises confidence that knowledge is being transmitted accurately and minimises obstacles to testing individuals' correct control of such knowledge.

The single-language system continues to operate for vast portions of humanity in a form little changed for centuries. Such is the case in the Chinese- and Arabic-speaking worlds, and in most of South Asia, though these cases differ in the degree of diglossic separation between an extremely conservative classical language, used for a limited range of religious and other functions, and a less conservative vernacular standard or set of standards. In Europe, the system whereby the West had Latin and the East Greek as their unique language endured for over 1,000 years, before being modified so that, while the basic one-language model remained in place, that one language came to be a standardised form of the national vernacular. This process took a long time to transpire, indeed it is still transpiring, and may never reach completion, as certain symbolic functions in law, religion and education continue to be reserved for the classical languages.

Initially, the main obstacle seems to have been getting people to believe that their vernacular ways of speaking were actually languages. Latin and Greek had 'grammar', as witnessed by treatises on the subject, and the variation in them was controlled by the fact that they were 'dead', since even Greek did not have native speakers of its classical form. This fulfilled (or perhaps determined) the expectations of what a language had to be, given the exigencies of maintaining and transmitting knowledge as outlined above. When one's 'enlightenment' was revealed by one's control of the Latin terminology for the highest philosophical concepts, it was difficult to imagine such knowledge being held and safely transmitted in a vernacular that was itself 'irregular' in two senses, exhibiting great variation from locale to locale (and even in the usage of a single individual), and lacking the formalised rules of a grammar book.

This is why, when Dante set out to imagine (or in his word, 'discover') an 'Italian language' at the start of the fourteenth century, the term he used for it was *volgare illustre* – *volgare* because it belonged to the ordinary people as well as to the learned, *illustre* because it could be the vehicle of enlightenment, of the highest knowledge. This, he realised, would take some work. *De vulgari eloquentia* laid out the work plan, and the *Divina commedia* then performed the result. Italian became the model that was followed in the creation of other 'illuminated vernaculars'. Once Dante had demonstrated that a vernacular could be not only a language, but a language of enlightenment, and could form the basis of a specifically *national* literary culture (even where the political nation did not exist, as, again, Italy would not for centuries to come), a new era opened in the politics of language in Europe. The first effect was simply that writing in the vernacular became semi-respectable, and more people – though still a small minority – began doing it. With movable type and print capitalism in the sixteenth century, it emerged that the potential market for books in the vernacular was more sizeable (though less prestigious) than for books in Latin. Profitability accelerated if large print runs were sold, which could happen only if a large audience could read the language.

This brought a new twist to the old language–power–resources nexus. While scholars and clergymen concerned themselves with enlightenment in the language, which the borrowing of words from Latin and Greek gave the impression of increasing, publishers knew that a certain economy between learned and popular language was necessary if the readership was to be wide enough to make a book profitable. Without profits, funds could not be raised to publish any more books, since those with the funds would invest them elsewhere. But something else was happening in the sixteenth century: the 'emergence' of the concept of the nation. I put the word emergence in scare quotes because it suggests a non-deliberate process, but in fact it is clear from the documentary record that vast efforts were undertaken by governments to get the populace to buy into the idea of the nation. The 'national language' was an obvious concept to seize upon to promote belief in the internal unity of the nation and its difference from its neighbours and rivals, at the most fundamental level, that of *knowledge itself*. Even if these ideas were not clearly articulated until the early nineteenth century (see for example Joseph 2004a: 109–15 on Fichte), they are implicit in much of the writing and cultural activity surrounding language from Dante through to the end of the eighteenth century – and nowhere more so than in those mostly northern European countries which took the nationalist route of breaking from Rome to form their own national church. Here again the obvious vehicle for reformed religious knowledge was found in the national language of enlightenment.

2.6 HOW NEW LANGUAGES EMERGE: FROM 'FALLING STANDARDS' TO 'WORLD ENGLISHES'

In the first decade of the twentieth century, when universalism seemed to be looming inevitably – either as Marxism, with its appeal to the working class, or as Esperanto or other universal language schemes, which offered a safe alternative to the middle class – Ferdinand de Saussure (1857–1913) noted a particular tension where language was concerned (see Saussure 1922: 281). On the one hand, the necessity of communication, or the 'force of intercourse' as he termed it, creates pressure for the diversity of languages to decrease; but on the other hand, the *esprit de clocher*, in Italian *campanilismo*, the feeling of local belonging, impels the local diversity of languages to increase. It is an especially interesting view for him to have taken at a time when his own brother, René, had recently become the head of the international Esperanto association. The Esperantists believed that one of the virtues of an invented tongue was that, being a rational creation, it would not undergo change over time as do natural languages, those relics of an irrational prehistory. Ferdinand taught, however, that an artificial language, once put into circulation, would undergo exactly the same history as a natural one, with change inevitable (ibid., p. 111). Unity or diversity would presumably be determined by the same balance between the force of intercourse and the *esprit de clocher*.

What we may term 'Saussure's tension' helps explain the emergence of World Englishes. If the USA and the UK shared exactly the same form of English, the imperative of intercourse would be satisfied, but that of identity would not. If they had two separate languages, the reverse would be true. But by having two forms of the same language – nearly mutually comprehensible but with a certain number of symbolically distinctive features – they have the best of both worlds. The same should be true for every part of the planet where the population develops its own form of World English.[10]

Yet it is rarely perceived that way, particularly during the early stages. In Joseph (2004a, Chapter 6) I have described at some length the current situation of the emergence of 'Hong Kong English', a form distinctive enough to be recognised by linguists, though not as yet by a significant number of English speakers in Hong Kong, for whom there is just 'good English' and 'bad English', the latter marked by all those distinctive features in which the linguist recognises a 'Hong Kong English'. The dominant discourse continues to be concerned with 'falling English standards' – the same discourse which Bolton (2003) and Evans (2003) show to have been going on in Hong Kong since the nineteenth century. The essential point to recognise is that 'falling English standards' and 'the emergence of Hong Kong English' are simply two ways of looking at the same thing, namely, language change that reflects in part the interference of the mother tongue, or *resistance* grounded in the mother tongue (see below, p. 53).

Whether or not the situation will change in the future so that a Hong Kong English comes to be recognised and celebrated by its speakers depends almost entirely on political considerations – how the people of Hong Kong (or possibly the south of China as a whole) come to perceive themselves in relation to the rest of China and to the world generally. If they should develop an identity comparable to that of Singapore – a nation-state independent of its neighbours and an important global broker for the goods they produce – then a sense of Hong Kong English comparable to that of Singapore English could develop. Of course, there are provisos: to begin with, not all Singaporeans recognise the existence of a distinctive Singapore English having a positive identity value for them, and are more inclined to talk about 'Singlish' and falling standards.

Brown (1999: 165–6), updating information initially collected in Tongue (1979), lists uses of prepositions or adverbial particles that distinguish Singapore English from Standard English.

Cases where Singapore English uses a preposition/adverbial particle, while Standard English doesn't

to consider about something	to cope up with something
to demand for something	to discuss about something
to emphasise on something	to list out items
to lower down the volume	to mention about something
to page for someone	to regret for something
to request for something	to say something out
to sell something away	to source for something
to stress on something	to tolerate with someone

Cases where Standard English uses a preposition/adverbial particle, while Singapore English doesn't
to butter someone (= Std Eng 'to butter someone up')
to deputise someone (= Std Eng 'to deputise for someone')
to side someone (= Std Eng 'to side with someone')
to mug the facts (= Colloquial British Eng 'to mug up [study] the facts')
to mug Shakespeare (= Colloquial British Eng 'to mug up on Shakespeare')

to dispose something	to meet an accident
to officiate a ceremony	to participate a game
to pick someone in a car	to tamper something

Cases where Singapore English uses a different preposition/adverbial particle from the Standard English one

in campus (on campus)	over Channel 5 (on Channel 5)
to hand/pass up homework (hand/pass in)	to put off a fire (put out)
to put up a show (put on)	to round up a lesson (round off)
to take out shoes (take off)	

Although these are features associated principally with spoken Singapore English – and in many cases with Hong Kong English and other 'Chinese Englishes' as well – Brown also cites instances of Singapore English preposition/adverbial particle usage (indicated in bold) in the country's leading newspaper, the *Straits Times*:

> [Name] was presented with an oversized cheque … He said with a wide smile: 'I'm going to frame it **up** and put it in my office'. (3 Jan. 1996)
> He says: 'You can never get through the telephone lines …' (= Std Eng 'You can never get through on the telephone'; 18 May 1996)
> [H]e said there was no issue **in** which it [the government] was not prepared to debate with the opposition. (14 Aug. 1996)
> Singaporeans have snapped up nearly twice as many **of** such cars in the first half of this year as they did last year. (15 July 1997)

It is true that the first two of these instances occur within a direct quotation, but the fact is that, in the past, the *Straits Times*, like most other newspapers, 'tidied up' the English of such quotations. That it no longer does this so regularly is a significant indicator of the rising status of Singapore English – even if, as may be the case, it represents a slip-up by a copy editor who neglected to catch it. It is on this rising 'slip tide' that new forms of English sail into port. They signal the gradual shift from the concern with falling standards to the perception that something new has emerged, something belonging to us.

The *Ausbau* process has been described by Kloss as following a particular order, now rather dated in view of the absence of references to the internet, or even to technical writing such as the texts of instruction manuals, which we now take more seriously than when he drew up his list. Yet the insights which informed it remain sound:

- *Pre-phase*: simple humour (jokes, amusing news snippets); untutored writing down of folk songs, children's songs, riddles, proverbs, etc.;
- *Phase 1*: lyric verses; humorous poems of all sorts, comic narratives, dialogue in novels and broadcast programmes;
- *Phase 2*: plays; serious prose narratives (not merely the dialogue sections); verse narratives (idyll and epic); short newspaper essays (the beginning of non-fiction literature);
- *Phase 3*: development of non-fiction literature: popular schoolbooks; short original essays (e.g., obituaries) involving the history of the homeland; popular magazines, sermons, radio programmes in simple, matter-of-fact prose;
- *Phase 4*: textbooks on all subjects; longer original works pertaining to the homeland; fully-fledged periodicals and magazines; serious broadcast programmes;
- *Phase 5*: longer original works on the most diversified subject matters; official community and state documents; entire newspapers. (My transl. from Kloss 1978: 52)

Various types of websites could now be added at each of the five phases, while mundane technical writing might well top Phase 5. It should be noted, however, that Kloss's schema involves value judgements about what is 'serious', 'popular', etc., which already open the way to significant disagreement; on top of which his order is particular to the cases he studied and cannot be universalised. Indeed it is unclear how much further one can generalise than to say that, at the present time, and in spite of recent technological developments, print and broadcasting probably remain more influential than anything else in achieving recognition of a new language and determining what its standards will be.

What we are observing with the emergence of World Englishes and the varied reactions to them is, in effect, the process by which all new languages emerge, apart from artificial creations such as Esperanto.[11] When motivated by the desire to claim a distinctive identity, which in modern times has usually meant a national identity, a cultural elite can perform the *Ausbau* tasks necessary to transform the perception of falling standards into the recognition of a new language. It is work that must be done first and foremost through writing, for reasons discussed in earlier sections of this chapter; and only when a critical mass of the educated and powerful within the identity-population itself accept that knowledge actually can be held and transmitted safely in the new language will its status be secure. But even that acceptance is a matter of persuasion and rhetoric, and is not dissociable from the political status of the language.

2.7 OPPRESSION AND IDENTITY

To close this chapter I shall return to the theme of 'them and us' introduced at the outset, in order to point out a queer fact about the nature of national linguistic identity. The more steps 'they' undertake to suppress our identity, the more motivated we are to maintain and even strengthen it. A very striking case in recent times has been that of Catalan (or Catalonian) identity in north-eastern Spain, including Barcelona, and extending into the area of France around Perpignan. Catalan had a flourishing literature in the late middle ages and early Renaissance, but was officially submerged by Castilian from the fifteenth century onwards following the completion of the reconquest of Spain from its Arab rulers and national unification under Ferdinand and Isabella. The Catalan dialects continued to be spoken, and the nineteenth century saw a Romantic revival of the literary language in parallel with that of Provençal in the south of France, which continued into the twentieth century.

But the revival of Catalan as an *Ausbau* language did not begin in earnest until the Spanish Civil War and its aftermath in the 1930s. Catalonia was the centre of the left-wing movement that briefly established an anarcho-syndicalist government in the region in 1936, and it continued to be the centre of resistance to the Franco government over the following decades. For Madrid, the suppression of the Catalan language thus had a clear political-symbolic motivation. For Catalans, in turn, the laws forbidding the use of the Catalan language made it the symbol for all their political and cultural aspirations. Retaining their language, using it despite the laws forbidding it, was a political and cultural imperative. Catalan attained its symbolic force from its suppression by the 'other' power. The efforts of the government in Madrid to promote Castilian had the effect of turning Catalan not just into the weapon of nationalist resistance, but into something giving the *frisson* of excitement that comes from a forbidden act and the defiance of a hated authority.

The 1930s to the mid-1970s were the years of the most intense suppression and the greatest vibrancy of the Catalan language. Its sharp polarisation to Castilian created an internal cultural cohesion, helping bring about the sense that the Catalan people were one in voice and spirit. After the death of Franco in 1975, they had their moment of triumph with the new constitution of 1978, which devolved powers to the seventeen regions of Spain, giving Catalans the right to use Catalan in official contexts for the first time.

Yet reports in the last few years suggest that Catalan has been losing some of its excitement value for young people in Catalonia, who now tend to perceive it as a required school subject – hence mildly 'oppressive' – rather than as a key element of a cultural nationalism. Not having fought for that nationalism, they take it for granted. Some of them prefer to speak Castilian when out of school, and English is popular in certain domains. Meanwhile, in the province of Valencia, to the south of Catalonia, a significant movement has begun to restore official recognition to Valencian – a language (or dialect) with less of an *Ausbau* heritage than Catalan, and, from the point of view of many Catalans, not enough *Abstand* from their language to justify a further split. To the partisans of Valencian, it is, ironically, the Catalans who have become the oppressors. But in view of the evidence that oppression is the mother of identity, it may, paradoxically, be the best gift an established culture can bestow upon an up-and-coming one.

SUGGESTED FURTHER READING

On political aspects of language and identity: Fishman (ed.) (1999), Murray (1999), Schieffelin, Woolard and Kroskrity (eds) (1998), Suleiman (2003), Wodak *et al.* (1999).

On the emergence of new languages: Ammon, Mattheier and Nelde (eds) (2003), Bolton (ed.) (2002), Chan (2002), Schneider (2003), Tsui and Andrew (eds) (2002).

On ideology and language standardisation: Androutsopoulos and Ziegler (eds) (2003), Blank (1996), Bonfiglio (2002), Cheshire and Stein (eds) (1997), Crowley (2003), Deumert and Vandenbussche (eds) (2003), Fisher (1996), Grillo (1989), Kroskrity (ed.) (2000), Linn and McLelland (eds) (2002), Wright (ed.) (2000). A much fuller bibliography on language and identity issues can be found in Joseph (2004a).

On language and print culture: Eisenstein (1993). On Foucault on language: Martín Rojo and Gabilondo Pujol (2002). On Kloss: Wiley (2002).

NOTES

1. Confusingly, the next chapter, Genesis 11, represents a distinct textual tradition, and begins 'And the whole earth was of one language, and of one speech', before recounting how God decided to 'confound their language, that they may not understand one another's speech', to prevent them completing the tower to Heaven they were constructing at the place subsequently known as Babel.

2. Latin continued to be used for books aimed at the international scholarly market.

3. This includes my maternal great-great-grandmother, born in Indiana, though admittedly the fact that she also insisted on flying the German flag outside her house didn't help matters. Her experience was powerful enough to have come down to me in the lore of my mother's family, who, though their origins lay in Alsace and Switzerland, always identified themselves as 'Dutch' – from *deutsch*, their language, rather than from their actual place of origin.

4. For a summary of key issues as they relate to applied linguistics, see Chapter 2, 'The politics of knowledge', of Pennycook (2001).

5. On Gaelic in Scotland see further Gillies ed. (1989), Joseph (2000b, 2004a: 212–15); and on its place in the historical development of Irish nationalism, Crowley (1996).

6. This is the same position taken by Chomsky (1986), but the conclusion Chomsky draws from it is bizarre and untenable. Because languages are ultimately political concepts, he dismisses them as 'unreal'. To this extent he is typical of his generation of linguists, along with DeFrancis. He claims further, however, that the only true reality is therefore what an individual speaker knows internally and intuitively about language (Chomsky calls this 'I-language' because it is individual, internal and intuitive). As shown in Joseph (2000a: 163–7), however, his I-language is in fact an abstraction of exactly the same order as the politically-based 'E[xternal]-languages' he trivialises as unreal.

7. On Bourdieu's views concerning 'cultural capital' see Bourdieu (1986). On Habermas' view that money itself is a development of language, see Habermas (1999: 235).

8. The philosophical approach of my 1987 book was conditioned above all by the (pseudo-) Darwinism then and now implicit in linguistics, which does not take seriously what people believe or say they believe, but only what they can be observed as doing that can be interpreted (by the all-knowing expert observer) as contributing to their (reproductive) interests (where ultimately anything in my interest can be interpreted as giving me some reproductive advantage). I now think that what people believe is ultimately more powerful than what I, from some imaginary objective position, might interpret as being in their self-interest.

9. For an exception which I believe supports this point because it seems so entirely dated in its class snobbishness, see the very interesting Sélincourt (1926).

10. For a survey of World English(es) and issues surrounding them, see Brutt-Griffler (2002). Erling (2005) offers an insightful critique of the various attempts at conceiving of world or international English.

11. Though even in the case of Esperanto a split occurred in the early twentieth century between purists and reformers, giving rise to the new language Ido in a process not all that dissimilar from the one just described.

Chapter 3

The social politics of language choice and linguistic correctness

3.1 HEARERS AS SPEAKERS

The preceding chapter looked into the political aspects of how different languages come to be recognised, as well as into obstacles to such recognition. This chapter will be concerned with the closely related question of the choices individuals make from among the ways of speaking available in their environment, with the focus on the political motivations and ramifications of their choices.

In §2.5 the point was made that, in traditional Christian doctrine, language differences do not really matter, being superficial in comparison with that inner language of knowledge that exists before any human language and is the same for all. As St Augustine (354–430) said in his Sermon on the Nativity of St John the Baptist:

> Here is an inner word, conceived in the heart – it is trying to get out, it wants to be spoken. You consider who it is to be spoken to. Have you met a Greek? You seek the Greek word. A Latin? You seek the Latin word. A Carthaginian? You seek the Punic word. Remove the diversity of listeners and the inner word itself, as conceived in the heart, is neither Greek, nor Latin, nor Punic, nor of any language. (Augustine 1863: 1304–5, my transl.)[1]

This might be considered an early version of Giles's Speech Accommodation Theory (see Shepard, Giles and LePoire 2001) or Bell's (1984) 'audience design', except that, whereas Augustine accords no significance to the choice of language, modern analysis sees it as important evidence that 'speaker' and 'hearer' are not polarly opposed roles. For any utterance, the hearer is not merely a passive recipient, but is partly responsible for the actual form the utterance takes, since speakers normally adjust what they say to suit the social–political reaction they anticipate from their audience. My choice of which language to speak, and of how to speak it – in the standard way, in a way marked for region, social class, educational level, generation, etc. – positions me vis-à-vis my interlocutors, whether I intend for it to do so or not. If the difference between us is wide, this fact can be very obvious, but it often takes much subtler forms, and can be masked by strong cultural forces, as described in the next section.

3.2 THE DENIAL OF HETEROGLOSSIA

Multilingualism and linguistic variation have characterised human societies at least since the time, long before history, when exogamy began to be practised. In the many cultures which require that marriage be with someone from another tribe, with women going to live with their husband's people, each wife's arrival adds to their multilingualism. Not only does she bring her own language with her, but over time, she learns their language – now hers as well – but speaks it in a way that reflects the influence of her mother tongue, plus the sorts of changes that characterise second-language use generally. She thus adds to the variation in the way her second language is spoken. Although most of the changes she introduces will disappear with her, some may spread and survive, first of all among her own children, on whom she is the first strong linguistic influence. As not every bride comes from a different outside tribe, there will be more support for the changes if a number of her own kinswomen have married in.

Even where exogamy is not a cultural requirement, it is proverbially true that opposites attract, whether or not there is a genetic-Darwinian basis to it in the reproductive advantage that comes from the mixing of different gene groups. If you have ever experienced hearing your mother tongue spoken with a foreign accent and perceiving it as sexy – and who hasn't, unless their mother tongue is so little known that few outsiders have ever attempted to speak it – you have heard that primal call of the exotic that guarantees that multilingualism and variation must always be the norm, *de facto* if not *de jure*.

Why not *de jure* as well? Mainly because of the strongly felt desire, discussed in §2.1, for each nation to have its own language, binding its members to one another as an in-group while also keeping all out-groups maximally distinct. The whole concept of 'a language' demands denial of the primal diversity of variation. The concept of a 'national language' further demands the denial of multilingualism, which is scarcely less primal. Perhaps the Coleridgean 'suspension of disbelief' is more appropriate than 'denial', because people never stop being aware of variation, even if their awareness simply takes the form of looking down on anything that deviates from the norm as bad or incorrect. And here is where the politics clearly enter – for whatever is identified as the good or correct form of the language empowers those who have it as part of their linguistic repertoire, and disempowers those who don't.

Even linguistics, the self-proclaimed scientific study of language, has tended over its history to treat languages as though they were unitary entities, either ignoring variation or relegating it to a secondary plane. A critical moment in the development of modern structural linguistics came in 1959, when Charles A. Ferguson (1921–98) introduced the concept of 'diglossia', originally with this narrow definition:

> a relatively stable language situation in which, in addition to the primary dialects of the language (which may include a standard or regional standards), there is a very divergent, highly codified (often grammatically more complex) superposed variety, the vehicle of a large and respected body of written literature, either of an

LIBRARY, UNIVERSITY OF CHELSEA

earlier period or in another speech community, which is learned largely by formal education and is used for most written and formal spoken purposes but is not used by any sector of the community for ordinary conversation. (Ferguson 1972 [1959]: 244–5)

The importance of Ferguson's article was that it put cultural politics right at the heart of how a language was to be defined and analysed. The core cases he examined were Arabic, Modern Greek, Swiss German and Haitian Creole. Other examples he cited were Tamil, Chinese, and Latin in relation to the emerging Romance languages in the Middle Ages and Renaissance. He specifically excluded the standard-language-plus-dialects configuration familiar from Western European languages as not encompassing the same level of 'divergence' either structurally or functionally. Standard French is used for 'ordinary conversation' in France, where it is not therefore in a diglossic relation which non-standard French dialects. In Haiti, on the other hand, only Haitian Creole is used in ordinary conversation, and therefore it *is* in a diglossic relation with Standard French. In such a case he called Haitian Creole the L ('low') and Standard French the H ('high') language.

Within a few years, however, Ferguson's narrow definition had been effectively abandoned. Those who used it found that the differences of linguistic structure were of trivial importance compared to the cultural–political factors implicit in the functional differentiation of L and H. The new 'broad' definition of diglossia, asserted notably by Fishman (1967), encompassed every case of a multilingual or multidialectal community where the varieties occupy different functional domains and have different levels of prestige. Subsequently it has become clearer that every linguistic community fits this description – 'monolingual' communities are a figment of the imagination, demanding the marginalisation or outright ignoring of anyone who speaks something other than the majority language, or speaks the majority language in a way that diverges from the general norm, or both. In the words of Patten (2003: 358),

There may be a few countries that can claim not to have any settled linguistic minorities – Japan, Korea, and Iceland are sometimes offered as examples – but even they are host to second-language teachers, foreign military personnel, refugees, and so on, that introduce an element of linguistic diversity into their societies.

Japan in fact has at least one clearly 'settled' minority, the indigenous Ainu.

A much more radical proposal than Ferguson's had been formulated 25 years earlier, then fallen into oblivion. Mikhail M. Bakhtin (1895–1975), writing in 1934–5, described the normal condition of language as being one of *heteroglossia*, where a multiplicity of different ways of speaking are constantly intermingling with each other. The 'unitary language' of both lay and linguistic discourse

is not something given but is always in essence posited – and at every moment of its linguistic life it is opposed to the realities of heteroglossia. But at the same time it makes its real presence felt as a force for overcoming this heteroglossia, imposing specific limits to it … (Bahktin 1981: 270)

In Bakhtin's Marxist schema, the tension between the unitary language and heteroglossia constitutes the arena of the class struggle where voices and signs are concerned
(this will be discussed further in §4.1).

Another powerful factor in this perception is writing, which, as shown in §2.3,
plays a crucial role in the historical recognition of languages. Written language has
the ongoing effect of effacing many of the levels at which variation in spoken
language is manifested – accent in particular, but also voice quality and intonation,
a level with particular importance for the signalling and interpretation of identity.
As you read these lines, unless you know me very well, the voice you hear speaking
the words in your mind isn't my voice, but yours, or some mental creation of yours
speaking in whatever accent, voice quality and intonation you choose for it. If you
heard me speaking the words orally, you wouldn't have this freedom which the
written word allows you. My voice would impose my particular variants.

But why do we generally perceive language as unitary rather than heteroglossic?
The reason is that our perception of language is, like all perception, only partial. If I
were equally focused on everything that was going on around me at any moment –
something impossible to imagine, let alone do – I wouldn't actually be 'focusing on'
or 'aware of' anything at all. Within language as in perception generally, focus
is selective, and usually aimed at one or the other of what linguists identify as the
'functions' of language: communication, representation, expression, phatic com-
munion, performances of various kinds. If we come away from a verbal exchange
with the perception that communication has taken place, then we perceive that we
have spoken 'the same language', regardless of how much linguistic variation a third
party might observe between us.

Such is our focus most of the time, even though we clearly do take in and interpret
much more than our interlocutor's 'message'. We make judgements about their
origins, social standing, education, upbringing – in short, their *identity*. Sometimes
we are quite aware of these judgements, yet even then, if we are left with the
impression of having understood each other, that communicative function can
occupy a central enough place that we suspend disbelief in non-variation and think
in terms of our having 'the same language'.

3.3 THE ROLE OF EDUCATION

If language and politics were a country, education would be its capital, the great
centralised and centralising metropolis that everyone passes through, from which the
country is run and where its future course is determined. On one level this has always
been true – for insofar as the politics of language, especially of 'correct' or 'standard'
language, are bound up with writing, they depend on a technology that demands
intense and sustained teaching before it is mastered. Even traditional master-and-
apprentice systems in arts that didn't necessarily entail writing still involved the
passing down of a specialised lexicon and discourse that both contained the
knowledge of the art and signalled one's mastery of it. The great classical languages,
Latin, Greek, Hebrew, Arabic, Syriac, Chaldean, Chinese, Sanskrit, Tamil and the

rest, were maintained and learned through formal systems of education bound up with a combination of religious practice and civil administrative practice, over the long centuries in which they were conceived of not even as the 'high' language in a diglossia, but as language *tout court*.

The emergence of vernacular standards in the European Renaissance depended entirely on the 'transferable skills' of people trained in reading and writing the classical tongues. Only very slowly did the new vernacular standards find their way into the curriculum, starting in the eighteenth century, getting the upper hand in the nineteenth, and finally relegating the classical languages to a marginal position in the twentieth – though it was still the case in the early decades of the twentieth century that for a doctorate in some continental universities one had to produce a second thesis in Latin in addition to the main thesis in the national language.

Starting in the 1860s, and running to near completion by the 1890s, universal education spread throughout Europe and the Americas, and eventually to their colonies. This transformed the very nature of education, from being a process reserved for a select few to one which everyone underwent, though to differing degrees, and through systems that never achieved the aims of social equality that motivated those who founded them. By the 1960s even the great Paolo Freire (1921–97), guru of the liberating potential of education, had to admit that, once educated and liberated, the formerly oppressed would become oppressors in their turn (see Freire 1970: 27). In the same decade Foucault (see §2.5, p. 34) popularised the view that 'knowledge' is itself a manifestation of power, and by the 1970s Pierre Bourdieu (1930–2002) and Jean-Claude Passeron were treating education as a system aimed essentially at reproducing existing social class differences (Bourdieu and Passeron 1977), an analysis far too well supported by their data to be dismissed as mere ideological positioning.

Bourdieu (1991) would argue that language plays the central role in the social reproduction that education carries out. Looking at regional differences in French in relation to the standard language, Bourdieu writes of the 'intimidation' felt by the student who has come to Paris from the provinces to do university studies. Bourdieu enquires into what exactly this intimidation is and where it exists. He describes it as a 'symbolic violence' that does not imply any 'act of intimidation' on the part of the Standard French speakers whose reactions to the provincial dialect make the newcomer feel intimidated. Bourdieu suggests as well that the non-standard speaker co-creates the intimidation, in the sense that it

> can only be exerted on a person predisposed … to feel it, whereas others will ignore it. It is already partly true to say that the cause of the timidity lies in the relation between the situation or the intimidating person (who may deny any intimidating intention) and the person intimidated, or rather, between the social conditions of production of each of them. (Bourdieu 1991: 51)

Some individuals from the provinces, in other words, will remain unaware of any reactions to which their dialect gives rise among Standard French speakers, in which case no intimidation can be said to exist. But they are the exception. Most highly-educated French people end up speaking Standard French, if not exclusively then in addition to their home dialect, from which one can infer that the feeling of intimidation is widespread.

Here then is one model for understanding how the spread of universal education encouraged the levelling out of dialect differences and helped make the 'national language', that dream of the sixteenth century, into a reality not just for a small elite but eventually for most of the population. Education created the necessary conditions for intimidation in those speakers who were inclined to feel it. Another, quite different model has however been put forward by the Anglo-German historian Eric Hobsbawm. Focusing precisely on the late nineteenth century, the period when universal education came into being, Hobsbawm notes that one social class in particular benefited from it: the lower middle class. The children of the small tradesmen and artisans who made up this class could, by passing examinations, enter into civil and colonial service and white-collar professions; and as they ascended from the lower middle class its ranks were refilled with children of the working class making their way up by the same process.

> The classes which stood or fell by the official use of the written vernacular were the socially modest but educated middle strata, which included those who acquired lower middle-class status precisely by virtue of occupying non-manual jobs that required schooling. (Hobsbawm 1990: 117)

These are also the people who become the mainstay of nationalism – not just by active flag-waving on symbolic occasions, but daily in the banal ways pointed to by Billig (1995), including their use of 'proper language' and their insistence on its norms, even in conversation with their own children. Hobsbawm believes that 'national identity' in the sense we usually think of it really goes back to Victorian shopkeepers and clerks who envied the feeling of class belonging enjoyed by both the upper classes, with their clubs and aristocratic titles, and the workers, who could locate their identity in socialism. Neither the aristocrats nor the workers needed education to maintain their position; neither worried about their language in the way that the middle class had to do, at least that very substantial portion of the middle class whose standing rested on their command of standard written and spoken usage.

There is not necessarily a contradiction between Bourdieu's and Hobsbawm's accounts. Both are describing how language shift toward the standard occurs among individuals with socioeconomic aspirations. But Bourdieu, in his structuralist-derived discourse aimed at understanding how our apparent 'choices' are guided by social forces, focuses on 'the social conditions of production' as embodied in our *habitus*, the dispositions acquired from infancy onward that incline us toward certain feelings and reactions. The forces which this model leads Bourdieu to perceive are negative ones, sticks rather than carrots. Hobsbawm, meanwhile, is furthering his recovery from Marxism by relocating language shift from 'conditions of production' (Bourdieu's term above, which by 1990 Hobsbawm would reject as vulgar-materialist reductionism) toward choices that individuals make, motivated positively by carrots that aren't exclusively economic. And it is positive forces that motivate those choices. Yet from the actual experience all of us have had of making important choices, we know that they are neither wholly determined by social forces nor made in isolation from them, and that both positive and negative considerations – carrots and sticks – play a role. Both accounts, in other words, may be right simultaneously.

By the same token, in certain circumstances the 'intimidation' and 'violence' through which the standard language is spread and enforced are not merely symbolic. During the first seven or eight decades of universal education, British and French children from Celtic speaking regions, or the French Basque country, and the children of Roma (Gypsies) and other minority groups whose languages were distant from English or French, were forbidden from speaking their mother tongue at school and were subjected to painful physical punishment if caught doing so. This matter will be considered further in the next section, but for now it is important to note that the education system provided the one mechanism through which shift to the national language could be effected. Children were in the hands of the institution at least five days a week, and there were few legal constraints on what the institution could do with them, stick-wise. Carrot-wise, their local communities were generally in step with the nationalising agenda, proud of the nation and its overseas empire, and certain that prosperity and progress lay with national language and identity, poverty and backwardness with the local.

Today, the schools in these same areas are doing their part – not necessarily very well or enthusiastically, and with varying degrees of government support – to rescue the minority languages they did so much to eradicate, but the main battle line has shifted to what it is elsewhere in Britain and France: standard versus non-standard English and French. Here, as in every country that has been a magnet for immigration in recent years, new issues of language choice have also come onto the agenda – the example of Latvia from §1.5 is a case in point. Without exception, education is at the centre of whatever language-and-politics debate arises. The reason for that should now be clear: it is through education that language and national identity are created, performed and above all reproduced. George Orwell famously wrote in *Nineteen Eighty-Four*: 'Who controls the past controls the future: who controls the present controls the past' (Orwell 1989 [1949]: 37). To which may be added: Who controls the schools controls the past, through the teaching of history; structures the present, through the powerful hierarchisation of individuals and communities entailed by language choice and the enforcement of language standards; and shapes the future, by shaping, or even by failing to shape, those who will inhabit it.

3.4 LINGUISTIC IMPERIALISM

The preceding section described how language functioned in the early decades of universal education in Europe and the Americas in the late nineteenth and early twentieth centuries. In the colonies of these same countries, the situation was complicated by the fact that for the language of education, a choice had to be made between the colonial language and the local vernacular, particularly if the latter was a language with a long literary tradition, as in China or India. Colonial language policies varied from period to period and at times became highly politicised in the colonies themselves, and more rarely in the legislatures of the colonial powers. But in general it is true to say that the policies of France and Britain represented two extremes, the former generally promoting the use of the colonial language in education, the latter the use of native vernaculars, with other colonial powers falling somewhere in between. Portugal was on the French end of the spectrum for most of its colonial history, while Spain followed a more pro-indigenous policy until the nineteenth century, at which point language policy both in the remaining Spanish colonies and in those that gained independence became increasingly 'assimilationist' (see Joseph 2000c).

This may seem surprising in view of the much publicised critique of English 'linguistic imperialism' led by Robert Phillipson, discussed below, but actual, in-depth study of Colonial Office documents, of which the most detailed is Evans (2003), shows beyond a doubt that, apart from brief periods which function as the exception that proves the rule, the British colonial administration in London did not support having colonial subjects educated in English. There are various ways of interpreting this fact, of which the most malign is perhaps also the most realistic: they reckoned that, if colonials mastered English, it would be difficult to deny them the administrative jobs in the colonial service that otherwise went to young men from Britain's own lower middle class. Again contrary to popular belief, for most of colonial history the colonies did not bring great wealth to the European powers but actually cost them money to run, with some spectacular exceptions like the Belgian Congo after the development of inflatable tyres accelerated the demand for rubber. The principal motives for the powers to maintain and expand their colonies were, first, to stay a step ahead of the other powers, and second, to provide opportunities for young men that they could not have had at home.[2] As Evans shows in the case of Hong Kong, the British government finally relented and provided English-medium education for Chinese children only after vehement and sustained insistence from the Chinese community, which realised full well what the value of English was in political and economic terms, and why the British were inclined to keep it to themselves.

Since the break-up of the European empires, the situation has changed surprisingly little where language is concerned. Indeed it has changed rather more in the old colonial powers themselves, as the result of large-scale immigrations since WWII, mainly from former colonies, South Asia (often via East Africa) and the Caribbean in the case of Britain, and North Africa in the case of France. Replicating their colonial policies of a century ago, Britain has been more inclined than France to support the use of mother tongues other than English in schools – though in 2005 Britain introduced an English proficiency requirement for new citizens, for the first time in history. In most former colonies the choice continues to be between local vernacular and the post-colonial language, with the latter, if it isn't English, increasingly in competition with English.

The point of the 'linguistic imperialism' critique is that this choice is not a fair one.

It forces untold millions across great swathes of Asia and Africa, and lesser numbers in the Americas and Oceania, to make a choice between their cultural heritage and their children's survival. This, the critique maintains, is not a choice at all. The power of the great world languages and cultures, particularly the English language and American culture, exerts a hegemony that forces the hand of people in poorer countries. If they believe they are making a free choice, then they are suffering from a typical example of what Marx called 'false consciousness'.

Not surprising, then, that the critique itself should have originated, not from third-world scholars (themselves likely victims of the false consciousness, according to the critique), but from a reformed 'imperialist', Phillipson, whose 1992 book did more than any other single work to put language and politics at the centre of the applied linguistics and English language teaching agenda. It argues that all education in a language other than the student's mother tongue is imperialistic, even if the motive of the educator is to help students rise out of poverty and obtain career opportunities: '[I]ndividuals with possibly the most altruistic motives for their work may nevertheless function in an imperialist structure. This might for instance apply to anyone concerned with educational aid ...' (Phillipson 1992: 46). Tove Skutnabb-Kangas, Phillipson's wife and research partner, expresses herself even more strongly: 'Schools are every day committing linguistic genocide' (Skutnabb-Kangas 2000: x). This English linguistic imperialism is embedded in the very structure of the education system and even the set-up of the classroom. The teacher, as the sole native English speaker or at least the English expert, stands before a roomful of students, who are seated (therefore in a lower position), and whose mother tongue is treated not as an asset but an obstacle to the goal of learning the 'valuable' language. Thus: 'the dominance of English is asserted and maintained by the establishment and continuous reconstitution of structural and cultural inequalities between English and other languages' (Phillipson 1992: 47). Phillipson has coined the word 'linguicism' to describe this form of inequality, its form echoing that of racism, sexism and the like. He defines linguicism as: 'ideologies, structures, and practices which are used to legitimate, effectuate, and reproduce an unequal division of power and resources between groups which are defined on the basis of language' (ibid.: 47). Phillipson variously calls English linguistic imperialism 'one example of' linguicism or 'a sub-type of' it. He makes clear that it is not limited to schools with 'English only' policies. Even multilingual schools are guilty of linguicism so long as they do not treat all languages equally – for instance, if mother-tongue education predominates in the earlier years, with the students making the transition to English in secondary school as preparation for university: 'Linguicism occurs ... if there is a policy of supporting several languages, but if priority is given in teacher training, curriculum development, and school timetables to one language' (ibid.). The initial response of the English Language Teaching (ELT) establishment to Phillipson's arguments in the 1980s was to ignore them on the grounds that, as ELT professionals, they were simply practising a well-established battery of techniques that research had shown to be most effective, and not 'doing politics'. By the time of the 1992 book Phillipson was puncturing this defence by further accusing ELT practitioners of hiding behind a cloak of 'professionalism', a term of abuse for Phillipson, who defined it as

> seeing methods, techniques, and procedures followed in ELT, including the theories of language learning and teaching adhered to, as sufficient for understanding and analysing language learning ... Anglocentricity and professionalism legitimate English as the dominant language ... (ibid.: 48)

In Phillipson's view, issues having to do with the form of Standard English to be taught in the classroom are bound up with cultural and linguistic imperialism as propagated under the guise of professionalism, as are issues of the method to be used in teaching. He gives the example of audiolingualism, which, he argues, by going against the tide of cultures whose traditional educational practices are heavily writing dependent, reinforces a linguicist structure which implies that our modern, expert professional practices are alone good, and your traditional ones worthless.

Phillipson grounds his critique within the Cultural Imperialism theory put forward by Galtung (1979). In this theory, imperialism is a relationship by which one society can dominate another, through four mechanisms: exploitation, penetration, fragmentation and marginalisation. Taking over the notion of *hegemony* from the Marxist theorist Antonio Gramsci (1891–1937), Galtung argues that these mechanisms do not have to be knowingly pursued by the dominators. The structure of relations may be such that the process takes place automatically – just as Phillipson maintains is the case with English language teaching. Galtung divides the world into dominating Centre and dominated Peripheries, but notes that the situation is actually more complex. As Phillipson explains,

> There are centres of power in the Centre and in the Periphery. The Peripheries in both the Centre and the Periphery are exploited by their respective Centres. Elites in the Centres of both the Centre and the Periphery are linked by shared interests within each type of imperialism and, it is claimed here, by language. (Phillipson 1992: 52)

The UK, for instance, is obviously a Centre country, but contains its own linguistic Periphery, including speakers of the Celtic languages and the languages of the Roma and more recent immigrant communities. Malaysia is a Periphery country, but contains its own linguistic Centre in the form of Malaysians with a mastery of English. These Anglophone Malaysians have in many cases gone to a Centre country for their higher education, then come home to 'exploit' their countrymen on the basis of their superior knowledge of English, which gives them a shared interest with the English-speaking Centre countries. From the Cultural Imperialism point of view, they are the enemy within.

But a phalanx of talented and eloquent scholars from the Periphery have lined up to reject Phillipson's model – which after all depicts them as suffering from a false consciousness at best, and at worst as traitors to their own cultures – or at least to propose amending the model in ways that still cut the legs out from under it. In the views of Bisong (1995), Makoni (1995) and Rajagapolan (1999a, b),[3] the ongoing existence of linguistic imperialism is a myth, an invidious myth that embodies a kind of imperialism every bit as bad as the one it purports to critique. Phillipson's notion that people in third-world countries are the objects of hegemonic forces that make it impossible for them to exercise any free choice, though intended 'for their good', is patronising in the extreme. By reducing them to pawns of a centre-controlled system it actually dehumanises them. Recapitulating anthropological views that were commonplace until the early twentieth century, it depicts a world in which only those belonging to the Centre are fully human agents with rationality and free will, while the peoples of the Periphery are mere patients, subject to the will of their masters in the Centre. Phillipson permits them to 'choose' only if the choice is of their traditional language – *his* choice for them – whereas if they choose a world language (or a more geographically restricted language that nevertheless is 'bigger' than the traditional one of their locale), they have been co-opted by the forces of the Centre, which is acting through them.

The particular shape of Phillipson's hegemony argument, denying as it does any possibility that someone from the Periphery could legitimately contest it, would seem to create an impasse such that one has either to accept Phillipson's worldview or reject it out of hand. Initially people in ELT and applied linguistics did indeed find themselves lining up on one side or the other. However, an alternative has emerged in the work of Canagarajah (1999a, b). He accepts Phillipson's view of a hegemonic linguistic imperialism that needs to be undone. But he rejects the notion that the only way to do this is to reject 'big' languages in favour of small traditional ones (or Phillipson's later suggestion, Esperanto). What Phillipson fails to see, in Canagarajah's view, is that people of the Periphery do not simply receive the Centre language in a passive way. Rather, they alter it – they speak it with an accent, which is to say with phonological carry-over (or interference) from their mother tongue, as well as with lexical and grammatical carry-over and with other 'interlanguage' features that cannot be traced back to the mother tongue, but that nevertheless distinguish their use of the language from that of its Centre 'home'. This active intervention in the form of the language is what Canagarajah calls *resistance*. Through it, the people of the Periphery *appropriate* the language, making it their own, while also gaining the power to use the language to further their own anti-Centre political agenda in the international arena, which they would never be able to do in their traditional language, restricted as it is to their own people.

A question to which Canagarajah's model gives rise is this: if someone speaks the L2 with an accent and other features distinguishing it from the Centre variety, but with no intention of 'resisting' – if, for instance, they have an accent despite a strongly felt desire to speak 'like a native', and experience their accent as a handicap they cannot overcome – does it still make sense to speak of 'resistance' and 'appropriation' in such a case? The question arises because the word 'resistance', when used in the context of human affairs, normally implies a wilful and deliberate political stance. It has no such implications in the context of resistance to disease, or electrical resistance, or water-resistant material or a problem that resists solution; but where language is concerned these do not seem apposite metaphors. In my view, the crucial point is that, if a whole community 'resists' the language in Canagarajah's sense – regardless of whether all, some or even none of them is doing so deliberately or is even aware of doing it – they have appropriated it for themselves at least in terms of linguistic distance (*Abstand*), and helped lay the ground for others eventually to make the political claim that their form of the language is a distinctive, appropriated, resistant one.

Canagarajah's approach does not make 'linguistic imperialism' disappear as a problem. But neither does it reduce the problem to an either–or choice between a Periphery language that alone can belong to Periphery people and express their thought and culture, and a Centre language that must always belong to the Centre. Nor does Canagarajah dehumanise Periphery people by denying that they have choice and agency. Perhaps most importantly, the linguistic imperialism model, by standing so aloof from the actual choices being made (whether freely or hegemonically) by Periphery people, has little chance of actually helping smaller languages survive. Canagarajah's model gives Peripheral peoples credit for having the courage to resist (whether intentionally or not) and the wit to do it in ways subtle enough to elude detection by people like Phillipson. This allows them a concept of ownership of the language (or significantly extends that concept) in a way that helps them articulate, in arenas beyond the local, what resources they need to keep their local language surviving – even if they also desire, for themselves and their children, the advantages that education in a larger language offers.

A different angle of attack on Phillipson's linguistic imperialism thesis has come from the Marxist linguist Holborow (1999). She targets all its blatant flaws on mostly the same grounds as non-Marxist critics such as Davies (1996), but adds to it the fact that, from her perspective, Phillipson's programme for combating linguistic imperialism is hopelessly reactionary. 'Phillipson's centre-periphery, north-south categorization', she writes, '… locks him into an anti-imperialist strategy of nationalism and the promotion of national languages' (Holborow 1999: 77), and nationalism is the traditional obstacle to social-class solidarity. Besides, implying that the spread of English will cause people to think in an Anglo-American way commits what for a modern Marxist is the ultimate post-modernist fallacy of attributing creative power to language. Holborow points out that language spread is more the result than the cause of cultural change, that the 'invading' language is more likely to change to accommodate the new culture than the other way round, and that the 'victims' of 'linguistic imperialism' are perfectly capable of using the imposed language as one of the most powerful tools for their own liberation from both imperial and class-based oppression.

3.5 LANGUAGE RIGHTS

Related to the linguistic imperialism critique is the idea of *language rights*, starting with a basic human right for a community, and perhaps an individual, to be allowed to use their mother tongue in public functions and to have their children educated in it, even though it is not the official or majority language of the place where they live. It is quite a recent concept, and actual language rights enshrined in law are few. As has often been pointed out, what are usually referred to as 'language rights' are more precisely *claims* for such rights, claims which imply that the rights exist in natural law and should therefore be enshrined in constitutional or statute law.

There are several reasons why such claims are a relatively recent phenomenon. Previously, linguistic minority groups tended to be more concerned with achieving either political autonomy (and perhaps re-unification with their mother country, if geographically adjacent) or full political and cultural integration into the majority society. Also, while the rights of groups in matters of language might be taken seriously, those of isolated individuals were not: it seemed to follow from democratic principles that it was up to individuals to conform to the majority, not the other way round. Finally, where education was concerned, the unspoken consensus seemed to be that the role of public schooling was to maintain the national culture and induct everyone into it. Foreign cultures would be studied as subject matter, but their ways of doing things, including language, could not be part of an education system funded by the taxpayer. If minority groups wanted education in their own language, they would have to pay for it themselves.

But the logical flaw in this last position played a significant part in shifting government views on minority education. For the fact is that members of minority groups are also taxpayers, and as such have the right within a democracy to a voice in how public education is conducted. Then, too, there is the fact that a particular 'minority' within a given country might not be a minority at all within a given *part* of that country. Scots is a minority language in the UK, but not in Scotland. Arguably the same is true of Welsh in Wales, even if less than 50 per cent of the population actually speak Welsh – but here the issue becomes complicated by questions of who is 'really Welsh' and who isn't, e.g. recent immigrants or even Welsh-born people whose parents moved to Wales from England.

With education the relevant focus is actually closer still, at the local level, and in any locale where a significant portion of the people who furnish the tax base want their children educated in Welsh, the current governmental ideology of increasing devolution would make it difficult to deny that they should be provided with public education in the language of their choice. And if the language in question is Punjabi, the same logic applies. The fact that it is not a 'heritage' language of the place is irrelevant – languages belong to people, not to places, and Punjabi is the heritage language of Welsh Punjabis.

More recently, the concept of language rights has been extended beyond education to cover every interchange involving a governmental or public agency. Until the 1970s, governments around the world operated on the basis that their official language or languages, as set by law or custom, would be used in dealing with the public.[4] Any member of the public who didn't know the official language, whether a recent immigrant, a deaf-mute, an aboriginal, a minority group member or a colonial subject, had to get an advocate to deal with the government on their behalf. Trials in which the defendant could not comprehend the language of the court proceedings have been commonplace throughout history, in Centre countries as well as Periphery ones, and are still a memory of just some twenty years' distance in places such as Hong Kong, where Chinese was not accorded any legal status until 1974 and English was the sole language of court proceedings until the 1980s.

Today, throughout most of the world, the presence of official courtroom interpreters is a matter of course and a defendant's uncontroversial right – though it is an extremely tricky business, given that differences between legal systems sometimes need to be bridged, and that the translation of implicit nuances in testimony is fraught with legal risks. Cooke (1995) offers a compelling study of the intricacies involved in the translation of a legal decision of the Australian courts in a case involving the killing of a white policeman by an aboriginal man. Only after a lengthy process of preparing initial translations into the aboriginal tongue and then having native speakers translate them back into English did it become apparent that there was a hugely important linguistic–cultural disparity: the English terms 'guilty' and 'not guilty' were being rendered in the aboriginal language by terms that meant the defendant was a 'good person' or 'bad person', rather than whether they had committed the particular crime with which they were charged.

The courtroom is probably the place where 'language rights' have proceeded the fastest because it is where the government potentially exercises its most oppressive power over individuals, sentencing them to life, or death. As the stakes lessen, so does the feeling that it is incumbent upon government to cater to individuals' linguistic needs. The City of Edinburgh Council offers an Interpretation and Translation Service that currently 'provides interpretation and translation facilities in approximately 40 community languages as well as Braille, tape, large print and British Sign Language'. It publishes its official information in a selection of these languages (notably Arabic, Bengali, Chinese, Italian, Japanese, Punjabi, Spanish, Turkish and Urdu) chosen according to the topic. The Council also provides education in Gaelic for children from nursery through to Higher Grade Gaelic in secondary school; for although Gaelic no longer has monolingual speakers, its value as a symbol of national identity remains high. There are, however, well over 100 languages spoken natively by smaller numbers of residents of the city. In this respect Edinburgh is typical of cities across Europe, the Americas and Oceania. A *de facto* official-language economy operates that will likely see the number of official languages expand in coming years, though this could change abruptly for political reasons, for instance if immigration and asylum policy should become even more controversial than at present.

In the last ten years some innovative perspectives on language rights have emerged from the work of two Canadian philosophers, Taylor (1994) and Kymlicka (2001, see also Kymlicka and Grin 2003, Kymlicka and Patten eds 2003). Kymlicka approaches the problem of language rights as one would expect a moral philosopher to do – by assuming that justice is the goal of any rational society, and enquiring into what justice would consist of where minority language speakers are concerned. Following the method developed by John Rawls (1921–2002) in his *Theory of Justice* (1971),[5] Kymlicka starts from the position that the most just solution would be equal language rights for all groups within a nation-state, in every sphere (education, government, broadcasting etc.). He then attempts to find a justification for any exception – cases where a given minority would itself benefit (along with the majority) by having its language *not* accorded full status. These would include cases where minority communities are too dispersed to form a coherent polity or identity group, and where moving to the majority language would actually allow them to pursue their political interests more effectively and to integrate into the society without significant harm to an identity that is unsustainable anyway.

But even admitting such cases, Kymlicka concludes that justice nevertheless demands multilingual language rights in every nation. A monolingual policy could never be justified in Rawlsian terms. Yet Kymlicka concedes that justice is in fact not the principal aim in every nation's development of a language policy. Alongside considerations of justice go ones of security that cannot be dismissed as irrational. Many Eastern European countries, including Latvia (discussed in §1.5 above) and others surveyed in Daftary and Grin (eds) (2003), have concerns about the survival of their independence that are at least partly legitimate, and where the major cause for concern is the existence within the country of a powerful minority that identifies itself with another state – usually the Russian Federation in this part of the world, but others as well, such as Hungary for the substantial Hungarian population of Romania.

Kymlicka's model allows for a moral balance between the interests of justice and security, to a surprising degree. He defends language 'purification' laws, such as the French Loi Toubon of 1994 restricting the use of English in advertising, broadcasting, the names of shops etc., or the laws passed in Nazi Germany aimed at ridding the language of foreign borrowings (on which see the extraordinary Klemperer 1949), on the grounds that they are a legitimate, and seemingly harmless, means of reinforcing the identity of the nation. The problem is that, in actual fact, language purification laws have always come in tandem with movements for racial purification, in the most extreme cases through genocide. True, this is guilt by association – purging the German language of words with non-Germanic roots cannot be equated with gas chambers. Yet it has proven to be such a reliable symptom of the racist mentality that one has to wonder how moral it is to ignore it or even accept it as Kymlicka would have us do.

Other questionable aspects of Kymlicka's position include the fact that the language rights of 'indigenous' minorities (the descendants of long-ago immigrants) turn out on the whole to have a stronger claim to moral legitimacy than do those of recent immigrants, which again is disturbing even if, logically, it can be shown to make sense within Rawls's model of justice. Part of the problem is that today we are much less inclined to think of nation-states as quasi-natural entities that are not open to question, as was the general way of thinking from WWI until the collapse of the Soviet bloc. Nations remain however the cornerstone of Kymlicka's thinking, and his conclusions depend upon our acceptance of their fixity.

These comments are not meant to diminish the importance of Kymlicka's work. He has made philosophers take seriously the political and moral issues surrounding language rights for the first time, and has given sociolinguists and applied linguists a new framework within which to think and talk about them. That is, after all, the philosopher's job – it is not to endorse comfortable positions or provide unchallengeable answers.

In the end, where does the current discourse of language rights leave us? 'Insecure' nations, meaning those with powerful minorities, seem to be morally entitled to suppress them in order to preserve the nation-state. Secure nations, however, are morally obliged to institute multilingual language rights for at least their coherent indigenous minorities, though not for just anyone who demands such rights. One wonders whether the outcome of this position will not be a never-ending circle, where the secure nations empower their minorities, only to find that the result is a feeling of insecurity (discovered and nurtured by the popular press, if history is any guide) among the previously secure majority, producing a moral obligation to backtrack on minority language rights, not just for the perceived security of the nation-state but to protect the minorities themselves from a political backlash. It does not seem like the ideal recipe for the long-term co-existence of languages and cultures, yet neither is it clear that a superior alternative is in the offing.

3.6 THE LINGUISTIC PERFORMANCE OF MINORITY IDENTITIES

Recent work on linguistic identity treats it as a 'performative' discourse, in which identities – those 'imagined communities', following Anderson (1991) – emerge between the 'claims' which we make (or indeed perform) in speaking, and the interpretations which others make of our claims. As a group of sociologists have asserted,

> National identities are not essentially fixed or given but depend critically on the claims which people make in different contexts and at different times. The processes of identity rest not simply on the claims made but on how such claims are received, that is validated or rejected by significant others. (Bechhofer *et al.* 1999: 515)

Nor, it should be added, can we neglect the identities that others project onto us. It is also important to make clear that the 'claims' in question are not restricted to explicit statements like 'I am Bengali', but most often take the form of what Billig (1995) has termed 'banal nationalism'. He defines it as

> the ideological habits which enable the established nations of the West to be reproduced. It is argued that these habits are not removed from everyday life, as some observers have supposed. Daily, the nation is indicated, or 'flagged', in the lives of its citizenry. Nationalism, far from being an intermittent mood in established nations, is the endemic condition. (Billig 1995: 6)

Billig criticises studies of nationalism for focusing too much on the 'passionately waved flag', and too little on 'routine flags', like the one hanging limp in front of the post office. The routine flag operates to reproduce banal nationalism precisely because it is a 'forgotten reminder' (ibid.: 8) – its significance is overtly 'forgotten' by observers, yet remembered in the depths of their mind. Billig's point is that studies of nationalism have perversely paid attention to the strongly asserted nationalism that is typical only of a small minority of people, ignoring the banal nationalism that is part of everyone's everyday life (strong nationalists included). What is more, he argues that this is part of

> an ideological pattern in which 'our' nationalism (that of established nations …) is forgotten: it ceases to appear as nationalism, disappearing into the 'natural' environment of 'societies'. At the same time, nationalism is defined as something dangerously emotional and irrational: it is conceived as a problem, or a condition, which is surplus to the world of nations. The irrationality of nationalism is projected on to 'others' (ibid.: 38)

In other words, *my* nationalism, *our* nationalism, is natural and good; but *their* nationalism is irrational and dangerous.

In Billig's view, 'an identity is to be found in the embodied habits of social life' (ibid.: 8), including language. In this he follows Bourdieu, for whom seeing identities as 'embodied habits of social life' is not in contradiction with the view quoted above that they 'are not essentially fixed or given but depend critically on the claims which people make in different contexts and at different times'. We take on new identities over the course of our lives; indeed, at any given moment each of us is capable of performing and claiming a range of identities, depending on the context we find ourselves in and the people we are with. What is more, the features associated with a particular identity are fluid, and shift over time. Rampton (1995) has memorably described cases of identity 'crossing' among young people in London, where features traditionally associated with Jamaican forms of English are taken on by Asian youths, and vice versa, and both are taken on by 'white' British youths, for whom they mark a generational identity, a 'cool' identity, their ethnic associations not entirely forgotten but heading toward being so.

In the case of linguistic minorities, performed claims of identity take multiple forms, which can be categorised under three main headings:

- performances in the minority language
- performances in the majority language
- code-switching between minority and majority language

Each of these can be further broken down. Performances in the minority language may be purely local in form, or in the standard form of the minority language, if such a form exists, either in speech or in writing. Gaelic speakers in Scotland are typical of 'old' language minorities in having a sense of locality associated with their particular dialect, but no real sense of a trans-local standard. Among communities who retain an immigrant identity after many generations, such as Italian Americans, Canadians or Australians, their awareness may be strictly of 'good' versus 'broken' Italian. Any distinctiveness of their form of the language, whether reflecting dialect divisions in the home country, or different forms of language change than have transpired in the home country, including influence from English, is viewed negatively by them and folded in conceptually with decreasing fluency from generation to generation.

On the other hand, the Arbëresh people whom Perta (2004) has studied, descendants of Albanians who emigrated to Italy beginning in the fifteenth century, and who have maintained a distinct identity over the centuries, have reacted strongly against recent proposals for their children to be educated in Standard Albanian, as used in the country they traditionally considered their homeland. The reason appears to be that the wave of 'new' Albanian immigrants who have crossed the Adriatic since 1991 have earned the wrath of the popular press, which depicts them as dishonest parasites. Hence the 'old' Arbëresh communities no longer want to be associated with the Albanian identity that for 500 years they claimed for themselves. Face to face with the new immigrants, the Arbëresh not only perceive their differences but also discover how much they have in commmon with the ethnic Italians whose peninsula they have shared for all these centuries, and whom in the past they have tended to resent as an oppressive majority. Now, only their particular Arbëresh dialect, not Standard Albanian, can be an acceptable vehicle for a minority identity performance – which raises certain obstacles when it comes to minority language education.

The majority language too can serve as the vehicle for a minority identity performance. In Britain, for example, second and third generation Indians and Pakistanis generally command, in addition to their 'heritage' language, a spectrum of ways of speaking English that range from being unmarked ethnically to being very heavily marked. They use this variation to perform their Asianness, not just to outsiders but with one another. In October 2004 I was a guest on a chat show on BBC Asian radio, alongside two young British Asian men, one of whom was there to express his 'cultural cringe' at hearing other Asians speak English in an ethnically marked way, while the other was arguing that your English should express 'what you really are'. As caller after caller kept condemning the first man – one even asking him why he doesn't go have his skin bleached white (see also Armour 2001) – I found myself genuinely surprised at the passions aroused in so many by this issue of ethnic performance in a language that outsiders might reckon not to be 'theirs', but the relic of a colonial imposition.

It is important to stress that both the Asian men on the programme, the one who sounded Asian and the one who didn't, were 'performing' their identity in the majority language. But it was different identities being performed. The man who sounded Asian was also quite capable of sounding 'English' if he chose to – so his performance in Asian English is, arguably, different in kind from that of his Pakistani-born father for whom English was a second language and who could not speak it without an accent no matter how hard he tried. We can speak less hesitantly of linguistic *resistance* in the case of the son, who is choosing not to use English in the majority way, than in the case of the father. But the counterargument can also be made, namely that every voice that contributes to heteroglossia within the majority language, willingly or not, is doing its part to resist linguistic and cultural homogenisation.

Finally, we have minority identity performance through code-switching between the minority and majority language. Code-switching is a complex topic in linguistics and specialists engage in fierce polemics over how to analyse it; for my purposes it is enough to assert that the mixing of majority and minority language takes different forms in different places. Having grown up in Michigan, I was used to the 'classic' mode of code-switching as described by studies of French-English bilingual Canadians and Spanish-English bilingual Americans, where there is a clear 'matrix' language, and switches into the second language occur at predictable syntactic or discourse boundaries. Moving to Hong Kong, however, I found myself submerged in an entirely different situation, where it is absolutely normal for Cantonese-English bilinguals to converse with code-mixing in every sentence, sometimes in the middle of a word, so that it was difficult or even impossible to identify a matrix language. Cantonese might appear to be the matrix one minute, English the next. This is not the pattern with *all* Hong Kong bilinguals – conversing in this way is generally interpreted by Hong Kong people as a mark of being educated and cosmopolitan, while still 'performing Chineseness'.

Living in Hong Kong I was myself a member of the ethnic and linguistic minority. It was important to me to learn enough Chinese that I could perform my identity as a certain kind of outsider, with at least a weak identity tie to the place, rather than another kind, who lives there for years without ever speaking anything but English. Such people reminded me of the Sicilian-American women I knew in my youth, who had come to Michigan in the early 1900s and still in the 1960s and 1970s could not, or would not, say a full sentence in English (or in Standard Italian, for that matter). On the other hand, those British and American colleagues of mine in Hong Kong who had fully embraced Chineseness and become really fluent speakers, seemed so tied to the place that one doubted they could ever leave it. This provoked a mixture of admiration, envy and fear in me – fear that I too might be so seduced by this extraordinarily attractive culture as to lose myself. Hence my ambivalent desire to be a majority language performer, but only up to a limit.

Of course, in this situation the 'minority' I belonged to was an oligarchy. Hong Kong was still a British Crown colony – and even today, English remains an official language and has lost none of its prestige. But Chinese is certainly not lacking in prestige, and its majority status is overwhelming, since well over 90 per cent of the population have it as their primary language. Rather different from this is the situation with the 'ex-colonial' language Russian in countries formerly under the control of the USSR, where members of majority ethnic and linguistic groups perceive themselves as under threat from minority groups. This may seem like a historically unusual situation, but across the world, culturally insecure majorities have been a growing trend. The more public the performances of minority identity become, the more the majority fear for the coherence of the national identity and the whole social fabric it underpins.

There is an inherent paradox in the fact that, because 'language rights' are accorded only to minority groups, who need them because their language is under threat and the majority language is not, the result can be that the majority now *perceives* itself as under threat because of the rights accorded to the minorities. Indeed, the majority's own language rights, having been taken for granted, are not given legal recognition or protection, the whole point being to erode them enough to create and maintain space for the minority language. But history has taught us repeatedly the dangers of brushing aside the rights and feelings of the majority. The likely result will be the rise of extreme political parties with a platform to shore up majority rights and limit those of minorities. It is in the interest of linguistic minorities to seek a balance, and self-destructive to position themselves in opposition to the majority – even if, on the moral plane, past injustices would seem to justify their doing so.

This discussion has ranged across a variety of different situations, and it would be a mistake to imagine that one single approach would bring improvement to all of them. Insofar as there is a theory for understanding and dealing with them, it is grounded in the fact that all these situations give rise to the same basic set of questions. It is the answers that differ from case to case. Several of these questions will be revisited, and possible answers to them sketched out, in §7.4 (points 6 to 11).

SUGGESTED FURTHER READING

On linguistic imperialism: Bolton (2003), Byram and Risager (1999), Eggington and Wren (eds) (1997), Fishman (ed.) (2001), Laforge and McConnell (eds) (1990), Mar-Molinero (2000), Ricento (ed.) (2000).

On ideological dimensions of language policy: Ager (2001), Ammon (1997), Annamalai (2003), Blommaert (1996), Blommaert (ed.) (1999), Cooper (1989), Coulmas (ed.) (1988), Cummins (2000), Dua (ed.) (1996), Gardt (ed.) (2000), Kaplan and Baldauf (1997), Landau (ed.) (1999), Mansour (1993), May (2001), Schiffman (1996), Spolsky (2004), Tollefson (1991), Tollefson (ed.) (1995, 2002), Weinstein (1983), Weinstein (ed.) (1990), Wodak and Corson (eds) (1997), Wright (2004).

On minority identities and language rights: Ammon, Mattheier and Nelde (eds) (2002), Crawford (ed.) (1992), Kibbee (ed.) (1998).

Case studies from particular countries are regularly published in the *Journal of Multilingual and Multicultural Development* and *Language Policy*.

NOTES

1. 'Inner word' here translates the Latin *verbum*, while 'word' translates the Latin *vox* (see Joseph 2005).

2. There were also genuine humanitarian concerns in the second half of the nineteenth century for saving Africans from the murderous slave trade still being run by the Ottomans and the Emperor of Zanzibar – anyone who doubts the sincerity of this motive should consider the strength of feeling still apparent today about the duty of people in the Northern hemisphere to relieve the suffering of Africans. However, the fact that the European powers had themselves only quit this trade a few decades earlier, combined with the clear evidence that

the 'scramble' for colonies was mainly motivated by European political concerns, and the fact that decolonisation did not immediately follow upon the abolition of slavery, makes the humanitarian aspects look, unjustly perhaps, like a smoke screen.

3. See also the similarly spirited and very thorough critique of Phillipson by Davies (1996), a 'Centre' scholar and the teacher of both Makoni and Rajagapolan; and Bruthiaux's (2000) thoughtful and thought-provoking study of the unfortunate lack of interaction between specialists in language education and development economics.

4. The USA, for example, has never had an official national language, although some states have official languages. The states which have legislated that English is their official language are listed here with the year in which the legislation was passed: Alabama (1990), Arkansas (1987), California (1986), Colorado (1988), Florida (1988), Georgia (1996), Illinois (1969, replacing a 1923 law that made 'American' the official language), Indiana (1984), Iowa (2002), Kentucky (1984), Louisiana (1807, passed as a condition of its admittance into the USA), Mississippi (1987), Missouri (1998), Montana (1995), Nebraska (1920), New Hampshire (1995), North Carolina (1987), North Dakota (1987), Oklahoma (2003), South Carolina (1987), South Dakota (1995), Tennessee (1984), Utah (2000), Virginia (1981, amended 1996), Wyoming (1996). Similar measures passed in Alaska (1998) and Arizona (1998) were declared unconstitutional by state courts. In 1989, New Mexico became the first state to adopt an 'English Plus Declaration', which declares the state's 'advocacy of the teaching of other languages in the United States and its belief that the position of English is not threatened'; similar measures were then passed by Oregon (1989), Washington (1989) and Rhode Island (1992). The only officially bilingual state is Hawaii, which in 1978 passed a constitutional amendment stating that 'English and Hawaiian shall be the official languages of Hawai'i, except that Hawaiian shall be required for public acts and transactions only as provided by law'. The other eighteen states not mentioned here have no official language.

5. Note however that Patten (2003) sees Kymlicka as standing in direct opposition to Rawls's basic principle that governments should maintain 'liberal neutrality' in the face of diversity, a principle which Patten himself claims to rescue with his own 'hybrid normative theory of language policy'.

Chapter 4
Politics embedded in language

4.1 STRUGGLE IN THE SIGN

The book credited with being the starting point of modern linguistics, Saussure's *Course in General Linguistics* (see above, §2.6), famously declares that *langue*, a language, is a social fact, and that social force holds the system together so powerfully that no individual can change the language. Changes occur in *parole* 'speech', and if eventually the community accepts the change, the whole system shifts to form a new *langue*. But the social space which language occupies for Saussure is not political: every member of the speech community possesses the language, he says, in identical form. There is no scope for one speaker to manifest power over another, since *langue* has no individual dimension. What individuals do is a matter entirely of *parole*.

Despite the apolitical nature of his analysis, the shadow of Saussure would loom large in subsequent attempts at a political account of language. If not reacting against Saussure's idealisation of a homogeneous speech community, such accounts are likely to be based on a methodology deriving from the structuralism he is credited with founding, or to be reacting against that very structuralism.

Nowhere did Saussure's *Course* have a deeper influence in the decade following its publication than in Russia, where it was initially received as consistent in spirit with the 'formalism' then in vogue. But over the course of the 1920s serious questions were raised about the commensurability of formalism with the basic Marxist view that every central facet of human experience is *social* in its origin and operation. The widest-ranging critiques of the structuralist approach to language were launched by Bakhtin (see above, §3.2) and members of the intellectual circle he led. The one who took on Saussure most directly was Valentin N. Voloshinov (1895–1936), in *Marxism and the Philosophy of Language* (1973, originally published 1929).[1]

For Voloshinov, Saussure's *Course* represents the most striking and thoroughly developed form of what he disparagingly terms 'abstract objectivism' (Voloshinov 1973: 58). It defines the boundaries of language to include 'not the relationship of the sign to the actual reality it reflects nor to the individual who is its originator, but the *relationship of sign to sign within a closed system* already accepted and authorized' (ibid., italics in original). Rather than deal with actual utterances, it considers only the language system abstracted away from them.[2] Voloshinov acknowledges that Saussure does at least move beyond the Romantic view of language as a facet of individual consciousness. Yet he refuses to engage with 'history', in the Marxist sense of what real people do (the 'base', as opposed to 'superstructure'), and this denies his approach any claim to genuine social substance in the Marxist sense. For Voloshinov,

> Every sign, as we know, is a construct between socially organized persons in the process of their interaction. Therefore, *the forms of signs are conditioned above all by the social organization of the participants involved and also by the immediate conditions of their interaction.* (ibid.: 21)

Signs are ideological by their very nature, and social existence is not merely reflected in them but 'refracted' by them. For the sign is not like a smooth mirror, but one with a cracked and irregular surface, created by the 'differently oriented social interests within one and the same sign community, i.e. *by the class struggle*' (ibid.: 23). When Voloshinov declares that 'Sign becomes an arena of the class struggle' (ibid.: 23), he makes language central to the 'base', a Marxist declaration that language and politics are inseparable, maybe even indistinguishable. '*Linguistic creativity ... cannot be understood apart from the ideological meanings and values that fill it*' (ibid.: 98).

No speech act is individual; they are always social, even if the addressee exists only in the speaker's imagination. And indeed, every word we utter is generated in interaction with an imagined audience in our mind, before any real audience ever hears or reads it. Thus, according to Voloshinov and Bahktin, language is inherently 'dialogic', and it is a fundamental error and illusion of 'bourgeois' linguistics to conceive of it as monologic, generated simply by the individual psychology of a speaker. The discrete systems that linguists normally study co-exist with a multiplicity of different ways of speaking that are constantly intermingling with each other, a condition for which Bakhtin (1981) introduces the term 'heteroglossia' (see §3.2, p. 45). This tension constitutes the arena of the class struggle where voices and signs are concerned.

Voloshinov's and Bakhtin's writings fell into obscurity until their rediscovery in the 1960s. By this time, many of their ground-breaking ideas had been arrived at independently by later Marxists, post-Marxists and even non-Marxists, and when their work began to be translated into French and English, they seemed perfectly contemporary despite the forty-year remove. Thus Voloshinov (1973) is not historically the master text for as much of modern thinking about language and politics as it might superficially appear to be, though it is still the most important book on the subject yet written. (For a fuller account of Marxist theories of language, see Minnini 1994.)

Saussure and Voloshinov offer two clearly differentiated modes for approaching the social and political in language. Saussure's is based on an understanding of the social as what binds people together, Voloshinov's as what keeps them apart. The latter accords better with what 'social' has now come to signify in sociolinguistics and the social sciences generally. The trouble with Saussure's analysis is that it demands a structural system that somehow precedes use, and doesn't delve into how anyone comes to have this system or what binds people together linguistically. The *Course* even contradicts itself by saying at one point that every member of the linguistic community possesses the language in identical form, and at another that everyone's knowledge is different, with the language representing the totality of all these differences, and not itself possessed by any individual. The trouble with Voloshinov's analysis is that, although it gives priority to use, it is so single-mindedly focussed on the 'class struggle' – understandably for its time and place – as to ignore all the other linguistic aspects of social and individual identity and the manifold ways in which language functions politically to separate and hierarchise people, and to bind them together.

The most interesting perspectives on language and politics of recent decades have come neither from linguistics or structuralism narrowly conceived, nor from orthodox Marxist thought,[3] but from combining what is enlightening in each. From Saussure, a recognition that our very way of talking about 'a language' implies a powerful social cohesion; from Voloshinov, that utterances come first, and that languages as abstract systems are artefacts of the analysis of politically contextualised utterances. From Voloshinov, a keen awareness of language as a field of political struggle; from Saussure, an admission that the arbitrariness of the link between signifier and signified, and the existential break between the signified (a concept) and things in the world, ultimately means that these political struggles are not directly tied to any sort of historical necessity, Marxist or otherwise.

4.2 STRUGGLE IN INTERACTION

The most important turn in the Marxist line has arguably been made by someone who is clearly post-Marxist, Jürgen Habermas (see Habermas 1999). He was trained in the Frankfurt School, which took as one of its intellectual starting points the reformulation of Marxist theory by Georg Lukács (1885–1971). By rethinking the relationship of theory to practice, Lukács led the way to a less deterministic and mechanistic form of Marxism than Marx himself had instituted. Linking theory to practice has been at the centre of Habermas's thinking, not least in what has been described as his 'leading idea', namely 'that human language and human communication in general already contain implicit intersubjective norms' (Jarvis 1999: 435). In these norms of everyday language use, Habermas argues, lie the grounds for universal values and principles – in short, for truth. Habermas's contribution has been less in analysing the political content of language use than in establishing why it should be the central topic of philosophical concern. Since the late Middle Ages philosophers have sought universal truth in logic-based theories of propositions and grammatical structures, while dismissing what people do with language as trivial. In arguing for the primacy of practice, Habermas has remained in the Marxist line, where the politics of language use is real, and its analysis trivial insofar as it is abstracted away from this reality.

Habermas would be the first to acknowledge that the crucial ground-work for his approach had been laid by people working on pragmatic approaches to language, from anthropologists such as Bronoslaw Malinowski (1884–1942) in the 1920s to philosophers such as J. L. Austin (1911–60) and John Searle in the 1950s and 1960s. The contributions of anthropologists and sociologists, and indeed of linguists, is less obvious because their concern was not overtly with refounding the nature of 'truth', but with explaining cultural and interpersonal behaviour. For understanding the political dimensions of language, the most central contribution was that of Goffman (mentioned in §1.3, p. 5), a sociologist who did his doctoral research in the late 1940s in the Shetland Islands, home to communities even more remote and inwardly-focused then than they are today, and so seeming to offer a laboratory for the study of interpersonal behaviour sealed off from all the 'noise' of modern urbanised society. From his research Goffman concluded that

> The human tendency to use signs and symbols means that evidence of social worth and of mutual evaluations will be conveyed by very minor things, and these things will be witnessed, as will the fact that they have been witnessed. An unguarded glance, a momentary change in tone of voice, an ecological position taken or not taken, can drench a talk with judgmental significance. Therefore, just as there is no occasion of talk in which improper impressions could not intentionally or unintentionally arise, so there is no occasion of talk so trivial as not to require each participant to show serious concern with the way he handles himself and the others present. (Goffman 1955: 225 [1972: 33])

By 'ecological position' Goffman means the positioning of the speaker's body relative to the interlocutors. Although his observations were made in the hothouse conditions of a small island society, he considered them to be universally applicable and simply more salient in the Shetlands than they might be in an urbanised environment. Here too, the structure of our 'self' links in directly with the way we organise our conversations:

> In any society, whenever the physical possibility of spoken interaction arises, it seems that a system of practices, conventions, and procedural rules comes into play which functions as a means of guiding and organizing the flow of messages. [...]
> The conventions regarding the structure of occasions of talk represent an effective solution to the problem of organizing a flow of spoken messages. In attempting to discover how it is that these conventions are maintained in force as guides to action, one finds evidence to suggest a functional relationship between the structure of the self and the structure of spoken interaction. (Goffman 1955: 225–7 [1972: 33–6])

For describing this 'structure of the self' Goffman landed upon the concept of *face*, generally associated with East Asian cultures. He defined it for his purposes as 'the positive social value a person effectively claims for himself by the line others assume he has taken during a particular contact'. A few years later, Brown and Levinson (1978) would make a distinction between *negative face*, the desire not to be imposed or intruded on, and *positive face*, the desire for approval; both types had already been described by Goffman, who correctly associated each with 'positive social value'. Members of any social group possess both kinds of face, and Goffman made clear that every act of speaking risks 'negative face':

[W]hen a person volunteers a statement or message, however trivial or common-place, he commits himself and those he addresses, and in a sense places everyone present in jeopardy. By saying something, the speaker opens himself up to the possibility that the intended recipients will affront him by not listening or will think him forward, foolish, or offensive in what he has said. And should he meet with such a reception, he will find himself committed to the necessity of taking face-saving action against them.

[...]

Thus when one person volunteers a message, thereby contributing what might easily be a threat to the ritual equilibrium, someone else present is obliged to show that the message has been received and that its content is acceptable to all concerned. (Goffman 1955: 227–8 [1972: 37–8])

It would be well into the 1960s before linguistics opened its gates to the sort of interpretive enquiry that Goffman had been pioneering, in part because a critical mass of linguists did not see 'discourse' – texts extending beyond the length of the phrase or sentence – as falling within their bailiwick. But already in 1958 two papers given at major linguistics conferences were signalling that structural linguistics had reached the end of its ability to suspend disbelief in language as an apolitical system evolved to fulfil the functions of communication and representation as efficiently as possible. One of these was Ferguson's 'Diglossia', discussed in §3.2; the other, 'The pronouns of power and solidarity', was co-written by a psychologist, Roger Brown (1925–97) and a Shakespeare scholar, Albert Gilman (1923–89).

4.3 DEFERENTIAL ADDRESS

Brown and Gilman (1960) presented the distinction between familiar and deferential (polite) pronouns of address (Spanish *tu* / *Usted*, French *tu* / *vous*, German *du* / *Sie*, etc.) as a system for establishing and maintaining interpersonal relations that is directly embedded into grammar. As an implicit critique of the structuralist view of the language system as autonomous and aloof from the mundane politics of *parole*, it is reminiscent of the then-forgotten Voloshinov's conception of language as the arena of the class struggle. However, Brown and Gilman consider only interpersonal relations and not the broader international order. They show how the *tu*-type forms are used to keep social inferiors in their place, but also to manifest tender intimacy to a child or a lover, political solidarity with one's peers, or a personal bond to God. They can, in other words, function to break down the social boundaries between individuals as much as to maintain them, the meaning of each utterance being dependent upon the surrounding political context. Brown and Gilman paved the way for research into such phenomena across a wide range of languages, and led ultimately to the 'politeness theory' of another Brown (Penelope), and her co-author Levinson (1978, 1987), discussed in the preceding section.

The languages of the world show a variety of strategies for creating polite pronouns, particularly in view of the fact that the number of personal pronouns in any language is limited, though the six or so of English (*I, you, he, she, we, they*, plus the more marginal *one* and *thou*) is on the low side. Arabic, for instance, has twelve. English and Arabic are unusual among modern languages in not having polite second-person pronouns – or rather, looking at Standard English from the historical point of view, *only* having a deferential pronoun, since the original non-deferential *thou* (cognate with *tu* and *du*) has become restricted to certain dialects of the north and west of England and a few relic uses such as in the Lord's Prayer. *You*, like French *vous*, was originally the second-person plural pronoun, and the use of the plural to refer to a single person is both the earliest recorded and the most widespread strategy for polite pronominal address. Head (1978: 191, n. 6), after examining a cross-linguistic corpus heavily biased toward Indo-European languages, concluded that pluralisation is the basic mechanism for deference, and that languages develop other devices only after passing through the pluralisation stage.[4]

In terms of Brown and Levinson's face-based model of politeness, one can see the deferential use of the plural as both a negative and a positive face strategy. Addressing someone as, in effect, 'you and yours', deflects the force of the speech act from the individual spoken to, making it less direct and less threatening. At the same time, it increases the 'size' of the addressee, as it were, implying that this person matters too much to be treated as a mere singular. At least, all this seems plausible in considering the *origins* of the polite form. When it has been in use for generations, fully con-ventionalised and institutionalised into the grammar of the language, it is less obvious that these implications remain operative. Still, even in the case of a language like French, where every speaker knows that *vous* is a plural as well as a polite singular, it is possible that some speakers, at least, feel something of this old force. Not so in English, however; even scholars who know the deferential origin of *you*, unless their mother tongue happens to be one of the rare dialects that conserve *thou*, do not feel its plural 'weight'.

The result is that interpersonal relations are not performed linguistically in the same way in English as in all those other European languages that have a polite form. In French, every time I talk to a person I am obliged to perform my relationship to them as intimate or distant by the choice of *tu* or *vous*. In English, I *can* perform my relationship to them as intimate or distant by calling them by their first name or by their title and surname, but generally I can also avoid this if I so choose. As Jakobson (1959: 236) famously pointed out, 'Languages differ essentially in what they *must* convey and not in what they *may* convey', and here we have a fundamental difference between English and every other modern Indo-European language in how the politics of interpersonal relationships are embodied in the linguistic sign.[5]

Although it seems that all these languages began by using the second-person plural as their deferential pronoun, there occurred historically what Burke (1993: 19–20) has described as the 'inflation' of polite forms. Once it becomes commonplace to address anyone of a certain rank with the plural, that form gets so conventionalised as a simple acknowledgment of rank as to lose any capacity for expressing truly *personal* deference. What then happened in many cases is the use of a noun phrase such as 'your grace' or 'your excellence' to designate a really distinguished person in a really deferential way; and then, since this grace or excellence is a quality possessed by the person rather than the person himself or herself, it is referred to in the *third person.*

It is thus that Italian, Spanish, Portuguese and Polish all came to use a third person singular form as the polite version of 'you',[6] as in Spanish *Como está Usted?* 'How are you', where the verb *está* is in the third person (cf. familiar *Como estás?*), and the pronoun *Usted* is held to derive from *vuestra merced* 'your mercy'. In Standard Italian, the corresponding question is *Come sta Lei?*, literally 'How is It?', the word *Lei* being originally the third person feminine pronoun, used to refer to the grace or mercy or majesty of the addressee (all these abstract nouns being feminine in Italian). German, Danish and Norwegian have taken the inflation of polite forms a step further, making the third-person *plural* the deferential form for addressing either an individual or a group. *Was haben Sie?*, literally 'What have They?', is how you ask someone politely what they will have, as opposed to the familiar *Was hast du?* The inflationary process cannot go any further than third-person plural, as no more deferential pronouns are available.

The *forms* of the polite pronouns are only the beginning, however. The real politics of interpersonal language use consists of deploying them, and withholding them, and in any given language the practices are complex and highly variable. With French, I have observed, just among members of my wife's family, cases in which:

- adults use *vous* to both parents, and receive *tu* back
- adults use *vous* to their father, and *tu* to their mother, and receive *tu* back from both
- adults and their parents always use *tu* with each other
- children use *tu* to their parents, *vous* to their grandparents, and receive *tu* back
- children use *tu* with both parents and grandparents
- spouses use *tu* with each other
- rarely, spouses use *vous* with each other
- very rarely (oldest generation only), wives use *vous* to husbands and receive *tu* back

As an observer, I find it difficult not to interpret differences in the relationships in parallel with the differences in pronoun usage, but am aware that these interpretations may not be valid. It is not necessarily the case, for instance, that someone who addresses her father as *tu* feels closer to him than does her brother who addresses him as *vous*, nor is it necessarily true that the brother respects their father more than the sister does. On the other hand, it takes no more than a casual remark to get all those involved to discourse at length on these differences and how they have changed over recent decades, which suggests that there is quite widespread awareness of the various practices and what they seem to mean.

One thing which speakers of languages with an active *tu/vous* type distinction are very aware of is any shift between the two forms of address made to them by another speaker. New acquaintances who address each other as *vous* can find that, as their friendship grows, a moment comes when the polite pronoun no longer feels appropriate, and one of them must initiate the shift to the intimate *tu*. The 'invitation' to switch may come as a direct invitation ('I think we've known each other long enough to use the *tu* now'), but is at least as likely to come indirectly through one of the persons simply starting to use the *tu* to the other. The reverse shift, from informal to formal, *always* comes, to my knowledge, indirectly; that is, I often hear people report their dismay when a childhood friend starts using the *vous* with them, but have never heard of someone being invited directly to make this switch.

If a switch from *tu* to *vous* is an unambiguous slap in the face, even the friendly switch from *vous* to *tu* threatens the invitee's negative face, and can be rebuffed. The *vous* provides a sort of emotional buffer zone within which one is safe, and it sometimes happens that the person who initiates the use of *tu* is further along in his or her own feelings of intimacy than the addressee is. Refusal of an invitation to switch to *tu* can again be direct or indirect – the invitee simply continues to use *vous*, perhaps with some gestural or intonational signs of distress thrown in, and the inviter generally gets the message.[7]

There are intermediate steps whereby the face threat of a switch from *vous* to *tu* can be mitigated. If a relationship has begun with each person using *vous* with the other and addressing the other with title plus surname, the switch to addressing each other on a first name basis can precede the switch to *tu*. In a language such as English, where the use of title and surname or first name is the only direct means available of signalling the personal–political status of one's relationship to another person, the available degrees of nuance are fewer.

Moving beyond the Indo-European language family, one encounters cases in which the politics of interpersonal relationships are embedded into language much more broadly than through pronouns and address forms alone. One of the most striking cases is that of Javanese. Home to 60 per cent of Indonesia's 200 million people, Java's population is approaching that of Japan, and is as large as that of the UK and France combined. The Javanese have a two-layered mother tongue, Ngoko (Low Javanese) being what they acquire first as infants, and Kromo (High Javanese) what they are socialised into, regardless of social rank, beginning in childhood. The differences between these two forms of Javanese are substantial, enough for some linguists and anthropologists (e.g., Siegel 1986: 309) to describe them as two distinct languages (though cf. §2.2 above on the limited validity of such assertions). The question 'Did you take that much rice?' would be in Low Javanese (where the first word, *apa*, indicates that the sentence is a question):[8]

Apa kowé njupuk sega semono?
?   YOU   TAKE   RICE THAT-MUCH

The same question in 'pure' High Javanese (Kromo Inggil, where *menapa* is the question marker) would be:

Menapa nandalem mundhut sekul semanten?
?   YOU   TAKE   RICE THAT-MUCH

Some relationship can be detected between the corresponding words at the two levels, except, interestingly enough, with the second-person pronoun, where *kowé* and *nandalem* are as distant as can be.

Siegel, who conducted his fieldwork in Solo (or Surakarta) in the late 1970s, has the following to say about Kromo:

> It seems … to have developed as a court language. What is remarkable about its development is that, though designed to mark differences of status within the Javanese feudal world, it has lost no ground in a period of nationalism and independence. It has done this by encompassing all new statuses. not just court officials but anyone with a recognized position of any sort is ordinarily entitled to be spoken to in Kromo. Thus government officials, army officers, and school-teachers, for instance, all persons considered to be, we might have once said, 'respectable', will usually receive this form of deference. In addition, the old are always deferred to. Every adult, in fact, is ordinarily given some degree of linguistically expressed deference. (Siegel 1986: 20)

The differences of 'degree of linguistically expressed deference' are quite fine-grained, and again appear particularly strongly in the second-person pronoun. In between the Low Javanese *kowé* and the pure High Javanese *nandalem*, we also find the following forms, listed by increasing degree of 'highness': *sliramu, sampéyan, panjenengan* (Holmes 2001: 244). Soepomo Poedjosoedarmo (1968) describes no fewer than nine distinct levels (though Siegel [1986: 311] cautions against reifying them into varieties). For the Javanese, the critical split comes between Ngoko (Low Javanese) and all the other forms. The latter all count as deferential, despite the differences in degree.

Other aspects must be taken into account besides vocabulary. Deference is also shown through the use of *alus* intonation. *Alus* is usually translated as 'refined', but Siegel (1986: 17) defines it more accurately as 'cajoling, pleasing, and without sharp edges'. The content of one's speech also matters – ideally, Kromo discourse should not be 'about' anything, or as little as possible, and it must not be about anything contentious.

> One can express anger only in Ngoko. If two acquaintances who normally speak to each other in Krômô should begin to quarrel, they will switch to Ngoko. If a younger relative quarrels with an older one (an uncle, for example), to whom he usually speaks in Krômô, he will use Ngoko. The expression of anger in Krômô sounds very odd to native speakers of Javanese, and in folk plays such as the ketopraq or dagelan this may be used as a device for getting laughs. (Soepomo Poedjosoedarmo 1968: 77)

Indonesian, the national language, is also in the linguistic repertoire of the Javanese except for those in the island's most remote corners, and although it is normally reserved for impersonal 'official' contexts, it can play a role in interpersonal linguistic politics, on account of its neutrality in the system of proper and improper behaviour.

A man told me that as a boy he used to quarrel with his brother. His mother forbade the brothers to speak Low Javanese to each other. Not until they realized they could use Indonesian did they begin to fight again. (Siegel 1986: 16)

By Siegel's interpretation, there is more going on in the sociopolitics of the Javanese language than the performance of interpersonal relations.

To speak some form of Javanese that is not Ngoko, even though it is not pure High Javanese (Kromo Inggil) but is linguistically almost indistinguishable from Ngoko, is still thought to confer recognition of the listener's social worthiness. One thus defers to the social order itself. (Siegel 1986: 21)

That is, the essential thing one performs is not deference of one individual to another, but a recognition, almost religious in spirit, of the social order's naturalness and permanence.

Does this make the Javanese case different from that of European languages with deferential address? Certainly the breadth and complexity of the Javanese system might induce one to think so. Yet it is worth noting that, when the leaders of the French Revolution and, copying them, the Russian Revolution, forbade the use of deferential pronouns along with titles, it was precisely because they believed that every such gesture propped up the social order they were determined to destroy. They did not consider that order to be either natural or inevitable, but did think that the politics of language played a significant role in maintaining it. In the event, the old pronouns returned, and the new order did not last.

4.4 GENDERED LANGUAGE

Robin Tolmach Lakoff's 'Language and women's place' (1973, 1975, 2004) began the contemporary discourse within linguistics that argues that languages, in both their structure and their use, mark out an inferior social role for women and bind them to it. The characteristics she identified as marking out women's language include the following (as summarised by O'Barr 1982: 64):

1. HEDGES: *It's sort of hot in here; I'd kind of like to go; I guess ...; It seems like ...;* and so on.
2. (SUPER)POLITE FORMS: *I'd really appreciate it if ...; Would you please open the door, if you don't mind?;* and so on.
3. TAG QUESTIONS: *John is here, isn't he?* instead of *Is John here?;* and so on.
4. SPEAKING IN ITALICS: Intonational emphasis equivalent to underlining words in written language; emphatic *so* or *very;* and the like.
5. EMPTY ADJECTIVES: *Divine, charming, cute, sweet, adorable, lovely,* and others like them.
6. HYPERCORRECT GRAMMAR AND PRONUNCIATION: Bookish grammar and more formal enunciation.
7. LACK OF A SENSE OF HUMOR: Women said to be poor joke tellers and frequently to 'miss the point' in jokes told by men.
8. DIRECT QUOTATIONS: Use of direct quotations rather than paraphrases.

9. SPECIAL LEXICON: In domains like colors where words like *magenta, chartreuse,* and so on are typically used only by women.
10. QUESTION INTONATION IN DECLARATIVE CONTEXTS: For example, in response to the question, *When will dinner be ready?*, an answer like *Around 6 o'clock?*, as though seeking approval and asking whether that time will be okay.

Several of these categories will be revisited in §4.6. As with deferential address and interpersonal relationships, gender politics is incorporated directly into the pronoun systems of English and many other languages, through the use of the masculine as the 'unmarked' gender (as in 'Everyone take his seat'), and similarly with many nouns, for example *actor* and *actress*, where any statement about all people who act will be about *actors*. The central importance of these forms is that they are virtually unavoidable in certain contexts (especially the pronouns), and thus force one to make a choice – *he* vs. *he/she* vs. *they*, for example – that is interpretable as connoting a particular gender ideology, whether or not that ideology is actually held by the person uttering the form.

Although the masculine bias in language is too evident to require demonstration, the survey of its manifestations across a broad range of unrelated languages by Pauwels (1998: 16–80) is nevertheless breathtaking. Her list of common features and issues in the linguistic representation of women and men fall into four categories:

1. The man (men or the male) is portrayed as the benchmark for all human beings; he is seen as the norm or reference-point. The woman (or women), on the other hand, is subsumed to be included in any linguistic reference to the man. The generic function for human agent nouns, including pronouns, is mainly expressed through nouns, pronouns and other linguistic practices which coincide with those referring to male human beings.
2. As a result of the above practice, the woman is largely invisible in language. However, if she is visible, her visibility is predominantly of an asymmetrical nature. She is made linguistically visible to show her 'deviation' or 'exception' from the male norm.
3. The linguistic portrayal of women is also one of dependence: grammatical and other features of language often contribute towards a view of linguistic dependency or derivation of the female element on (from) the male (e.g. derivation of feminine forms from masculine forms).
4. The linguistic representation of both sexes is often highly stereotypical. Women are primarily portrayed as sexual creatures (e.g. the 'madonna–whore' polarity) whereas men are more likely to be portrayed as 'rational' creatures. (Pauwels 1998: 34–5)

Examples of Category 1 have been given in the first paragraph of this section, where the word *actress* also illustrates Category 3: it is derived from the 'unmarked' form *actor* by the addition of the feminine suffix *-ess*, and speakers are aware of this through the existence of a whole series of such unmarked and marked terms, notably *prince/princess*, which figures prominently in the stories through which young children get socialised into this dyad. Although *prince/princess* shows no sign of weakening, *actor/actress* does – many newspapers now use only *actor*, in a return to pre-eighteenth century usage – and some other pairs such as *author/authoress* have progressed still further along this road.

So has *master/mistress*, though it remains a particularly important example as a clear representative of Category 4, *mistress* having the sexual connotation of extramarital paramour that *master* lacks entirely; and also, though most English speakers are unaware of it, as the source of *Mr (mister)*, *Mrs (missus)* and *Miss*, the last having originated as a shortened form of *mistress* in the seventeenth century. The *Mrs/Miss* distinction again illustrates Category 4 in that it forces one to designate a woman's marital status, which *Mr* does not do with regard to men.[9] The alternative, marital-status-unspecific title *Ms*, which has gained considerable ground over the last thirty-five years, has in fact been around much longer than most people suspect: in 1949 the linguist Mario Pei wrote that 'Feminists … have often proposed that the two present-day titles be merged into … "Miss" (to be written "Ms."), with a plural "Misses" (written "Mss.")' (Pei 1949: 78). But it did not enter general cultural awareness until 1971, with the launch of the American magazine *Ms.*, pronounced *miz*.

Pauwels' Category 2 is actually rather difficult to disentangle from Category 3, since, in the majority of cases, the way in which the female 'is made linguistically visible to show her 'deviation' or 'exception' from the male norm' is precisely by 'derivation of feminine forms from masculine forms'. This is not to deny the importance of what is expressed in the two categories, merely to suggest that it can be less confusing to think of them as working in tandem. The word *actress* first appeared early in the eighteenth century, when women were regularly appearing on stage for the first time, thus constituting exceptions to the previously all-male norm – but only for so long as the former norm whereby boys played women's parts was vividly remembered. Certainly by the late twentieth century it was unlikely that there were more actors than actresses in the English-speaking world, yet the form *actress* survived.

How then to distinguish *actress* from, say, *mayoress*, given that female mayors have always been and still are exceptional?[10] Complicating matters further, *mayoress* meant only 'mayor's wife' until the nineteenth century, and was still cited by the *OED* with this meaning as late as 1989. But in the mid-nineteenth century, cities in the USA began electing women mayors, and using *mayoress* to designate them, making the term ambiguous between a meaning that was an exception to the male norm (a female mayor) and another that was not exceptional but was dependent in another sense on the male (mayor's wife).

Pauwels' Category 4 is also illustrated by a seemingly universal tendency to have a lexical and metaphorical 'double standard' for males and females where sex and rationality – body and mind – are concerned. From amid the myriad of examples she offers I shall cite just two. First, the 'semantic asymmetry' that lurks beneath the surface of certain words:

For instance, it is very likely that native speakers of English attach different meanings to the following gender-paired phrases:

> He is a professional: i.e. he is a member of a respected profession.
> She is a professional: i.e. she is a member of the 'oldest' profession (prostitute).
> He is a secretary: i.e. he works for an organisation.
> She is a secretary: i.e. she does typing and general office work for a person.
> He is a tramp: i.e. he is a homeless person, drifter.
> She is a tramp: i.e. she is a prostitute. (Pauwels 1998: 51)

Pauwels (ibid.) also notes similar cases in Japanese as pointed out by Hiraga (1991: 52):

> Yogoreta otoko: a dirty man, i.e. a man who is physically unclean.
> Yogoreta onna: a dirty woman, i.e. a promiscuous woman.
> Kegare-nak-i seinen: a pure young man, i.e. pure of mind.
> Kegare-nak-i otome: a pure young maiden, i.e. pure of body (a virgin).

The second point is Pauwels' (1998: 66) discussion of claims of sexism inherent in the Chinese writing system, as previously made by Ng and Burridge (1993) and others. The radical 女 *nü* 'woman, female, feminine' is the basis of a set of characters denoting actions or qualities with negative connotations, including:

- 姘 *pin* 'to cohabit or have illicit sexual relations'
- 妒 *dù* 'to be jealous'
- 嬻 *dú* 'to slander or humiliate'
- 嫌 *xián* 'to quarrel, hate suspect'
- 媟 *xiè* 'indecent'
- 妄 *wàng* 'absurd, outrageous, ignorant, stupid'
- 女 *lán* 'covetous, greedy'

One might argue that the presence of the radical in the written character is strictly a historical residue and does not betray anything about the present-day beliefs of those who use the characters. Such arguments were made for many years concerning the use of the masculine form as generic in the European languages, where ultimately a consensus has emerged that this does not wash, and that to perpetuate the usage could only hold back the attainment of gender equality, if it has any effect at all.

Less clear, however, is whether the status of the Chinese examples is akin to that of *authoress*, a case of derivation implying exceptionalism that can easily enough be read as perpetuating a belief that real authors should be male, or to that of *history*, a word that for some feminists carries a connotation of male dominance of the academic field it denotes, despite the lack of any historical link to *his*. With *authoress* there are two arguments for replacing it by *author*, one historical, the other the forward-looking view which says that calling everyone 'author' regardless of their gender will help mould society toward a genderless conception of that profession.

For replacing *history* by *herstory* or *theirstory*, only the latter argument applies.

Pauwels' assessment is that, broadly speaking, change has been occurring in all the categories she has identified, though at nothing like the same rate across all languages and cultures. A change in the Chinese characters described above is difficult to imagine happening at any time in the foreseeable future; the same is true with regard to the inflectional morphology of languages like Italian or Spanish that not only mark the gender of nouns and pronouns but reinforce it by marking as well the gender of the adjectives and articles that accompany them. In the Italian sentence *i piatti e le tazze si sono rotti*, 'the dishes and cups were broken', there are five markers of gender, two of which, the article *i* and the final *-i*, show that *piatti* 'dishes' is masculine, another two, the article *le* and final *-e*, showing that *tazze* 'cups' is feminine, and the last, the final *-i* of *rotti* 'broken', showing that any combination of masculine and feminine nouns, even ninety-nine feminines plus one masculine, takes a masculine agreement marker. One can imagine this agreement rule loosening up so that, for instance, the majority of nouns in a mixed group determine the gender of the participle or adjective that modifies them all.[11] That would represent a very substantial shift in the internal political culture of the Italian language. But the loss of the gender system entirely would represent something else again – the end of the Italian language as we know it, and the beginning of a new language.

Lakoff's pioneering work was soon followed up by Thorne and Henley (eds) (1975), Spender (1980), and an increasingly voluminous literature that fed into a movement to change usage, so that now it is more common to say 'his or her' or use 'their' as a singular pronoun, a usage formerly considered solipsistic but now on its way to acceptability. Lakoff's identification of features occurring more frequently in women's than in men's English received independent support from conversation analysis data (Sacks 1992; Sacks, Schegloff and Jefferson 1974; Tannen (ed.) 1993) showing that in discussions involving both men and women, the occurrence of interruptions is very unequal, with women many times less likely to interrupt men than the other way round.

This in turn led both to the discourse analyses of women's language practised by Tannen (1994), and to the more politically oriented work of Cameron (1992, 1995). Tannen (1990), an international best-seller, would give rise to a very considerable industry of personal and marital therapy based upon the notion that men's and women's different modes of conversing box them into separate cultures, the walls of which need to be broken through in order for genuine communication to occur and the politics of marriage to be kept peaceful and productive. This is wholly inimical to the Marxist view that gender differences are trivial, class distinctions being the only ones that matter (see Holborow 1999: 97–148). But even many non-Marxists question whether it is ultimately in the interests of women or other 'powerless' groups (see next section) to insist on their cultural difference, rather than working for integration.

4.5 'POWERLESS' LANGUAGE

O'Barr (1982) argued that in fact the features of women's language which Lakoff identified are not primarily distinguished by gender belonging, but by social politics, being connected to powerlessness. O'Barr did not dispute that, in general, women wield less power in society than men do, but pointed out that the features in question occur with greater frequency in the language of women *or* men who occupy low-prestige jobs and are less well educated, than among persons of the same sex with a higher level of education and more prestigious employment. O'Barr's particular concern was with the effects which forms of language perceived as 'powerless' and 'powerful' produce in the courtroom situation. His data show that juries generally give more weight to testimony that does not include the features Lakoff pointed out, although this depends somewhat on their preconceptions of where the witness testifying ought to be on the sociolinguistic scale.

O'Barr analysed 150 hours of tape recordings of courtroom proceedings in North Carolina, focusing on six witnesses, three women (A, B, C in the chart below) and three men (D, E, F). He counted the occurrences of 'women's language features' in the speech of each, with the result shown in Table 4.1. Explanations and examples of most of the features can be found in the list on pp. 73–4 above, though not on that list are intensifiers ('Forms that increase or emphasize the force of assertion, such as *very, definitely, very definitely, surely, such a*', O'Barr 1982: 67) or hesitation forms ('Pause fillers such as *uh, um, ah*, and 'meaningless' particles such as *oh, well, let's see, now, so, you see*', ibid.).

Table 4.1   Frequency distribution of 'Women's Language Features' in the *Speech of Six Witnesses* (adapted from O'Barr 1982: 67)

	Women			Men		
	A	B	C	D	E	F
Intensifiers	16	0	0	21	2	1
Hedges	19	2	3	2	5	0
Hesitation forms	52	20	13	26	27	11
Polite forms	9	0	2	2	0	1
Use of *sir*	2	0	6	32	13	11
Direct quotations	1	5	0	0	0	0
Other[12]	4	0	0	0	0	0
Total (all powerless forms)	103	27	24	83	47	24
Number of answers in interview	90	32	136	61	73	52
Ratio (powerless forms per answer)	1.14	0.84	0.18	1.36	0.64	0.46

Man D is the most 'womanly' of the six in his linguistic performance, while the most 'manly' is Woman C, who is in fact Dr C, a pathologist and the only one of the six with professional status. These facts, together with the wide variation he turned up among both the men and the women, were behind O'Barr's move to reconceive these features as indicative of powerless language rather than of women's language. O'Barr's findings have been taken as suggesting that the fairness of trial by jury is compromised by the inherent politics of language, though it is not at all clear that any attempt at remedying this would be equitable, or indeed possible.

Of course, O'Barr's interpretations too are open to question. His decision to include in his data the 'Use of *sir*' by witnesses to the lawyers questioning them – not one of Lakoff's features, though arguably falling under '(super)polite forms' – has skewed the results considerably. Removing this feature from Table 4.1, the Ratio for the three men would drop respectively from 1.39 to 0.87 (Man D), from 0.64 to 0.47 (Man E) and from 0.46 to 0.25 (Man F). It would no longer be the case that Man D is the most 'womanly' of the six; Woman A would far outrank the others in this regard, and Lakoff's interpretation of the features would look much less dubious. The striking 'anomaly' of Woman C would remain, and the powerfulness conferred on her by her professional status would continue to be the obvious explanation for it. But the balance of interpretative weight accorded to the gender factor would perhaps settle to somewhere in between what Lakoff and O'Barr have each accorded to it. These issues will be re-examined toward the end of the following section.

4.6 THE POLITICS OF LANGUAGE CHANGE

As was mentioned in §2.5 (p. 33), all languages are constantly changing, and most cultures invest a great deal of resource in intervening to ensure that the changes occur at a differential rate among various groups within the population. Some emerge as more conservative than others, and this furnishes the basis for the differential distribution of resources and responsibilities. Societies operate within a very real economy based on language change.

Here is at least one sense in which we might understand Voloshinov's view (§4.1) that the linguistic sign incorporates the class struggle within it. No one would deny that 'variation' characterises all communities of language users at all times. Some might conceive of it as good and bad usage rather than variation, but it is variation all the same.[13] Every time I use a linguistic sign, what I utter is actually one of the variants of its signifier. This is what I offer up for interpretation, and my interlocutor interprets not just the signified that corresponds to this signifier, but along with it, where the particular variant I have used stands in the intersecting hierarchies of change – conservatism vs. innovation, powerfulness, and all those elements that contribute to 'class'. Consider the following exchange:

A: So what does Milligan think of your report?
B: He says the thing is the boss doesn't like it.
B': He's like the thing is is the boss is just so not liking it?

On some abstract level B and B' are 'saying the same thing'. But it is hard, initially at least, to interpret B and B' as being the same person – parent and offspring, more probably. Knowing the power of audience design (§3.1), it is possible that B' is a particularly linguistically accommodating parent responding to a question from his or her offspring A, or vice versa. But I, personally, am not so accommodating, and cannot imagine myself uttering B' except to imitate someone else's speech. It embodies six features which I do not believe I ever use, but hear with great frequency and have seen attested by others in the speech of middle-class native speakers from across the English-speaking world, the frequency increasing as the speaker's age drops from 50+ to 25 or younger:

- the so-called 'new quotative' *be like* (often followed by a glottal stop and a pause) to introduce an embedded main or independent clause representing reported speech (or pseudo-reported speech, indicating a general attitude rather than actual words spoken – *she's like, yeah right*).
- the doubling of *is* in phrases such as *The thing is, The trouble is, The problem is*, and so on, producing *The thing is is, The trouble is is, The problem is is*. This began to be remarked upon by linguists on The LINGUIST List, the internet bulletin board, around 1991, and is now very well attested.
- the use of *just*, or *so*, or *just so* in unmarked declarative sentences expressing a value judgement. By 'unmarked' I mean that there is no independent basis, apart from the *just so* itself, for saying that these sentences are emphatic in some way, especially for those speakers who seem rarely to express a value judgement, however anodyne, without *just so*: *It's just so nice that you could come, I'm just so happy to see you, We just had so much fun, It's just so cold out today*.
- the use of *so* before a present participle – *I am so enjoying this*, or indeed *I am so not enjoying this*. It cannot be entirely disconnected from the preceding feature, the extension of *(just) so*.
- the extension of the present progressive to verbs such as *like* that have not traditionally taken it. *I'm enjoying this* is something which I often say; *I'm liking this* is something which, again, I could say only in imitation of a different kind of English from my own. Trappes-Lomax (2005) has linked this change to the McDonald's advertising campaign slogan *I'm lovin' it*.[14]
- the use of rising intonation at the end of declarative sentences, making them sound like what in Standard English would be questions. *My computer crashed? I don't know what to do? I'm just like, so frustrated?*

Attentive readers will have noticed that the ongoing changes in English discussed in this section overlap with the features of women's language, or powerless language, as listed on pp. 73–4. Feature 10 of that list is precisely the use of rising intonation in declarative sentences. The use of 'emphatic *so*' is included under the heading 'speaking in italics'. Possibly *the thing is is* is a case of 'hypercorrect grammar'.

I shall return to this last line of explanation further on. First, however, I want to explore a rather different explanatory strategy – different because it considers neither the structure of the sentence nor how it is managed nor what it expresses in terms of meaning content, at least as we usually conceive it. Instead it takes the view that a crucial function of *The thing is is* is to mark the speaker as a member of the sub-community of English speakers who say *The thing is is*. And likewise with the other features. Belonging to this sub-community has a potential identity value to it for just so long as not all members of the larger community say *The thing is is*.

Linguists usually think of language change in terms of a two-tiered process of innovation followed by spread. The language community comes into play only in the second phase. The innovation begins with an individual, and it is there that all the modes of explanation laid out above are aimed. By this view, spread will occur inevitably if the change is well enough motivated within the structure of the language itself. The extent and rate of spread is something for the sociolinguist to measure, and while the role of sub-communities is recognised as an important factor in the spread of change, it is not ordinarily proposed by linguists as a primary reason for a change occurring.

But there are good reasons for turning this around, and saying that a change will spread if and only if the linguistic sub-community identity it defines coincides sufficiently with other defining features of that sub-community, non-linguistic as well as linguistic. In other words, the place to look for the primary explanation of change is not the language, but the speakers – the whole language-producing human beings, not patterns of what they produce that have been abstracted away from them. The 'meaning' of any innovative feature in language is first and foremost what it means to be someone who does or doesn't use it – how such persons are perceived by themselves and others. The primary difference between *He says the thing is the boss doesn't like it* and *He's like the thing is is the boss is just so not liking it?* is in the speaker, not the text. This is not to claim that the two sentences 'mean' exactly the same thing (as declarations abstracted away from their speakers), even though we might predict with accuracy that the one and the other are what person x and person y might say in a particular circumstance. The pragmatic force of some of the extra elements, for example, might be very significant. But however we characterise the difference in their meaning as sentences, this is secondary to the totality of how we interpret speakers x and y themselves on the basis of their using or not using these particular pragmatic elements.

Of course, speakers do not in most cases make a deliberate choice to use *the thing is is*, etc. But then, one thing which linguistic pragmatics has made us very aware of is the commonness of 'indirect speech acts'. We do not usually bring conversations to a close by saying 'I've talked to you long enough, goodbye', but by switching from asking questions to making comments on the conversation itself, shortening our utterances, and so on. In §4.3 I discussed how, in languages which have an active *tu/vous* type distinction, the 'invitation' to switch from the formal to the informal form may come as a direct invitation, or by one person simply starting to use *tu* to the other. What I want to suggest here is that when someone in conversation with me says *The thing is is*, this is an indirect invitation to me to say it as well, just as the use of *tu* is.

Admittedly the case of the pronouns is special because it has been so strongly institutionalised and ritualised as marking the precise nature of the relationship between two people. With the innovations, it is instead a matter of marking one's group or sub-community belonging, which still impacts on the relationship with the interlocutor. In both cases, the issuing of the indirect invitation may or may not be something the issuer is aware of – one can slip into the *tu* without ever planning to or even realising it, though again the likelihood of awareness is greater here than with the innovations because of the ritualistic factor. But finally it does not matter; for if the uttering of *The thing is is* is 'unconscious', then, even if the perception of it and response to it are also unconscious, there is no reason to think that all these unconscious processes are somehow insulated from one another. We are still dealing with direct reactions.

If I accept the 'indirect invitation' to say *The thing is is*, I mark myself as belonging to the same group as my interlocutor. If I do not accept, I mark myself as not belonging, which my interlocutor may interpret as a deliberate refusal or a failure from ignorance, or may not interpret at all. But it is unlikely that the sum total of all the acceptances or refusals I give, together with all the other signals I send intentionally and unintentionally, is going to escape interpretation. Indeed, it is from them that the other person is going to construct her image of who I am, at a deeper and more powerful level than from the 'rational' contents of the words I speak.

Before leaving the case of *tu* and *vous*, it is worth noting that when a change becomes sufficiently widespread, it can be the individuals who have resisted the change who form a distinctive minority sub-community. This has happened very markedly in the history of English, where the distinction between informal *thou* and formal *you* retreated in favour of the innovation of using *you* to everyone except God. But the Quakers, refusing the invitation to this innovation, became a linguistically distinctive sub-community outside those English dialect regions that retain the *thou–you* distinction for people.

Now to come to the logical difficulty. I am saying that the principal factor to be considered in understanding why so many people say *The thing is is* is that they want to belong, or project themselves as belonging, to the group of people who say *The thing is is*. Is there not a logical circularity here? If we define a linguistic identity according to the way people speak, how can we then turn around and use that same identity to explain why they speak as they do? In part the answer is that 'the group of people who say *The thing is is*' have a great deal more in common than that particular structure. The linguistic innovation itself, like linguistic identity generally, is a kind of emblem that people use to interpret whether they will have the same likes and dislikes, can understand and trust each other, or more crassly, how much they can get from the other.

In Chapter 2 of Joseph (2004a) I have argued that, together with other animal species, we have evolved into instinctive overinterpreters of underspecified data. This means that we determine a lot more about each other on very little contact than a rational analysis would permit us to know; indeed, a lot of what we determine in this way is wrong, but a phenomenal amount of it is accurate enough for our purposes. When I hear someone say *just so* in two or three successive sentences, I instinctively draw a lot of conclusions about the person, that will vary according to how well the general associations I make with *just-so* speakers accord with how this individual looks, dresses, speaks and otherwise behaves. It is largely on this basis that I evaluate the truth or falsity of the assertions they make to me in the words they utter. This, again, is why linguistic identity matters so much. It comes into operation *before* the functioning of language as a tool for representation and communication, and *determines* that functioning, rather than being some kind of second-level gloss.

As I said, this is part of the answer to the objection that linguistic identity provides a circular explanation for what happens in language. The data of linguistic identity are subjected to massive overinterpretation that connects them with other aspects of mind and behaviour, and these connections can in fact be investigated empirically to determine just what non-linguistic associations people make with particular linguistic features. The rest of the answer is that the overinterpretation that is intrinsic to the functioning of linguistic identity does indeed operate with a con-siderable amount of logical circularity. For instance, suppose I associate final rising intonation in declarative sentences with 'powerless' speakers, because my experience has been that non-professional people use it more than professional people. I then hear it used by an expert medical witness in a legal case, and my reaction is that he is less sure of his facts than he purports to be. I may be right or wrong, but my reaction is based on a logical circle:

Non-professional people say x
Dr A says x
Dr A is insufficiently professional

The logical flaw here is actually contained in the first proposition: from my ex-perience of hearing only non-professional people say x, I have determined that x is a marker of non-professional identity. The fact that I associate rising intonation with questions, and questions with lack of information, reinforces the connection. But it is circular nonetheless, just as circular as it would be to assume that someone must be an authority on what they are talking about just because they have the title 'Doctor'. To be a proper syllogism it would have to have this form:

Only non-professionals say x
Dr A says x
Dr A is a non-professional (in spite of the title)

– but it is impossible to imagine anything that 'only non-professionals say' outside the bounds of the professional lexicon.

I am not claiming that the conclusion drawn about Dr A on the basis of intonation patterns is necessarily mistaken. The complexity of linguistic identity is such that this conclusion, although untenable by the strictures of predicate logic, may be perceptive and astute and help to prevent a miscarriage of justice. It may also be silly and misguided and help to thwart justice – such is the complexity and power of language in its political dimension.

On the other hand, looking back from today, when those features that looked like 'women's language' to Lakoff in 1973 and 'powerless language' to O'Barr in 1982 have now spread to become normal features of the English of anyone under the age of twenty-five, what can we conclude? That the denizens of the English-speaking world have become more feminine, or less powerful? Or that, for these changes-in-progress, women rather than men were in the vanguard, and people in professional and other 'powerful' positions were, characteristically, conservative enough in their usage to refuse the implicit invitation to take on these innovations? This appears a far more cogent explanation. It also serves to caution us against taking Voloshinov too literally. To imagine that class struggle, or any other political struggle, is 'fixed' in the linguistic sign is to attribute too little power to the capacity for reshaping the sign by the person who receives and interprets it, and to ignore the fact that this interpretation extends beyond the utterance to the speaker. What Lakoff took to be a fixed system of signs constituting 'women's language' has turned out to be a fluid system of signs, interpretable in various ways, including political ways, and where the politics of gender plays a more oblique part than Lakoff's particular optic made it appear.

SUGGESTED FURTHER READING

On ideological aspects of linguistic politeness: Bargiela-Chiappini (2003), Beeching (2002), Christie (ed.) (2004), Eelen (2001), Hickey and Stewart (eds) (2005), Kienpointner (ed.) (1999), Locher (2004).

On language and gender: Cameron and Kulick (2003), Holmes and Meyerhoff (eds) (2003).

On powerful/powerless language: Grob, Meyers and Schuh (1997), Harris (1997, 2001), Lakoff (1990, 2000), O'Barr (2001), O'Barr and O'Barr (eds) (1976), Shapiro (ed.) (1984), Thornborrow (2002).

On linguistic form and personal and social identity: Mühlhäusler *et al.* (1990), Suleiman (2004).

On political aspects of language change: Joseph (2000d), Thomason (1999).

On Bakhtin on language: Crowley (2001).

A number of journals serve the areas covered in this chapter, among which *Discourse and Society* and the *Journal of Pragmatics* regularly feature relevant work.

NOTES

1. Here, as in certain other works by those close to Bakhtin, his ideas are so closely interwoven with theirs that it remains unclear to what extent Bakhtin should be considered the co-author or indeed the author (see Todorov 1984).

2. For Saussure's part, he had insisted that the language system is not abstract but concrete because it is 'psychologically real' for speakers (see Joseph 2004b: 64–5).

3. In continental Europe, significant contributions to a Marxist account of language would be made by Ferrucio Rossi-Landi (1921–85) and Michel Pêcheux (1938–84) (Rossi-Landi 1975, 1983, Pêcheux 1982).

4. See further Joseph (1987b: 261–3), and for a study looking in greater depth at practices in

four languages (Portuguese, Georgian, Norwegian and Arabic), Braun (1988). Within Indo-European, the origins of deferential use of plural for singular, in the first as well as the second person (the 'royal we'), is best attested within the Latin-Romance branch, beginning with Latin documents of the early Christian era (see Maley 1974). Romance historical linguists have long connected this usage with rule by joint emperors – a rather unusual connection for linguists to make, given that political factors are rarely invoked in explanations of grammatical change. Still, the *ad hoc* nature of this particular explanation gives cause for dubiety (see Joseph 1987b: 261).

5. As noted in Joseph (1987b: 262), certain modern Italian and Daco-Romance dialects never developed deferential address, and in a range of Breton dialects, *c'hwi*, originally plural, has undergone the same changes as English *you*, ending up as the sole second-person pronoun.

6. I refer here to the standard languages, there being considerable variation among dialects in the polite address forms used. For details see Joseph (1987b: 262–3, Table One).

7. I found myself in such a situation when, on a visit to Quebec in 1992, I was conversing with a native speaker of Quebec French and misinterpreted her use of the impersonal *tu* (comparable to the English impersonal *you* in *You never know*) as an invitation of this sort. When I then addressed her as *tu*, it was clear from her shocked reaction that she received *my* invitation as completely inappropriate, and she went on addressing me as *vous* until she could slip away.

8. The examples are drawn from Holmes (2001: 244).

9. On the other hand, in British English, *ladies* does not force one to designate a woman's social status, as its male counterparts *lords* and *gentlemen* do.

10. In January 2001, 12 of the USA's 100 largest cities had women mayors or city managers, while 203 of the 978 cities with more than 30,000 residents had women mayors (information from <http://www.gendergap.com/governme.htm>, citing Bureau of the Census, U.S. Department of Commerce for the first figure and Center for the American Woman and Politics and the United States Conference of Mayors January 2001 directory for the second).

11. That the University of Geneva, Saussure's old stomping ground, has recently begun advertising for "Postes de professeur-e ordinaire ou adjoint-e"; French speakers whose reactions I have sought do not find the 'bisexual' *adjoint-e* shocking or objectionable but do tend to react strongly against the optional addition of feminine *-e* to the noun *professeur*, traditionally masculine even when the referent is a woman.

12. Here I conflate O'Barr's two categories 'Witness asks lawyer questions' and 'Gestures', for each of which Woman A performed two occurrences.

13. And some (like me) would shy away from 'variation' as suggesting the deeper existence of something invariant that then gets 'used' in a variable way, when in truth the different ways of speaking are the first and primary reality. But that just makes the point even stronger.

14. In Trappes-Lomax's view, the slogan only works because it picks up on a change that is already potentially ready to happen, perhaps already present in the most 'advanced' usage. This has been confirmed to me by Sarah M. Hall, who writes that 'I have noticed in recent re-runs of *Friends* on TV (pre-dating the McDonald's ad) that they occasionally use the "I'm loving this" type of construction' (email to the author, 30 Nov. 2005).

Chapter 5

Taboo language and its restriction

5.1 SWEARING

The word *taboo* is a borrowing from Tongan, first introduced into English by Captain James Cook (1728–79) in the second volume of his *A Voyage to the Pacific Ocean* (2nd edn, 1785; see further Gray 1983). Not only is the word modern (outside Polynesia), but so is the concept of a category of words whose most salient feature is that, whether on grounds of profanity or obscenity or political offensiveness, they are 'forbidden' in the minds of speakers, those who use them as well as those who don't. The concept's modernity is signalled by the exoticness of the word *taboo*, implying as it does that perspectives gained from encounters with 'primitive' peoples can deepen our understanding of our own civilised cultures, a hallmark of modernist thinking. But it is ironic that Polynesian languages, with few exceptions, do not have swearing, as neither do any of the American Indian languages.[1]

Modern too is the idea that those who use taboo words do so principally because they *are* taboo. This view developed and spread quickly through the nineteenth century, becoming ubiquitous in twentieth-century treatments of language.[2] Indeed it has become such a commonsense notion that it's difficult to place ourselves outside it and see it as a historical product. For us, where swearing is concerned, taboos are made to be broken. The semantic significance of the words seems to be a secondary consideration. The primary one is that the taboo words signify forbiddenness, the social force that restricts what an individual is free to do, and impropriety, another social determination of what is allowable behaviour for persons desiring social acceptance. The breaking of the taboo signifies various things, depending on the context, about the person breaking it. It can signify rebellion against social force generally, in which case it is the verbal equivalent of random vandalism, as when adolescents smash down tombstones in a cemetery at night, or against a particular social force such as is found in one's family or workplace. When directed at an individual, it is less like vandalism than like a well-aimed punch.

However, most of the swearing I hear around me does not appear to be performing any of the functions just described, but instead has the rather more positive function of *bonding* people through their mutual abrogation of the taboo. Groups of students who have just finished their exams and are feeling on top of the world integrate taboo words into their conversation with no less frequency than aggrieved coal miners do. Anyone who failed to join in with the swearing would be holding themselves back at the margins of the group, just like the refusers of innovative forms discussed in §4.6. In the case of swearing the language involved tends to be historically venerable ('Anglo-Saxon') rather than innovative. But just as the perception of a form as new requires awareness of an older norm from which it deviates, perception of a form as taboo demands awareness of the social norm that it defies. Over time the force of this social norm may be less keenly felt, and the taboo words may gradually become conventionalised into a norm for the sub-group for which it functions as an identity marker. Eventually, awareness of the words' taboo nature can even disappear, as has happened for example with French *con*, originally 'vagina', but now meaning 'stupid', and with few speakers under the age of about fifty having any awareness of its once strong taboo status.

Modern linguists operate with a catch-all classification of taboo words because, for us as speakers, there is such an active concept covering a wide variety of locutions. Yet we are engaging in anachronism if we project it backwards much beyond the nineteenth century. Traditionally, the distinction in speech acts between swearing, cursing and obscenity (or 'bawdy talk') was enormous. Indeed we can't even separate out obscenity – when people talked bawdy they were making assertions or asking questions, which happened to be on topics that were appropriate in limited contexts only. John Disney (1677–1730) makes the following distinctions:

- **Obscenity**: '*Obscene Talking*, and lewd *Poetry, Books,* and *Pictures*; which assault the chastity of the Mind, and inflame Imagination in a very dangerous way.' (Disney 1729: 2)
- **Cursing**: 'Cursing is the declarative Act of wishing some terrible Evil to another.' (ibid.: 196)
- **Swearing**: 'Swearing, call it *vain*, or *Prophane*, (for they are much the same, what difference soever the *Jewish Rabbies* made …).' (ibid.: 194)

Disney is unusual in discussing obscene language at all, but the quotation shows how he immediately casts it into the context of 'Poetry, Books, and Pictures'. He has a separate and much longer chapter on 'play-actors', for it was the stage with its representations of obscene behaviour that was the real lightning rod. As the page numbers indicate, the discussion of obscene language in Disney is far removed from his treatment of swearing and cursing – his book is organised in a way that builds up to the most serious crimes, and swearing, cursing and play-acting are at the pinnacle.

In the seventeenth century and still into the nineteenth, 'swearing' meant swearing an oath, either to the truth or falsity of something or to the keeping of a promise. This was an important and solemn discourse function, and great consternation arose because oaths were increasingly being sworn over the most trivial matters. In the words of one of the most widely circulated eighteenth-century works on the subject, by the Bishop of London, Edmund Gibson (1669–1748):

[Scripture] ought to teach all Christians to use it [the Name of God] sparingly and reverently; not to bring it too familiarly into any of their Discourses concerning the Affairs of this World, much less to mix it daily and hourly (as the common Swearers do) with their Sports and Passions, their Riots and Excesses.

2. The same Thing is to be said of the Name of *Jesus Christ* ... And yet how little this is remembered or regarded by many careless and profane Christians, who allow themselves in a wicked Habit of bringing the sacred Name of JESUS and CHRIST to express their Wonder, and confirm their Promises or Purposes, in the most slight and trivial Matters. (Gibson 1760: 6–7)

For whatever reason, it had become normal to *intensify* what was said by including oaths that didn't really mean what they appeared to mean. Discursively, it is the same sort of intensifying function that we can currently observe happening with the *just so* speakers discussed in §4.6. What is the meaning of 'by God' in *By God, it's hot today?* How does this sentence differ from *It's hot today?* Hearing the sentence with 'by God', we interpret the speaker as experiencing a more intense discomfort. The speaker might also have said *It's awfully/mighty/jolly/bloody hot today*, or indeed *It's just so hot today.* Very few people nowadays would interpret the 'by God' as occupying another linguistic class altogether, that of a sacred oath by which the speaker solemnly asserts the truth of the proposition *It's hot today*.

As we go back in time, however, the proportion of people who did interpret it this way rises. There were also people for whom swearing appears to have been bleached of its literal oath function outside a formal context such as a court of law. But no one seems to have understood what was happening in the way I've just described it, not even Dan Michel, who in the *Ayenbite of Inwyt* (1340) acknowledged that some people swear

By habit [or custom], as at each word. For some are so evil taught that they can say nothing without swearing. They hold God in great unworship [contempt] when all day and for nought him call to witness of all that is said, for swearing is no other thing but calling God to witness, and his mother and his holy ones [halzen]. (Cited by Montagu 1967: 123)

Though habitual, the swearing is taken to have its full and literal meaning in the speaker's intention. The words meant what they meant, and the lack of any semantic connection between that meaning and the context in which they were used simply made the swearer guilty of a breach of the First Commandment, against taking God's name *in vain* – because no one could imagine a context in which it might be necessary to invoke the sacred name to assert something so banal and self-evidently true or false as *It's hot today*.

By the sixteenth century a great profusion of oaths was recorded in the literature. The following is a selection of just some of those containing the word *God's* – but of course oaths on Jesus Christ, the names of saints, pagan gods, parts of one's body and words like *cock* and *giz* that sound like God or Jesus were no less common:[5]

by God's blessed angel, God's arms, God's limbs, God's body, God's bodykins, by God's (precious) bones, God's bread, by God's dear brother, by Goddes corps, by God's cross, by God's precious deer, by Goddes dignitee/dentie/dines, by goddys dome, by God's fast/vast/fate, Gods fish, by God's foot, God's fury, for Goddes herte, be godes grace/by God's grace, by God's guts, by God's heart/hat, God's (precious) Lady, God's lady, by God's lid [eyelids], God's life, God's light, God's Lord, for Godes love, God's malt, God's nails, God's good mercy, be godes name/o' God's name, Godsnigs, by God's passion, for/o' the passion of God, by God's pity, by goddys pyne, By Gods precious/God's precious, God's sacrament, Sacrament of God, for God's sake, God's santy [sanctity], by God's side, (by) God's soul, (by) God's will, God's word, (by) God's (glorious) wounds, God for his passion. (Swaen 1898: 30–34)

Moving up to the late seventeenth century, and to the newly emergent social class of the *beaux* or dandies, we have the following sample of their way of discoursing furnished by Daniel Defoe (1660 or 1661–1731). Note that the nature of the 'swearing' has expanded to include self-curses like *God damn me* and *let me die*.

I must descend a little to Particulars, and desire the Reader a little to foul his Mouth with the Bruitish, Sordid, Sensless Expressions, which some Gentlemen call Polite *English*, and speaking with a Grace.

...

[Tom:] Jack, *God damn me* Jack, *How do'st do, thou little dear Son of a Whore? How hast thou done this long time, by God?* – And then they kiss; and the t'other, as lewd as himself, goes on;

[Jack:] *Dear* Tom, *I am glad to see thee with all my heart, let me dye. Come, let us go take a Bottle, we must not part so; prithee let's go and be drunk by God.* –

This is some of our new florid Language, and the Graces and Delicacies of Stile, which if it were put into *Latin*, I wou'd fain know which is the principal Verb. (Defoe 1697: 241–2)

It is surprising that Defoe considers Jack's bit 'as lewd as' Tom's, since Jack hasn't done any 'swearing' by modern lights. But in fact each of them has sworn two clear oaths – in Tom's case, *God damn me* and *by God*, and in Jack's case, *let me dye* and *by God*, plus another quasi-oath for Jack, *with all my heart*. Tom's *Son of a Whore* and Jack's invitation to get drunk are both lewd and balance each other out, though neither is 'swearing' in Defoe's terms. But keep in mind Defoe's closing remark about the 'ungrammaticality' of the language – I'll be coming back to this.

Just how bad was swearing reckoned to be in this period? Edward Stephens (d. 1706) put it in the same league with witchcraft and devilry:

Prophane SWEARING, is ... an affected Ornament of Speech and Gallantry, ... A Crime so *Unnatural, and intirely Diabolical*, without any Natural Disposition to it, but merely of Diabolical Impression, that the Common Swearer may reasonably be reputed an Associate with that Cursed Prophane Company of Witches, and Confederates with the Devil, and ought to be abhorred by all Sober People, and Punished in the next degree to that accursed Crew. (Stephens 1695: 14)

The terms used by Stephens to describe swearing go far beyond Defoe's complaint about grammar. In saying that there is no 'Natural Disposition' to swearing, he apparently means that it serves no *functional purpose*. It is a mere 'Ornament', an accessory or adjunct, and an 'affected' one, that is, artificial and deliberate. Stephens clearly believes that common swearers are choosing their words, and thus choosing to profane the sacred name. Virtually the same opinion is ventured by Disney, except that he does suggest a possible functional purpose for swearing.

> Swearing by God, or Christ, in ordinary Conversation, is highly Shocking and Offensive: because those venerable Names, which should never be *thought of* without the utmost Reverence,) are undiscriminately and profanely tossed about, to patronize a rash, (perhaps a false, or wicked) Resolution; an idle and uncertain Story, and perhaps a Lye; to serve an unaffected Ornament of Speech; or as an Expletive, and By-word, to supply the want of Sense ... (Disney 1729: 194)

At the end of this passage we have a hint of the modern concept of the 'pause filler', the 'by-word' that is uttered to fill a gap in the continuous meaning of one's utterance ('supply the want of Sense'). This does not make swearing any less shocking or offensive to Disney, but it does open up the possibility that it is not always *deliberately* sacriligeous. That seems to be the significance too of the fact that, where Stephens called swearing 'an *affected* Ornament of Speech', Disney says exactly the opposite, 'to serve an *unaffected* Ornament of Speech' – not deliberate.

Stephens and Disney agree that swearing has sense, that it means what it appears on the surface to mean; otherwise it could not 'supply the want of Sense', as Disney put it. As the eighteenth century progressed, however, the idea emerged that maybe this swearing really has *no sense at all*. The first step was to recognise that the sacrilege might not be deliberate; the next was to recall, as suggested by the *Ayenbite of Inwyt*, that it might be a matter of habit. An anonymous treatise by 'A Soldier' published in 1752 introduces the idea of 'habitual' swearing, though without any indication that this might mitigate the crime.

> But come in the third Place to a yet greater abuse of this great and feared Name, altogether unworthy of a rational Creature. These are I mean customary and habitual Swearers and Blasphemers of God, whose Tongues surely are touched with the virulent Poison of Hell who cannot express three single Words, or a whole Sentence without tearing and prophaning that sacred Name, as if they had been made for no other End at all, but to propagate Blasphemy against God; and introduce the Language of the bottomless Pit among the Children of Men ... (Anon. 1752: 9)

Bishop Gibson too ascribes common swearing to habit:

> Consider how Men fall at first into the Custom of Swearing; that it is never taken up (as all wise Designs are) with Consideration, or upon a Foresight of any Benefit that is likely to arise from it; but is usually owing to profane Company, and suffered to grow into a Habit through a supine careless Humour ... (Gibson 1760: 16)

Arguably, if 'A Soldier' is right and it is the language of Hell itself that we hear from the mouths of common swearers, for it to become a habit is *even worse* than if it is occasional and deliberate. Habit is the absence of reason – it is therefore more animal than human in nature. This seems to be the view shared by Bishop Gibson, but he adduces another contextual factor that pushes his understanding toward the modern view:

> Another Aggravation of the Guilt of Common Swearing, is, the Frequency of it; that it is repeated every Day, and every Hour, nay, almost every Minute, after it is grown into a Habit. Oaths flow from such Men without Thinking, and are a constant and almost necessary part of their Mirth, Passion and Discourse. (Gibson 1760: 15)

What the Bishop recognises is that swearing is a part of *mirth*, just as, in the quotation on p. 87 above, he linked it with the swearers' 'Sports and Passions, their Riots and Excesses'. He cannot conceive of any reason why anyone should *enjoy* swearing, but to his credit he sees that it is so and admits it – and the immediately recognisable truth of his observations may help explain why his little book, intended 'to be put privately into the Hands of Persons who are addicted to Swearing', had gone through twenty printings by 1760 and would continued to be printed into the early nineteenth century.

5.2 THE LANGUAGE POLICE STATE

On the pragmatic level, Gibson pointed to a secular problem with common swearing that might have made an impression even on those who had grown immune to being preached at:

> [W]here Swearing is grown into a Habit, it breaks out equally upon any Occasion, or no Occasion : and in Cases where there is most Occasion; that is, when they cannot easily make themselves believed, it stands them in no Stead; because none will believe him the more for Swearing, who is known to have lost all *Reverence* for an Oath. (Gibson 1760: 19)

Non-profane oath-taking was still a very serious business in the eighteenth century, more so than today, where in secular societies it is normally only in courts of law that we are asked to swear to the truth of our declarations, on penalty of perjury. (It is also the case, though less explicitly, when we sign a claim form for expenses, insurance claims and the like.) Common swearers could not be trusted to take their oaths seriously, making them risky people to do any sort of business with. Indeed, technically, they were criminals.

Within the English-speaking world, Scotland pioneered legislation against profane swearing and cursing. Disney (1729: 201) records concerning the Scots that

> Donald VI, their King, (about the year, 900.) made a Law, that those who were guilty of rash or common swearing [by *God's*] or cursing by the *Devil's* name, should *have their Lips seared with a red-hot Iron.*

Previously, any such punishments had been left to ecclesiastical authorities. With modern anti-swearing legislation too, it was Scotland that led the way in 1551, some fifty years before England. Cursing was made a capital offence, but only if directed at God or one's own parents, and only if one was not 'distracted', i.e. deranged (Grant 1700: 46, 48). Profane swearing, along with curses not directed at God or one's parents, were still criminal acts, but the punishment was limited to fines, with some provision for imprisonment and placing in stocks.

> Abominable *Oaths*, and detestable *Execrations*, particularly Swearing in vaine by GOD's Blood, Body, Passions, and Wounds; Saying Devil Stick, Gore, Rost, or Rieve, them; and *such other Execrations* : are Punished as in the Act Which is Ratified : [Act 16, Parl. 5. Q.M.] … And that all *House-Holders Delate* Transgressors within their Houses, under paine of being punished *as Offenders* themselves. (ibid.: 46–7)

The last sentence is especially noteworthy. Those who ran public houses – just the sort of place where the 'sports, riots and excesses' that induce common swearing abound – had to arrest anyone who swore, or risked being turned in themselves. The fines were considerable, and doubled for a repeated offence; and informers got a share (ibid.: 47–8). Montagu (1967: 131) states that 'The records of the local authorities from Glasgow to Aberdeen testify to the vigor and resolution with which the campaign against swearing was being prosecuted toward the latter part of the [sixteenth] century'.

It was the original language police state, and everyone had an interest in it, whether as a common swearer or a potential informer – or as the innocent victim of an informer who had misheard something, just wanted the money, or was out for revenge. How, after all, could you prove your innocence when charged with profane swearing, if there were no witnesses? All you could do was to swear an oath, that, by God, you had not sworn. But, as Gibson noted, as an accused common swearer your oath's sincerity was less likely to be believed. It is not even clear that your accuser was obliged to repeat the oath he claimed to have heard you swear – technically, he would have been subject to prosecution had he done so, since the law provides no exclusion for *quoting* a profane oath.

In England, the laws do not seem to have been applied with quite so much success, except during the Commonwealth and Protectorate (1649–60), when Puritanical mores were in the ascendant. Thereafter, complaints about the failure to enforce the laws are common, as are attempts at emending the laws themselves. By the end of the century, Stephens is complaining about people's unwillingness to turn 'informer' (1695: 10). In general, writers in this period are glad that the monarchy has been restored and happy to have seen off the Commonwealth and Protectorate, but, they repeat, at least back then the swearing was kept down. What is more, soon after the Restoration, London was hit with the calamities of the plague (1664–5) and the Great Fire (1666), creating a long-lasting sense that the nation was under a curse, and was being punished for the sinfulness of its people. This is reflected in Stephens' depiction of swearing as 'an epidemical Sin in this Nation', and he goes on to say:

[W]hat a load of Guilt doth lye upon this Nation upon the score of this one particular ... [T]hough this be a *Christian State*, yet is the whole Nation in a very *sinful State*, and hath great reason to fear some very severe *Judgment of God* for the Punishment and Correction thereof. (Stephens 1695: 10–11)

Similarly, Edward Fowler (1632–1714) explains that it is incumbent upon every citizen to upbraid common swearers for their sin, for the salvation of the nation as a whole (Fowler 1692: 16). Stephens too makes the point that not just the common swearers are to blame, but that everyone shares in the 'National Guilt' (1695: 9).

The language police state that appears to have functioned for a decade or two in the seventeenth century had broken down in England, and would soon do the same in Scotland. Yet there remained, besides the general fear for the nation, a more concrete worry about the threat which common swearing posed to the law. Modern rules of evidence were not yet developed; as indicated earlier, the oath remained the primary guarantor of truth. And common swearing was seen as diluting the sacred magic of the oath, removing the fear of God from the words.

But the *political* Reason, why *Magistrates* are highly concerned to suppress Common Swearing, is, that it naturally leads to *Perjury*; which is destructive to the Safety, and all the Interests of Mankind ... The Common Swearer must undoubtedly (in the Course of such a Habit) very often swear to what he knows or believes to be *false*; and oftener still to *Uncertainties*, or what he does not know to be true ... (Disney 1729: 196)

Moreover, common swearing was coming increasingly to be perceived as constituting a threat to *reason* itself. A number of the seventeenth-century writers quoted here associate swearing with the passions, traditionally the opposing force to reason, yet most take it for granted that the swearer is acting on deliberate choice. The Scots law which exempted 'distracted' persons from capital punishment for cursing clearly takes the presence or absence of reason to be an entirely separate matter from the use of profanity. The strongest voice associating swearing with unreason is Defoe's – we saw in §5.1 his remark on the swearing of the Dandies that 'if it were put into *Latin*, I wou'd fain know which is the principal Verb'. Language without grammar is language without reason. Defoe further says of common swearing:

'Tis a senseless, foolish, ridiculous Practice; 'tis a Mean to no manner of End; 'tis Words spoken which signify nothing; 'tis Folly acted for the sake of Folly ...; Whoredoms and Ravishments, Adulteries and Sodomy, are committed to please a vicious Appetite, and have always alluring Objects; ... but this, of all Vicious Practices, seems the most Nonsensical and Ridiculous; there is neither Pleasure nor Profit; no Design pursued, no Lust gratified, but is a mere Frenzy of the Tongue, a Vomit of the Brain, which works by putting a Contrary upon the Course of Nature. (Defoe 1697: 247–8)

One would hardly have found Bishop Gibson or any of our other divinely-minded writers making the argument that at least whoring, rape, adultery and sodomy *make sense* – hence swearing, which doesn't, is a worse sin than any of those. Significantly too, Defoe holds that, whereas common swearing is a heinous crime against nature, obscenity ('bawdy talk') is not a crime at all, but merely an impertinence, a breach of manners. He makes this clear in a part of his discussion where, having established the criminality of swearing, he goes on to add to the arguments against it the fact that it is *also* an impertinent breach of manners. In this regard he compares it to two other such breaches, which however are *not* crimes:

> [T]his sordid Habit, even those that practice it will own to be a Crime, and make no Excuse for it; and the most I cou'd ever hear a man say for it, was, That *he cou'd not help it.*
>
> Besides, as 'tis an inexcusable Impertinence, so 'tis a Breach upon Good Manners and Conversation, for a man to impose the Clamour of his Oaths upon the Company he converses with; if there be any one person in the Company that does not approve the way, 'tis an imposing upon him with a freedom beyond Civility; as if a man shou'd *Fart* before a Justice, or *talk Bawdy* before the Queen, or the like. (ibid.: 248–9)

It is surprising that 'talking bawdy before the Queen' would have been considered merely an impertinence in this period, akin to letting a fart in court. Admittedly, this is from a man who also thinks that saying *Let me die* is worse than committing rape, but it is confirmed by the difference in how profanity and obscenity were treated in law.

Defoe's proposed solution to the threat to reason posed by common swearing was to found a language Academy, which would set the example which 'must sink this Crime' (ibid.: 249). The proposal was never put into practice, any more than was the satirical 'Swearer's-Bank' devised by Jonathan Swift (1667–1745) to fund the government of Ireland by rigorously collecting the fines for swearing that remained on British law books through the eighteenth century (Swift 1720).

To summarise, swearing (*stricto sensu*) and attempts to suppress it occupy a central place in the political history of English. Swearing was the subject of endless legislation and condemnation, because it was seen as ruinous to the soul, public morality, the law, the nation, and rational thought and language. The modern category of 'taboo language' leads us anachronistically to conflate swearing with obscenity in describing periods when the latter was nothing like such a serious concern. The attempts at eradicating swearing were the first organised, sustained attempts at policing language. Their significance for the history of language standardisation calls for further attention, and the evolution of 'swearing' into a general category of taboo language demands further study for what it may reveal about changing concepts of language generally.

The 'language police state' did not end with the repeal of laws against common swearing. Its modern counterparts will be discussed later in this chapter. Nor has concern with swearing ended. Jim O'Connor of Illinois has had great success with his book *Cuss Control* (O'Connor 2000), which went into its third printing within two months of its publication, and his 'Cuss Control Academy', through which he offers presentations and workshops for individuals and workplaces aimed at reducing the level of swearing (in the broad modern sense).[4] Many of the points which the Academy cites under the heading 'What's wrong with swearing?' are ones which few people, including inveterate swearers, would disagree with:

Swearing Imposes a Personal Penalty: It gives a bad impression. It makes you unpleasant to be with. It endangers your relationships. It's a tool for whiners and complainers. It reduces respect people have for you. It shows you don't have control. It's a sign of a bad attitude. It discloses a lack of character. It's immature. It reflects ignorance. It sets a bad example.

Swearing is Bad for Society: It contributes to the decline of civility. It represents the dumbing down of America. It offends more people than you think. It makes others uncomfortable. It is disrespectful of others. It turns discussions into arguments. It can be a sign of hostility. It can lead to violence.

Swearing corrupts the English language: It's abrasive, lazy language. It doesn't communicate clearly. It neglects more meaningful words. It lacks imagination. It has lost its effectiveness.

O'Connor acknowledges that cursing has a certain value – 'it is one of the ways we express ourselves and communicate' – but argues that it has lost much of its expressive and communicative value through rampant overuse. That is undoubtedly true. Yet if all the negative attributes O'Connor cites are right, and swearing is no longer very effective for expressing and communicate certain things, then a couple of difficult questions arise: why does anyone swear, and why does anyone care? Humans are rational creatures, mostly, and though we do irrational things, it is normally only in other people's perspective, or in hindsight, that they are irrational – they usually seem right at the time. Although swearing 'makes you unpleasant to be with' for some people, it is apparent that nowadays most people actually find it quite enjoyable. Otherwise they would not pay to see top comedians who routinely use the most taboo words, or expect those same words in the movies they go to see or, in Britain, the television they watch after 9pm. Nor would they choose friends who use the same kind of language and give them positive reinforcement for it by laughing at their dirty jokes and bonding with them over their mutual breaking of linguistic taboos. For every relationship that swearing endangers, it strengthens twenty more.

How does this bonding happen? Again we can look to the familiar and polite personal pronouns for an analogy. Using *tu* with someone (other than the archaic use to a social inferior who gives *vous* in return) performs intimacy, if it is another adult, or paternalistic caring if it is a child, which is also a kind of emotional investment. Before the twentieth century, the mutual use of *tu* between a man and a woman who were not members of the same immediate family signified a sexual intimacy between them; when the man and the woman were not married, it involved the breaking of a taboo. When we break a taboo with someone, we bind ourselves to them through a mutual interest in protection, through the intimacy of a shared indiscretion and a shared secret. If I use a taboo word in conversation with one of my colleagues, it functions as an invitation much as the first use of *tu* does; if the colleague responds with taboo words of his or her own, we relate to each other henceforth with greater intimacy; if the invitation is refused, then potentially with greater distance.

In the mind–body dyad with which we operate, dirty language belongs to the body. It is evoked by bodily passions and it alludes to bodily functions. The mind is, or should be, the locus of pure knowledge and pure language, where 'pure language' is ambiguous between the senses of *clean* language and *good* (i.e. correct) language. Errors of language are likewise intrusions of the body upon the mind – the fact that we speak of 'slips of the tongue', for example, indicates that we think this way. In the politics of language, the head rules, the body follows. A limited amount of mild cursing is all right – it shows that one is human. But in excess it brings one down to the level of an animal.

Swearing represents a remarkably uninnovative segment of the English lexicon. From Victorian times through the 1960s the regular euphemism for dirty words was 'Anglo-Saxon' terms, which indeed the bulk of them are. Yet the average speaker considers them 'slang', thus putting them into a category whose prototypical members are recent innovations that are expected to have a short lifespan.[5] On p. 48 I cited what Hobsbawm (1990) had to say about the Victorian lower middle class and the desire to be the most 'proper' citizens of the empire. In Hobsbawm's view this accounts for the bundling together of 'correct English' and national identity. To this we can add 'clean' English, allowing a little bit of terminological anachronism, and remembering again what was said in §2.5 about the necessity for a modern national language to demonstrate its worthiness as a vehicle of knowledge, in the traditional Christian sense. Foul words, dragging in the body, reeking of putrid matter, 'corrupt' the language, and so threaten the nation.

5.3 THE POLITICS OF (SELF-)CENSORSHIP

Words can be offensive for reasons other than profanity or obscenity. We saw in the discussion of the Expurgated Scrabble Players' Dictionary in §1.6 that words referring disparagingly to particular groups of people were treated in just the same way as vulgar, obscene and profane words. For many of the words listed on p. 13 – DAGO, GOY, GRINGO, MICK, NANCY, NIGGER, PAPIST, POMMIE, POOFS, REDSKIN, SPIC, SQUAW, WETBACK, WOG, WOP, YID – there is a general consensus that they are offensive and cannot be used in public discourse, except (as here) to refer to the words themselves rather than the people they are meant to designate. For certain words, it is not so obvious: I have already discussed the cases of JESUIT and JEW, and alongside JEW we can put SHKOTZIM and SHIKSA as words that are not obviously derogatory. REDNECK too does not seem so derogatory as to belong in the same list with NIGGER, since it has never been used to keep a whole class of people down within a racist system. But perhaps that is not the right criterion to apply, and any term that a group of people does not use or recognise for themselves should be treated as offensive *prima facie*.

On the other hand, it is rarely if ever the case that all members of a group agree on exactly what term ought to be used to designate their group, and even if there is a broad consensus today, it may well change in a few years' time. Yet when more than one such term is in use, any of them is liable to cause offense to people who prefer another. In the northern USA in the early 1960s, *black* was an offensive term; older and working class people of colour used the term *colored people*, the younger and middle class used *Negro* (a word that caused discomfort to many because it was 'the same word' as *nigger*). Later in the decade, *black* came to be embraced – *Say it loud, I'm black and proud!* – and while *Negro* remained acceptable, *colored* did not. Within a few years it had become a racist designation. In the early 1970s, *Afro-American*, a term with a history going back to the late nineteenth century, came to be the 'received' term alongside *black*, and *Negro* receded to the racist margins along with *colored*. By the 1980s, *Afro-American* had ceased to be used, and *black* was the one acceptable term; but late in that decade *African American* came into vogue, and *black* began to be sidelined. In the 1990s, *person of color* became the fashionable term – *colored people* was by now completely archaic – and *black* began to be suspect. Today it is generally acceptable to use *black* as an adjective but not as a noun, since referring to people as *blacks* would offend by implying that their race, rather than their humanity, is their defining characteristic. In French, meanwhile, *les nègres* and *les noirs* have both become politically dubious terms, and the acceptable alternative is, ironically enough, *les blacks*.

Comparing the rate of use of the 'ultimate taboo' words *nigger* and *fuck* in the American media in 1994–5, Lester (1996) found that the former occurred much more frequently, 1,389 times compared with just 9 instances of *fuck*. This was the period of the O. J. Simpson trial, in which the use of *nigger* by a police officer who was a key prosecution witness became an issue. Lester also counted instances of the two words outside the context of the Simpson trial, and still found a huge difference: 3 occurrences of *fuck* to 742 of *nigger*. Still more surprisingly, he found that, of the small number of stories containing the word *fuck*, 72.7 per cent were on the broadcast media, and just 27.3 per cent in print media, whereas of the large number of stories containing *nigger*, the proportion was reversed, with 31.5 per cent on broadcast media, and 68.5 per cent in print.[6] While one hesitates to draw grand conclusions based on so few occurrences of one of the two words, it is striking that *nigger* is apparently so much more acceptable in print than in spoken language, while the same does not hold for *fuck*, which however is much more taboo overall (or at least was so ten years ago).

Language need not be profane, obscene or racial to be offensive. Terms indicating any group of people who have historically been discriminated against – handicapped people, for instance – are liable to become taboo and replaced with other terms, which again will have a short shelf-life because of the sensitivity of what they designate. Most of us try to avoid offending others when we can help it, and it is sometimes frustrating to use what one believes to be the acceptable term, only to discover that it is no longer 'politically correct'.[7] For publishers of school textbooks and standardised tests, not to have the acceptable language of the moment can mean financial disaster.

Ravitch (2003) has examined the rules which publishers and testing agencies have developed since the 1970s to restrict the use of language by the authors of textbooks and tests.[8] What she has found is stunning in its scope. Whole topic areas are taboo, because the bias and sensitivity panels which review the texts and tests have decided that they might be upsetting to some students. Virtually every text dating prior to 1970 has something in it – subject matter, language, the presence of outdated stereotypes – that is sure to offend someone either on the right or the left of the political spectrum, so such texts are either omitted or bowdlerised. Publishers look to the Texas State Board of Education to define the limits of what is acceptable to the right, and to its California counterpart for what is acceptable to the left.[9]

Although originally it was enraged parents and school boards that were doing the censoring by taking away the public procurement on which the sales of books and tests depend, the situation has changed so that now it is the publishers who 'self-censor'. But it is still censorship from the point of view of authors, who are told what cannot be talked about (dinosaurs, for instance, since acknowledging their existence implicitly raises questions about Biblical chronology and evolution) and what words cannot be used, and must accept this as the price of publication.

Ravitch's 'Glossary of Banned Words' (2003: 171–83), keyed to show the source publication for each ban, includes 404 items. They do not include any of the obvious obscenities, profanities or racial epithets – these are so plainly beyond the pale as not even to merit banning. Some of the items she cites are ones that it is perfectly reasonable to avoid, such as *the little woman* for wife, but many more seem to reflect an extraordinary degree of sensitivity, in some cases bordering on the absurd, and where it is difficult to see how the 'acceptable' alternative is any better. Below I have selected forty entries from Ravitch's 404:[10]

> **Able-bodied** (banned as offensive, replace with *person who is non-disabled*) [SF-AW]
>
> **America/American** (use with care, because it suggests 'geographical chauvinism' unless it applies to all people in North America, South America, and Central America; refer instead to *people of the United States*) [SF-AW, HM, HAR₂, NES]
>
> **Arthritic patient** (banned as offensive, replace with *person who has arthritis*) [SF-AW] – also **Paraplegic** (*person with paraplegia*)
>
> **Blind, the** (banned as offensive, replace with *people who are blind*) [SF-AW, HM, HAR₁, NES, ETS₁, ETS₂, RIV] – also **Deaf, the** (*people who are deaf* or a *person with loss of hearing*) [SF-AW, HM, NES, ETS₂], **Deaf-mute** (*person who can't hear or speak*) [SF-AW, HM, HAR₁, NES]
>
> **Bubbler** (banned as regional bias, replace with *water fountain*) [AIR] – also **Pop, Snow Cone, Soda**
>
> **Cassandra** (banned as sexist, replace with *pessimist*) [AIR] – also **Suffragette** (*suffragist*) [MMH, SF-AW, HAR₁, HAR₂, NES, ETS₂], **Tomboy** (no alternative suggested) [SF-AW, NES, AIR]
>
> **Courageous** (banned as patronizing when referring to a person with disabilities) [ETS₂] – also **Special** [SF-AW, AIR, ETS₂]
>
> **Devil** (banned) [AEP] – also **God, Hell**

Dialect (banned as ethnocentric, use sparingly, replace with *language*) [SF-AW]

Dogma (banned as ethnocentric, replace with *doctrine, belief*) [SF-AW] – also **Extremist** and **Fanatic** (*believer, follower, adherent*); **Dissenter** and **Heretic** [ETS₂], **Sect** (unless it separated from an established religion) [SF-AW, ETS₂]

Down's syndrome (banned as offensive, replace with *Down syndrome*) [ETS₂]

Fat (banned, replace with *heavy, obese*) [AEP]

Insane (banned as offensive, replace with *person who has an emotional disorder or psychiatric illness*) [SF-AW, HM, NES]

Junk bonds (banned as elitist) [ETS₁, ETS₂] – also **Regatta** [ETS₁], **Yacht** [ETS₂]

Majority group (banned as offensive reference to cultural differences) [ACT] – also **Minority group, Subgroup**

Middle East (banned as reflecting a Eurocentric worldview, replace with *Southwest Asia*; may be acceptable, however, as a historical reference) [HAR₂] – also **West, Western** (replace with reference to specific continent or region)

Normal (banned as offensive, replace with *a person without disabilities*) [SF-AW, ETS₂] – also **Disabled, the** (*people with a disability*) [SF-AW, HAR₁]

Senility (banned as demeaning, replace with *dementia*) [APA]

Pace the American Psychological Association, not a single non-psychologist I have asked expresses a preference for *dementia* over *senility* as a term to be applied to a loved one suffering from the condition. Oops – *suffering from* is offensive in this context; I should have written *having*. As for the terms *pop* and *soda*, either of which gives an advantage to students living in the region to which it is restricted, they are doubly proscribed by virtue of appearing on the list of 'Foods to avoid in textbooks', as compiled by the California State Nutrition Unit, 1981, and cited in Holt, Rinehart and Winston's *Guidelines for Literature Selection*, 1984 (Ravitch 2003: 196). Other insufficiently nutritious foods whose names children must not be exposed to are butter, coffee, honey, salt and sugar – though, bizarrely, the same document declares hamburgers, hot dogs, pizza and tacos to be acceptable foods.

Over the course of this chapter we have followed the rise and growth of the category of taboo language, from constraints against profanity, to obscenity, to racial designations and terms indicating physical or mental difference, to terms indicating any kind of difference, and ultimately to any language that might be received by one group of people differently than by another. The next section will consider the role of language within 'hate speech', a category of discourse that has come in recent years to be outlawed in many countries, raising difficult political questions for the general democratic principle of freedom of speech.

5.4 HATE SPEECH

The fact that the linguistic taboos discussed in §5.3 are enforced by state school boards qualifies them as official censorship, even if, technically, it is 'voluntary' or 'self'-censorship by publishers hopeful of winning lucrative contracts. These taboos do not have *de jure* status – no one will be prosecuted or sued for using them. Unless, that is, they form part of a discourse that qualifies as 'hate speech', a term whose origins the *OED* places in the USA in the late 1980s (a few years after 'hate crime', possibly its model), and which it defines as 'speech expressing hatred or intolerance of other social groups, esp. on the basis of race or sexuality'. Action to control hate speech appears to be incumbent upon the governments of the 153 nations by virtue of a panoply of international treaties and covenants on civil rights and racism that nearly all countries have signed up to and most have ratified. One of the core provisions is Part 2 of the following article of the International Covenant on Civil and Political Rights (ICCPR):

Article 20
1. Any propaganda for war shall be prohibited by law.
2. Any advocacy of national, racial or religious hatred that constitutes incitement to discrimination, hostility or violence shall be prohibited by law.

This seems quite straightforward, but legally, it presents no end of difficulties. How does one determine whether or not a particular example of advocacy constitutes incitement? Must actual discrimination, hostility or violence be proven to have taken place? Or does a tendency to provoke these things suffice – and if so, to provoke *whom*, exactly? What, in other words, is meant by 'incitement'? Where does the boundary lie between 'hatred' and criticism? And what exactly constitutes 'discrimination'? Finally, what is 'advocacy' – must the speaker or writer *intend* what they say to be advocating hatred, or is it enough simply for it to have that effect?

These questions matter seriously because of other civil and political rights protected by the same convention, particularly Part 2 of the immediately preceding article:

Article 19
1. Everyone shall have the right to hold opinions without interference.
2. Everyone shall have the right to freedom of expression; this right shall include freedom to seek, receive and impart information and ideas of all kinds, regardless of frontiers, either orally, in writing or in print, in the form of art, or through any other media of his choice.
3. The exercise of the rights provided for in paragraph 2 of this article carries with it special duties and responsibilities. It may therefore be subject to certain restrictions, but these shall only be such as are provided by law and are necessary:
   (a) For respect of the rights or reputations of others;
   (b) For the protection of national security or of public order (*ordre public*), or of public health or morals.

Parts 1 and 2 together make clear that this convention recognises an absolute freedom of thought, but not of expression. Part 3 then spells out what the limitations on expression are, and Article 20 adds two more limitations that do not obviously fall out from 19(3) – if they did, then Article 20 would not be necessary. As Gelber (2002) has noted, it is particularly Article 20 that a number of liberal-democratic countries, including the UK, Australia and the USA have signed onto only with reservations specifying that it will not be allowed to abridge their traditional rights of free speech.

Every state that is a signatory to the treaty must fashion its own particular laws for carrying out its declared principles. Gelber's (2002) study focuses on New South Wales in Australia, where the laws adopted are similar to those elsewhere in Australia, and in the UK and the USA, except that only Australian law provides for civil as well as criminal remedies.[11] Examining the attempts at applying the NSW law from its inception in 1989 through 1998, Gelber makes clear that it fell far short of its aim. Not one of the sixteen cases she examines resulted in action being taken against the 'hate speaker'. In most instances the complaint was withdrawn by the person who had made it, either because the complainant didn't want to spend the time necessary to pursue the matter, or decided that the hate speaker was such a committed racist that no actual progress would be achieved, or received threats, or simply moved and lost contact with the Anti-Discrimination Board. In other cases, the Board found the speech in question 'unlikely to pass the hatred threshold', or was unable to proceed by NSW law because the complainant himself or herself wasn't a member of the particular minority being vilified in the hate speech.

Gelber makes a strong and convincing case that the problem isn't a superficial one stemming from some detail of the NSW law or some aspect of how it has been applied. Rather, it lies at the heart of the way in which international law has conceived of hate speech, the harm that it does, and how that harm should be prevented and remedied. She offers an alternative approach that, in my opinion, is headed in the right direction, though below I shall be raising some questions about the analysis and reasoning that underpin it. Gelber's view is that hate-speech laws are misguided insofar as they either attempt to suppress or punish speech, which puts them in conflict with the basic human right to self-expression, or else to measure harm done purely in terms of actions *outside* speech (e.g. the 'discrimination, hostility or violence' of ICCPR Article 20(2)). Drawing on Austin (1960), Searle (1968), Habermas (1984) and Butler (1997), among others, she argues that hate speech itself constitutes discrimination and violence, directly causing psychological harm, and propagating and perpetuating discriminatory domination.

Because the effects of that domination include 'silencing' the victim (Langton 1993), the remedy which Gelber advocates is for government to provide 'the educational, material and institutional support which would enable the victims of hate speech to speak back, a capabilities-oriented approach' (Gelber 2002: 117). She sketches out a programme aimed at showing members of the vilified community how to assess the 'validity claims' of the hate speech, following Habermas, then to compose a response, the validity claims of which are superior (as they are bound to be in reality – the assistance needed is mainly rhetorical in nature). Gelber is able to claim that this remedy entirely obviates the collision with free-speech rights that existing hate-speech laws cannot avoid. Indeed, it has the effect of promoting *even more* free speech, and in the best of circumstances, dialogue that will lead to a productive outcome for all concerned. However, even where the hate-speaker is a confirmed racist, the principal harm done to the minority individual and community – silencing – will be undone by empowering them to speak.

I mentioned above that I did not accept all the points of Gelber's analysis. In her determination to prove beyond doubt that hate speech does not need to provoke damage because it is itself an inherently damaging act, she leaves herself open to a *reductio ad absurdum* whereby segregation and slavery could be defended as really no worse than saying something hateful. She repeatedly makes fun of Rauch's (1993: 27) suggestion of saying to a victim of vilification, 'Too bad, but you'll live', and while I share her disdain for its seeming flippancy, it is nevertheless true that the suffering caused by a racial epithet (I speak here as someone who has endured them), while real, is less serious than if one has been properly addressed but denied access to a school, enslaved, or fallen victim to genocide. We who specialise in language and discourse are prone to thinking that the reality of words is more concrete than the average person takes it to be. In Gelber's case this also manifests itself as a surprising literalism in her analysis of actual hate speech cases.

> Case F concerns a[n Australian aboriginal] woman … who was the target of the following comments from occupants of another vehicle at a service station: 'You black slut', 'You're nothing but a coon', 'I've shot worse coons than you' … What were the truth claims raised in Case F? In this case, the utterance sought to convey a state of affairs within which the recipient was posited as inferior. The speaker's use of the word 'coon' reflected a derogatory, culturally racist meaning of the word. There seems little doubt that the term 'coon' is understood by members of the speaker's and hearer's community as an offensive slang term for a person of colour. The use of the word also suggested that the recipient was comparable with a 'racoon', an animal assumed to be of a lower order than human beings, and furthermore an animal which may be hunted, trapped, killed and regarded as a pest. The use of the word 'slut' indicated a claim that the recipient was sexually promiscuous. The use of this personally derogatory term implied that her sexual activities were morally denounceable, a claim which reinforced the inferior state the perpetrator held the recipient to be in. (Gelber 2002: 69–71)

First of all, no one can read this without their heart going out completely to the victim, and feeling anger and disgust at her abusers – one pities them for their lack of basic humanity, but that does nothing to mitigate their behaviour.[12] That said, how much further does Gelber's Habermas-inspired analysis take us? I am not at all sure that these Aussie rednecks make any association between *coon* the racial term and *coon* the animal; the history is not straightforward, given that when *coon* was first applied to negroes in American English it was also being applied to members of the Whig party and, in some places, to people generally (the *OED* cites Frederick Marryat, *A Diary in America*, Ser. I. II. 232, 1839: 'In the Western States, where the racoon is plentiful, they use the abbreviation 'coon when speaking of people'). The etymology of the term hardly seems relevant.

Similarly, when the woman has been called 'You black slut', it seems silly and pedantic to speak of 'a claim that she was sexually promiscuous', hence 'morally denounceable'. Surely no such claim was in the mind of the speaker, who simply chose the most hateful and hurtful word available. When a driver comes careening down my street and nearly knocks me over, and I yell, 'Slow down, asshole!', am I raising a truth claim that the driver is the opening of an alimentary canal? Such discursive power as the word *asshole* possesses derives in part from its literal associations, but mainly from its having become conventionalised as a moderately taboo word for someone the speaker doesn't like or thinks is behaving badly. So too with *coon* and *slut* – drawing out the analysis does not enlighten, but only misses the essential point of hate speech, which is to express hate, using, in most cases, not carefully chosen words raising intended truth claims (and intent does have to be proven for any charge of hate speech to stick), but blunt weapons, and the blunter the better.

An important point that Gelber does not take up (nor do others writing about the subject) is the key role of labels and epithets – national, racial, religious or just broadly derogatory – in making a particular utterance identifiable as hate speech. In Case F, the epithets are clearly at the heart of the utterances, indeed the whole point of the utterances is to allow the epithets to be hurled. The cases which the NSW Anti-Discrimination Board found unlikely to pass the 'hatred threshold' were ones that described Asian immigration as a threat to social cohesion; not only did the absence of epithets make it difficult to demonstrate that this qualified as hate speech, but the fact that it was directed at 'immigration' rather than 'immigrants' tended to put it in the category of legitimate political opinion. It has been suggested (e.g. by Matsuda 1993) that what we are seeing in these latter cases is a 'sanitising' of racist discourse, producing an 'elite racism' that appears humane but has the effect of making fundamentally racist policies palatable to a large, politically moderate segment of the population (Twomey 1994, Van Dijk 1995).[13]

An experience I had during the writing of this chapter brought home the particular power of the 'broadly derogatory' blunt-weapon word. On the morning of 7 July 2005 four bombs went off in London, three in the Underground and one on a bus. The online edition of the *Washington Post* opened a discussion board about the topic, and the first message to go up, from a reader in Switzerland, excoriated the British for being too lenient with Muslim radicals prior to September 2001, so with regard to the victims of the bombing, the writer said that he was not going to waste any of his sympathy on this 'scum'. Now, in this case, there was a genuine problem with a truth claim: the author of the message was asserting that those who died were 'scum', villainous, worthless people, because they were British, and therefore bore responsibility for fostering Islamic terrorism. The mistake in the truth claim is simply this: the people on London public transport are not British. Some are, but others are tourists, students, businesspeople and others from abroad who just happen to be in London. Even if one were to accept that being British makes one 'scum', the simple fact of being on London public transport cannot rationally be taken to do so. Hence this is not legitimate political opinion; there is a political opinion behind it, but it has been put in a way that is illogical and hurtful, and difficult to construe as other than *intentionally* hurtful, because of the use of the word *scum*. Had the writer said that he wasn't going to waste any of his sympathy on these 'people', although the logic would not have improved, I doubt that there would have been nearly so many messages of disbelief and scorn as followed until the original message was taken down by the *Post*.

There is scope for further investigation of the role of particular types of language in the identification of hate speech and in understanding its effects and how to deal with it. One doubts, however, that such investigation will alter Gelber's basic conclusion, which is that existing approaches to hate speech are fundamentally unworkable. As with the laws against swearing in the seventeenth and eighteenth centuries, there is a basic problem with their formulation that makes them difficult to execute. The speech that the laws are attempting to stop – swearing then, hate speech now – is execrable to the majority. We do not want to hear it, we do not want others to have to hear it. Yet when it honestly represents what a person believes, we cannot give the state the power to prosecute that person for what they think, feel, opine, nor indeed for expressing their genuine thought, feeling, opinion. Gelber's solution, to make the state responsible for empowering those on the receiving end of the hate speech to talk back, is realistic and would probably prove about as helpful and workable as a hate-speech policy could. On the other hand, we ought to admit that it is something entirely different in kind from outlawing hate speech. Ultimately, it is therapy for the victims, a useful therapy that promises to undo much of the harm of the hate speech in the best cases – though in others it might leave the victims feeling doubly harrassed, if they found themselves struggling to meet the state's expectations for breaking out of their silence.

5.5 THE RIGHT TO HEAR NO EVIL?

The present-day discourses of political correctness and hate speech are focused on the *recipients* of the speech. The same was not true of the concern with swearing in earlier centuries. Then what was at stake was the relationship of human beings to God. When we find Defoe expressing concern about the effect upon the hearer, he portrays it as a mere breach of manners, as opposed to the 'crime' being committed against reason itself – his secularised version of God. Today, even the Texas State Board of Education, with its strong religious commitment, has no fear of the wrath of God being visited upon the nation because the theory of evolution is propounded in textbooks; not that such a fear is completely non-existent in Texas, but it is restricted to a small minority. For the majority, their worry is for the children reading the textbook, and the effect on their religious faith. With hate speech, those who would outlaw it have no doubt whatever of its falsehood, yet fear that its recipients – including members of the vilified minority group – will come to believe it is true, or at least will internalise the message subliminally. (This connects with the topic of propaganda anxiety, discussed in the next chapter.)

In the Middle Ages, language was conceived of primarily in terms of man's relationship to God. It was the medium in which divine knowledge is transmitted, and any subsidiary use for communication among people (which in any case was likely to be in the vernacular rather than in 'language' proper) was strictly secondary in nature. Although the man–God relationship loses none of its importance in the Renaissance, we find greater expression, alongside it, of concern with how language relates to the nation. In parallel to this, because the 'nationalisation' of language changes the relationship of 'language' (heretofore Latin, henceforth a panoply of emerging vernaculars) to knowledge, logic and the mind, we find concern expressed with these relationships as well, which peaks in the Enlightenment.

The role of language in the relationships of human beings to one another comes to the fore, not in writings about language, but in language itself, specifically in the redistribution of personal pronouns for deferential and non-deferential address, as discussed in §4.3. This linguistic phenomenon is not found in any ancient languages; it begins in the Middle Ages, apparently first with very restricted use, then gradually spreading throughout the feudal system. It seems first to have become controversial with the Reformation, as the question arose of whether God should be addressed deferentially or informally – various Christian sects took various positions for various reasons, and still today many of these differences remain. That the question should have arisen and been highly controversial is not surprising, given the intense concern in the period with the role of language in the relationship of man to God.

More surprising, perhaps, is how slowly the role of language within human relationships manifests itself as an intellectual or theoretical concern. It is there as a subsidiary issue, for instance in discourses about what form the language of poetry should take, what should be the official language, what is proper usage (*le bon usage*), whether a universal written character might be devised, and in John Locke's (1632–1704) concern with how 'understanding' can be improved (Locke 1690). But in none of these cases is the principal issue 'communication' from one human being to another; rather, it is the relationship to something absolute – beauty and, above all, truth, whether or not one equates truth with God or treats them separately. It is implicit, too, in rhetoric. But overt discussion of how human beings position themselves relative to one another through language is rarely met with before the later eighteenth century, when we find it taken up by Thomas Reid (1710–96), the pre-eminent figure of the Scottish 'common sense' school (Reid 1788). In the nineteenth century it becomes a part, albeit marginal, of the new 'general linguistics', notably in Whitney (1867), who in the view of Alter (2005) was principally influenced by an early education in which the Scottish philosophy was dominant (see further Joseph 2002: 30–2). But it is really in the 1890s and after that the 'social' nature of language becomes a major theme – and this almost certainly connects with the experience of universal education, which gave impetus to the renewed focus on standard languages after 1880, into which new concern with nationalism fed.

As the central role of language within human communication, relationships and identity was coming to the fore, its role in the man–God relationship was receding, to become the specialised concern of divines. I want to caution against over-simplifying the historical changes outlined here – if it is true, as I am proposing, that there was a general shift of emphasis away from how language links us to God, toward how it links us to mind, truth and nation, and eventually to other people, socially at first, then individually, it must be remembered that *all* these concerns have always been there, but in differing degrees. There are many today for whom the man–God link must always be the most important issue, and I do not mean to suggest that they are somehow stuck in the Middle Ages; it is just that what was once a general overriding concern has become a more specialised one, for the time being anyway.

In Joseph (2004a, Chapters 2–3) I have sketched the history of how concern with language and identity developed within twentieth-century linguistics and adjacent disciplines; read in conjunction with Joseph (2002, Chapter 5) on the history of sociolinguistics, this gives an account of scholarly interest in the interpersonal role of language that I shall not repeat here. Its political manifestations include the efforts to control hate speech and to eliminate objectionable language from school text-books that have been reviewed in this chapter. These developments suggest that a new linguistic ethics is in the process of emerging, one in which every individual has an implicit right of protection from being hurt by others, not only physically, but verbally; and in which the state has the obligation to intervene in the ongoing development of the language by preventing children from being exposed to language that is racist, or, more broadly, suggestive of any inherent difference among people, or broader still, connected to anything that a socialpolitical consensus deems harmful.

Another aspect of this emerging 'right' is to be found in the Data Protection acts that have become enshrined in the law of most nations within the last few years, part of the impetus for which is the view that it is unjust for individuals to have potentially harmful information about them kept by public agencies and passed around among agency officials. The reality, however, is that people get around the acts by resorting to oral rather than written means of communication, thus decreasing rather than increasing the accountability of the process. There is a real problem here that deserves a real solution, but the Data Protection acts do not look like solving it any more than anti-hate-speech legislation is succeeding at preventing hate speech. Both suffer from the same basic flaw that underlay anti-swearing legislation in times past – they overestimate the amount of control that can be exercised over language, at least in any state that also wants to promote basic freedoms of thought and opinion and to regulate only behaviour that directly and palpably harms others.

In the seventeenth century almost everyone agreed that swearing directly and palpably harms others as well as the swearer, by drawing down the wrath of God upon the nation. Today, most people would agree that hate speech harms the individuals at whom it is directed, and the minority group to which they belong, and perhaps too the nation as a whole; they disagree however about the nature of that harm, and whether it only becomes real harm if, as the ICCPR suggests, the hate speech incites 'discrimination, hostility or violence'. In another hundred years, will concern about hate speech seem as antique as that about swearing? Or will the view of 'harm' evolve toward universal acceptance of the view that speech itself constitutes real harm rather than just a provocation to it? Either is possible; my hunch is that the former is slightly more likely than the latter, just because the latter would mean ever increasing conflict with those basic rights to freedom of speech that we sometimes show signs of not caring about anymore, until some government proposal actually threatens to impinge upon them in a way that affects us as individuals – at which point we are suddenly prepared to fight to the death for them, goddammit.

SUGGESTED FURTHER READING

As the subject matter of this chapter has not been so widely studied by applied linguists as has been the case with the three preceding chapters, much of the relevant literature has already been cited above. It is worth noting, however, that Montagu (1967) remains unsurpassed as a study of taboo language, despite a sometimes heavy-handed psychologism that is very much of its time, and that the linguistic aspects of hate speech are thoroughly covered by Gelber (2002), which provides ample guidance to recent critical and philosophical literature on the topic.

NOTES

1. See Geertz (1968) and Siegel (1986) on the Javanese 'psychological disorder' known as *latah*, in which the sufferer, when startled or upset, involuntarily utters taboo words. This appears to happen only when the sufferer is in the presence of her social superiors. Geertz, studying the phenomenon during fieldwork in the early 1950s, found that it only affected middle-aged and older women, and particularly those who had formerly worked as servants for Dutch families. Geertz and Siegel offer various psycho-political explanations; neither considers the possibility that it may simply represent learned behaviour, since Europeans routinely swear when startled or upset. The early history of swearing in Dutch is covered by Swaen (1898).

2. Particularly noteworthy examples include Jespersen (1922: 240) and Ullmann (1957: 43); also Graves (1927), Montagu (1967), Andersson (1990) and Hughes (1991).

3. Clearly many of these – all the ones including body parts – refer implicitly to God the Son, since the Father has no body. The list given here was inspired by Montagu's (1967: 116), which however is riddled with inaccuracies. Concerning my personal favourite from the list, *God's malt*, it comes from *Gammer Gurton's Needle*, Act II, Sc. 1 (line 254), set at the ale-house door. The *OED* records no other meaning for *malt* than the familiar current one.

4. Commenting on Ross (1960), a study of swearing among a group of young male and female zoologists on an expedition to Arctic Norway, Montagu (1967: 87) wrote, 'As was to be expected among members of the middle class, the words used were blasphemous rather than obscene'. This aligns with my own childhood memories of the 1960s, when, in my family milieu, profanity was perfectly normal and acceptable in adult speech, but obscenity was not. The only adults I ever heard say the word *fuck* were workmen. In the intervening years, however, the class (and gender) distribution has shifted considerably.

5. Among the innumerable pieces of spurious history to have spread via the Internet is one currently cited as fact on many websites, according to which a landmark in the history of taboo language occurred on 4 April 1900, when the then Prince of Wales (soon to become King

Edward VII), having been shot by an anarchist, is supposed to have said, 'Fuck it! I've taken a bullet'. The main problem for the story's credibility, besides the fact that no documentation is ever offered for it, is that the shot missed and the Prince was unharmed. But it is clearly a story that, for some reason, people want to believe, perhaps because it gives the word a royal pedigree.

6. This last set of figures includes also occurrences from 1985, which Lester included for diachronic comparison and which his presentation does not allow to be factored out. However, the overall trend for 1985 was not different from that for 1994–5. Lester also gives the figures for broadcast vs. print occurrences with the Simpson trial factored out: stories with *fuck* are 66.7 per cent broadcast, 33.3 per cent print, and stories with *nigger* are 18.5 per cent broadcast, 81.6 per cent print (these have been rounded up and so do not add up to 100 per cent).

7. The *OED* defines *politically correct* as 'conforming to a body of liberal or radical opinion, esp. on social matters, characterized by the advocacy of approved causes or views, and often by the rejection of language, behaviour, etc., considered discriminatory or offensive'. The term, which originated in the USA in the early 1970s, is not one a person applies to his or her own views (unless ironically), but always to those of other people whom one perceives to be enforcing a 'received' view. It is, obviously, itself a very politically charged term.

8. For some interesting insights on Ravitch (2003) from a French linguist-*cum*-historian of ideas still recovering from twelve years of living and raising his children in California, see Courtine (2004).

9. How exactly this self-censorship works in the UK and other English-speaking countries remains obscure, but it assuredly does operate – the USA is by no means unique in this regard.

10. Sources: ACT = *Fairness Report for the ACT Assessment Tests, 1999–2000* (ACT, 2000); AIR = American Institutes for Research, *AIR Principles for Bias, Sensitivity, and Language Simplification*, Fall 2000; APA = American Psychological Association, *Publication Manual*, 4th edn (APA, 1994), pp. 46–60; ETS₁ = Educational Testing Service, *Overview: ETS Fairness Review* (ETS, 1998); ETS₂ = Educational Testing Service, *Sensitivity Review Process: Guidelines and Procedures* (ETS, 1992); HAR₁ = Harcourt, *Striving for Fairness* (unpublished document, for internal use by publishing company, 2001); HAR₂ = Harcourt Horizons, *Editorial Guidelines* (unpublished document, for internal use by publishing company and reviewers of its textbooks, 2001); HM = Houghton Mifflin, *Eliminating Stereotypes* (Houghton Mifflin, 2001); MMH = Macmillan McGraw Hill, *Reflecting Diversity* (1991); NES = National Evaluation Systems, *Bias Issues in Test Development*, 1991; RIV = *Bias and Sensitivity Concerns in Testing* (Riverside Publishing, 1998); SF-AW = Scott Foresman-Addison Wesley, *Multicultural Guidelines*, 1996.

11. This is significant because the standard of proof is not as high in civil proceedings. The USA stands somewhat apart from the other two because of the especially strong protection of free speech guaranteed by the First Amendment to the Constitution.

12. The outcome of the case was that the complainant moved residence and was uncontactable, so the file was closed (Gelber 2002: 168).

13. Again, one needs to exercise caution with such suggestions, which can have the unintended effect of diluting all attempts at dealing with racism by blurring the line between clearly racist discourse on the one hand, and, on the other, moderate xenophobia that,

however repulsive to most of us, nevertheless does not exceed the bounds of legitimate political opinion, the expression of which must be protected. See further Leets, Giles and Noels (1999), which cites evidence that utterances such as 'your sort' are more often perceived as racist when uttered by members of ethnic minorities.

Chapter 6

Rhetoric, propaganda and interpretation

6.1 RHETORIC VERSUS TRUTH?

The origins of rhetoric as a formal technology of persuasion through language are closely bound up with the origins of democracy in fifth century BC Athens. It did not appear out of nowhere – already in monarchy, wise rulers surrounded themselves with advisors who represented different interests and were not like-minded, and whose job is was to convince the ruler that the particular course they were advocating was the best one. Subjects too had to persuade the ruler, or a functionary delegated with authority by the ruler, of the justness of any petition they might make, or the unjustness of any charge levelled against them.

Still, with democracy came a sea change. The power to persuade became ultimate power, and instruction in the art of persuasion was not long in being put on offer. The first teachers of the subject were given the name Sophists (roughly, wise guys) by their enemies, those who thought that persuasion should come purely from stating the truth, and not from any 'art', the purpose of which could only be to persuade others of what is *not* in fact the case. The best remembered of their enemies is Socrates – himself a teacher, but of dialectic, a form of enquiry aimed at reaching the truth rather than persuading. In modern terms, Socrates was training philosophers and theologians, while the Sophists were preparing lawyers, advertising and PR types, spin doctors and politicians.

In view of how much of his writing is taken up with his teacher Socrates ranting against the Sophists, it is hardly surprising that Plato never produced a manual of rhetoric. But his student Aristotle did. His *Rhetoric* opens with an implicit apology for its very existence. It points out that we all employ rhetoric, the persuasive use of language, generally in trying to demonstrate the truth or rightness of what we want the other person to accept. There is nothing wrong, Aristotle insists, with such persuasion or the rhetoric that brings it about, whatever the context. The problems begin when we try to persuade by appealing to *emotion* rather than reason, particularly in the context of a legal proceeding.

> It is not right to pervert the judge by moving him to anger or envy or pity – one might as well warp a carpenter's rule before using it. … [M]embers of the assembly

and the jury find it their duty to decide on definite cases brought before them. They will often have allowed themselves to be so much influenced by feelings of friendship or hatred or self-interest that they lose any clear vision of the truth and have their judgement obscured by considerations of personal pleasure or pain. (Aristotle, *Rhetoric* I.1, Roberts transl. [1924])

Yet, Aristotle insists, even those who agree with him about the immorality of persuasion via the emotions need to study the rhetorical means of such persuasion, so that they will recognise when and how it is being done by others, and be able to fight back.

> Rhetoric is useful because things that are true and things that are just have a natural tendency to prevail over their opposites, so that if the decisions of judges are not what they ought to be, the defeat must be due to the speakers themselves, and they must be blamed accordingly ... Further, we must be able to employ persuasion, just as strict reasoning can be employed, on opposite sides of a question, not in order that we may in practice employ it in both ways (for we must not make people believe what is wrong), but in order that we may see clearly what the facts are, and that, if another man argues unfairly, we on our part may be able to confute him. (ibid.)

The cleverness of this rhetorical self-defence argument borders on the Sophistic. Arguing that an honest man must master rhetoric to protect himself from rhetoricians is reminiscent of calling military units 'peacekeeping forces'. The problem Aristotle keeps tacit is this: how can one be sure that the person who studies rhetoric with such clear moral motives will not, in time, succumb to the temptation to use it toward immoral ends?

Aristotle gives one further reason for the study of rhetoric, in which the moral line appears quite blurred:

> Moreover, before some audiences not even the possession of the exactest knowledge will make it easy for what we say to produce conviction. For argument based on knowledge implies instruction, and there are people whom one cannot instruct. Here, then, we must use, as our modes of persuasion and argument, notions possessed by everybody, as we observed in the Topics when dealing with the way to handle a popular audience.

The 'notions possessed by everybody' include pain and pleasure, and above all, happiness, the chief end of all human actions. Aristotle is giving his backing to general appeals of this sort as the only possible means of persuading *hoi polloi*, the people one cannot instruct. He would not necessarily have disapproved of those television advertisements that are all about establishing a mood – the sort where you don't even know what product is being advertised until its name appears at the end – the sort admired by an arty elite, sneered at by a middle class that sees them as evidence of the dumbing-down of society, and probably tolerated with a vague annoyance by the rest of the population. But one can be fairly sure that they produce the desired results – increased sales of the product – or the genre would have died out years ago.

Certain types of language produce particular rhetorical effects, examples of which we have encountered throughout Chapters 4 and 5, such as the effect of racial epithets and generally deprecatory words such as *scum* (§5.4). Word choice is not the only way to create rhetorical effect: word order and sentence construction are another powerful means, as are repetition, rhythm, and all the other classic tropes that make for effective style. In spoken language there are still other means, including voice quality, pitch, volume, speed, modulation and even vibrato, rarely used today but commonly heard in recordings of speeches from the early decades of the twentieth century. These linguistic resources combine with features of content to produce effects in the hearer that extend beyond the logic of the argument, considered objectively.

Would language be better if it were devoid of rhetoric, so that the plain truth of what was being said were immediately obvious? Certainly there are abundant cases of deliberate obfuscation – 'spin' – where speakers, whether government officials or misbehaving children, state facts in a way that foregrounds what is to their advantage. In such cases there is a clear need to restate the 'plain' facts, and to expose the vested interests that have led to their being masked. More and less neutral ways of stating facts and making arguments exist – yet rarely, if ever, could one point to an *absolutely* neutral way of stating a fact or making an argument. As I write these words, I am looking out of the window at a cloudy sky; it might seem a neutral statement to say *It's a cloudy day*. But 'cloudy day' has negative connotations, and in fact it has been so sunny and hot for the last week that it is a relief to have it overcast and cooler, and some rain would be welcome for the garden, though rain isn't usually welcome. No neutral way exists of stating this state of affairs, and *It's a cloudy day* isn't neutral because its normal implications do not apply.

To state the truth usually requires some rhetoric. Yet rhetoric also permits bending the truth. As Aristotle taught, to be able to do either effectively – and to recognise which is being done by others when they are trying to persuade us – demands an understanding of rhetoric. Ultimately, then, it's true that even those who would eliminate rhetoric in favour of plain speaking are in as much need of studying how rhetoric works as are those who want to bend language to their own advantage.

6.2 LANGUAGE, THOUGHT AND REALITY

For Socrates and Plato, reality lay beyond the reach of mere language. Their view of the relationship between language and reality was the basis for the medieval vernacular one described in §2.5. What they most feared about the teaching of rhetoric was the Sophists' premise that man (not the divine) is the measure of all things – hence that reality is for us to create, and the persuasive use of language is our means of creating it.

This essential split between, on the one hand, believers in a reality that stands apart from human perception and cognition, and on the other, those who think that reality is actually structured by perception and cognition, would re-emerge in the Middle Ages in the debate over 'universals'. The question would take the form of whether a category such as *cat* really does exist independently of individual cats and of our mental concept of a cat, as the Platonic and mainstream Christian view has it; or whether what truly exists are individual cats, in which the category of *cat* has an 'immanent' existence; or whether the category of *cat* is the product of our sensations, that is, our perception and cognition of the individual animals. These three positions would come to be known respectively as realism, nominalism and conceptualism. The first has Plato as its ancient predecessor, the second Aristotle, and the third the Stoics.[1]

Each of these positions implies a different role for language. For realists, language is a mere garment draped upon thought, with no effect on its content. Language simply encodes a reality which exists independently of it. For nominalists, language potentially has a greater importance, as the bridge between the universals that are immanent in individual entities and the knowledge of those universals in human minds. For conceptualists, the role of language is fundamental – for even if universals are rooted in sensations that all humans share, it is with their naming that they really come to exist, and it is through language that they are shaped and spread.

As we come into the Renaissance and modern thought, these medieval views of the relationship of language to thought and reality persist, albeit in new guises. The 'mere garment' view continues essentially in the form described in the preceding paragraph, while in opposition to it there emerge two other positions, each of which assumes that language exerts a shaping influence upon thought. One of them regards such influence in an essentially positive light, and sees language as a sort of magic key to understanding the thought of an individual or an entire culture. The third view regards the influence of language upon thought in an essentially negative light, with language as the source of metaphysical garbage that gets in the way of clear, logical thinking (see further Joseph 2002: 75–80).

Linguists of the nineteenth and twentieth centuries mainly followed the magic key line, which does after all give a privileged place to the study of language as the key to broader cultural and intellectual understanding. The tradition of analytic philosophy has been the main stronghold of the metaphysical garbage view. But there have been crossovers among linguists, who tend however not to give up magic key rhetoric entirely even when entering into metaphysical garbage discourse. Edward Sapir (1884–1939), the doyen of twentieth-century anthropological linguists, was very much of the magic key persuasion in his early work, including his 1921 book *Language*, where he wrote that 'Language and our thought-grooves are inextricably interrelated, are, in a sense, one and the same' (pp. 217–18); 'Language is the most massive and inclusive art we know, a mountainous and anonymous work of unconscious generations' (ibid.: 220). But his rhetoric would change abruptly after he read *The Meaning of Meaning* (1923) by C. K. Ogden (1889–1957) and I. A. Richards (1893–1979), a wide-ranging book aimed at addressing the power of 'Word-Magic'. Ogden and Richards believed that words possess the power to engender 'hypnotic influences' (p. 132) which make symbols appear directly bound to referents, and they saw this as the basis of almost all human deception and misunderstanding – including that particularly dangerous misunderstanding which is the arbitrariness professed by philologists such as Saussure, according to whom 'it is "all a matter of words"'. This Ogden and Richards call 'linguistic nihilism' and 'scepticism', and they declare:

> The best means of escape from such scepticism as well as from the hypnotic influences which we have been considering, lies in a clear realization of the way in which symbols come to exercise such power, and of the various senses in which they are said to have Meaning. (ibid.)

Already in his review of *The Meaning of Meaning* its impact on Sapir's thinking about these matters is evident:

> To a far greater extent than the philosopher has realized, he is likely to become the dupe of his speech-forms, which is equivalent to saying that the mould of his thought, which is typically a linguistic mould, is apt to be projected into his conception of the world. Thus innocent linguistic categories may take on the formidable appearance of cosmic absolutes. (Sapir 1924: 154 [1949: 157])

As shown in Joseph (2002, Chapter 4), this shift in perspective was crucial to what would become known as the 'Sapir–Whorf Hypothesis', one of the most widely known ideas to originate in modern linguistics.[2] No one can say definitively what the 'hypothesis' is – the term, and nearly all the attention that has gone to the idea itself, were posthumous. Its different interpretations include what is generally called the 'strong' version, that 'one's perception of the world is determined by the structure of one's native language' (*New Shorter Oxford English Dictionary*, 1993, under 'Whorfianism'), and the 'weak' version, that 'the structure of a language partly determines a native speaker's categorization of experience' (ibid., under 'Sapir–Whorf Hypothesis').

Benjamin Lee Whorf (1897–1941), who was Sapir's protégé, famously analysed expressions of time in an American Indian language, Hopi, and concluded not only that the Hopi conceived of time in a completely different way from speakers of what he termed SAE ('Standard Average European'), but that the Hopi conceptions were actually closer to those developed by modern physicists.[3] With Whorf the 'metaphysical garbage' approach to language and thought really comes to the fore, as he critiques SAE as the source of conceptual blinders that the language structure imposes on speakers.

Whorf's writings (1956) have served as the touchstone for modern linguists arguing that languages have a deep connection to the thought and culture of the people who speak them. Chomsky and other linguists of 'universalist' bent have never had any time for the Sapir–Whorf Hypothesis. Cognitivists who have tried to test the hypothesis have turned up results that admit of various interpretations. Yet linguists arguing for the importance of protecting and preserving 'endangered languages', or simply explaining why language matters in the understanding of identity, have been highly prone to falling back upon Whorfian statements that every language divides the world up differently, and that language is essential, not accidental, to cultural formation, cohesion and transmission.[4]

To a large extent, Ogden and Richards (1923) represent the reaction of traditional British empiricism to Continental idealism, where empiricism grounds reality in what the senses (hence the body) can perceive, while idealism distrusts the senses as a source of illusion and ultimately relies on reason (hence the mind) to determine what is real. The continuity with the medieval debate on universals is apparent, at least in retrospect, though modernist discourse with its implicit ideology of continuous progress masked this for many at the time (and still does so today). On the Continental side, neo-conceptualism had reached a high water-mark with the writings of Friedrich Nietzsche (1844–1900). Originally trained as a philologist, Nietzsche abandoned the close study of classical texts to pursue much broader philosophical issues – but his early obsession with language is no doubt connected to his mature view that reality exists only through its structuring in language. Just to show that the British–Continental divide is anything but clear-cut, the high water-mark of nineteenth-century neo-realism is Karl Marx (1818–83), Nietzsche's countryman; still, Marx spent more than half his life in Britain and produced all his major works there.

These nineteenth-century debates have very direct resonances in present-day applied linguistics. The Marxist view underlies (in name at least) a fair range of current approaches, including those deriving from M. A. K. Halliday (see below, p. 126) and most of whatever goes under the name of 'critical'. Orthodox Marxism is strictly wedded to a 'mere garment' view of the relationship of language to society, culture and thought. Even Voloshinov, who, as we saw in §4.1, maintained that the class struggle is embodied in the linguistic sign itself, did not believe that by changing language one could make any difference to that struggle; the direction of influence is strictly one-way. Nietzsche provided the inspiration for those 'post-structuralist' philosophers such as Foucault, who, from the 1960s, would again maintain that knowledge is a historical product and indeed a political one. What essentially distinguished Foucault from his Marxist counterparts was his belief that the objects of knowledge, including language as well as the concepts that constitute its signifieds, are not produced by subjects thinking, speaking and acting intersubjectively.[5] Rather, Foucault believed, the objects of knowledge are produced by 'power' itself, with which they have a mutually constitutive relationship.

> We should admit that power produces knowledge …; that power and knowledge directly imply one another; that there is no power relation without the correlative constitution of a field of knowledge, nor any knowledge that does not presuppose and constitute at the same time power relations … In short, it is not the activity of the subject of knowledge that produces a corpus of knowledge, useful or resistant to power, but power–knowledge, the processes and struggles that traverse it and of which it is made up, that determines the forms and possible domains of knowledge. (Foucault 1977 [1975]: 27–8)

Foucault is sometimes misrepresented by his opponents – a category that runs the gamut from Marxists to conservative anti-relativists such as Margaret S. Archer (see §7.1) – as holding that neither power nor knowledge nor any other reality is anything but a mere linguistic construct. His critique of Western thought is actually much more subtle and powerful than this. Power, operating through language, determines the parameters of what is knowable (the *episteme*), which change from epoch to epoch. What has however led to dissatisfaction among many people who were initially inspired by Foucault to focus on language and power is that, beyond a certain point, thinking in terms of 'power' thus abstracted becomes an obstacle to understanding who exactly is doing what to whom, and how.

It plays too into a widely-held but false dichotomy according to which only those 'in power' actually have and make choices, while the vast majority of people only think they are making choices when in fact they are simply living out inevitabilities forced upon them by the power structure. Since this is essentially the Marxist view, it is ironic that Foucault has become the focus of so much Marxist scorn in recent years. Present-day Marxist linguists such as Holborow (1999) see the 'post-structuralists' and 'post-modernists', rather than capitalists, as their principal intellectual opponents.

6.3 PROPAGANDA ANXIETY

The impetus for Ogden and Richards to write *The Meaning of Meaning* was their experience of WWI, and their belief that the war had been fought largely with propaganda, through the distortion of abstract words such as 'freedom', 'democracy' and even 'victory'. This belief was very widespread at the time. In Joseph (2002, Chapter 9) I have argued that this period saw a popularisation of the 'metaphysical garbage' view of language, initially in the English-speaking world but eventually well beyond, in the form of a 'linguistic mind control cultural discourse frame'. It endures to this day, and has been the subject of most vivid discussion in times of intense international conflict. It takes the form of anxiety about propaganda, especially that generated by governments, but also by commercial interests.

Although propaganda has a centuries-old history, a shift in the discourse concerning it began in 1914. *The Times* and the *Daily Mail*, both then owned by Viscount Northcliffe, advocated British entry into the war, and were accused by pacifists as operating in a government–press conspiracy. In Anthony Smith's words,

> The Northcliffe newspapers depicted the work of German soldiers in images which are the familiar material of horror stories: babies being lifted on bayonets, nuns raped on tables. Public sentiment was whipped into a frenzy of anti-German hatred. (Smith 1973: 30)

From the government's point of view, there was a pressing need to convince men to volunteer for the armed forces, to create public support for forced conscription, and to persuade the USA to enter the war, which it did not do until 1917.

Repressed during the war, when resistance to government policy could land one in prison (as happened to Bertrand Russell), 'propaganda anxiety' broke out openly after the Armistice, in Britain and abroad. British propaganda was blamed by resentful Americans for their entry into the slaughter, and Woodrow Wilson's Democratic party lost the presidential election of 1920 to Republicans campaigning on the slogan 'The War Was a Fraud'.[6] German writers, meanwhile, convinced themselves that they had been defeated not by British might but by British propaganda. Smith (1973: 42) notes that 'In *Mein Kampf* Hitler was to write that he learned all his own propaganda techniques from British methods during the war'.

At least two additional factors were at work stoking the fires of propaganda anxiety after WWI. One was widely acknowledged: the beginnings of radio broadcasting. The first commercial broadcast in Britain was in June 1920, sponsored by none other than Northcliffe's *Daily Mail* (Gorham 1952: 23), which became the major player in the early development of British radio. In the USA, the first daily radio broadcasts began in August 1920, with commercial sponsorship initiated some two years later. In Smith's view,

> The experience of the propagandists of the First World War coupled with the ensuing reaction against the black art they had perfected were among the profoundest influences on the men who came to lay the foundations of broadcasting in the early nineteen-twenties. (Smith 1973: 31)

The result in Britain was the birth of 'a new kind of state monopoly' (ibid.: 56), the BBC, in 1923, the same year in which *The Meaning of Meaning* was published. Their aims were obliquely connected, in that both were directed at preventing a sort of verbal anarchy, as radio was perceived as being in America, where government interference in broadcasting was limited to the assigning of airwave frequencies. Ogden would later call radio 'the most powerful standardizing force the world has yet seen' (Ogden 1944 [1934]: 8). A very similar comment occurs in a book on broadcasting published a year earlier: 'It must, of course, be admitted that broadcasting is a huge agency of standardization, the most powerful the world has ever seen' (Matheson 1933: 17–18). Perhaps both Ogden and Hilda Matheson (1888–1940) heard someone say this on the radio?[7]

The new reality of disembodied voices entering ordinary people's home from some central broadcasting authority coincided with the diffusion of the notion of the 'unconscious mind' into middle-brow, then general cultural awareness. This began in the early 1920s and accelerated over the following decades, thanks in part to radio itself. What made propaganda so frightening was never the fear of succumbing to it oneself, but of vast numbers of less intelligent people falling victim to linguistic mind control. The growing awareness of Freud's theory that our actions are ruled by an unconscious mind made the danger seem all the greater.

By the time of WWII, Eric Arthur Blair (1903–50) was writing pieces under his pen name George Orwell claming a link between the power of propaganda and the structure of language (e.g. Orwell 1944). In a more famous article of two years later, he wrote that

> Modern English, especially written English, is full of bad habits which spread by imitation and which can be avoided if one is willing to take the necessary trouble.

If one gets rid of these habits one can think more clearly, and to think clearly is a necessary first step towards political regeneration ... This invasion of one's mind by ready-made phrases ... can only be prevented if one is constantly on guard against them, and every such phrase anaesthetizes a portion of one's brain. (Orwell 1946: 252–3, 263)

The linguistic 'bad habits' consist of strings of words that form well-worn patterns, coercing their users to think in certain ways. 'Clear thinking' demands that one start from mental images, visualising things then finding words to describe them. Starting with words is likelier to produce purely abstract thinking. The detachment of language from observable reality is what makes it possible for a political party to maintain an orthodoxy among its followers, and in the most extreme cases, to dupe those it wishes to enslave. If the party uses language in a way that prevents concrete mental pictures from being called up, people will not understand what is happening to them, and they cannot rebel against what they do not understand. Orwell is not against abstract thinking so long as it is grounded in observable reality. Too great a distrust of abstractions can have catastrophic political consequences of its own. Tyranny and freedom, after all, are abstract concepts, yet resisting the one and defending the other is a matter of life and death.

As indicated in §6.2, Ogden and Richards (1923) were inspired by a belief that WWI was the result of the misuse of complex abstract words, and that any hope of future world peace depended upon the ability of thinking people to control the meanings of such words so that they could not be abused. It is thus very much a part of the propaganda anxiety story. Ogden's and Richards's other great joint project, Basic English, proceeded directly out of the principles outlined in the chapter on Definitions in *The Meaning of Meaning*. Basic was a set of 500 English words, later expanded to 850, in which Ogden claimed any idea could be expressed. Its 'two chief purposes' were 'To serve as an international auxiliary language' and to 'encourag[e] clarity of thought and expression' (Ogden 1944: 4). The latter aim, largely forgotten now, ties it directly to *The Meaning of Meaning*. Richards wrote in 1943 that

Neither those who learn English nor those who teach it as a foreign language have in general any feeling that they are submitting to or furthering a process of intellectual subjugation. On the contrary, they are more likely to feel that they are helping themselves or others to resist such influences. (Richards 1943: 13–14)

English – here meaning Basic – is the language of intellectual freedom, the immunisation against propaganda.[8] Whorf was aware of Basic English and dubious about the linguistic principles behind it, yet credited it with a 'crude but vast power to change the thinking of tomorrow' (Whorf 1956: 82).

It was also during the great wave of post-WWI propaganda anxiety, in 1921, that Alfred Korzybski (1879–1950) first sketched out his General Semantics, which traces many of the world's problems to an 'Aristotelian' bias embedded in Western languages – a very central metaphysical garbage outlook (see Korzybski 1921, 1933). One of General Semantics' many adherents, Stuart Chase (1888–1985), produced the widely read *The Tyranny of Words* in 1938. It presents Korzybski, Ogden and Richards as the 'Three human beings [who] to my knowledge have observed and reflected upon the nature of meaning and communication for any considerable period' (Chase 1938: 10). Chase goes on to assert that the core problem of the modern world is 'abstract words and phrases without discoverable referents', such as 'The Aryan Fatherland'. It is, he says, 'a semantic blank. Nothing comes through' (ibid.: 14).

Criticising Chase, Orwell (1946) would point out the danger of a distrust of abstract terms so extreme that it made it impossible to recognise fascism, removing any possibility of combating it. But General Semantics grew into a big business, which is still around, though like Basic English its glory days are behind it. Those days have come in times of war, hot and cold. For General Semantics one of the supreme moments was in 1941 when *Language in Action* by S. I. Hayakawa (1906–92) was chosen by the Book-of-the-Month Club, a decision no doubt strengthened by pre-war propaganda anxiety in the USA and yielding sales in the hundreds of thousands.[9] As an appendix it contained Whorf (1940), giving the Sapir–Whorf Hypothesis its first mass exposure in the year of Whorf's death.

6.4 NEWSPEAK

Athenian democracy gave the impetus for rhetoric. In the 1930s, modern dictatorships – Hitler on the right, Stalin on the left – transformed propaganda anxiety from a concern about the abuse of rhetoric within democracies to dread of a much more pervasive mind control that threatened to turn whole populations into slaves, indeed robots, subservient to the will of a Führer.

The ancient Roman coinage of the word *dictator* to denote the office of an absolute ruler presupposes a culture in which laws are normally constructed and executed in a dialogic manner, but in which the dialogic is also seen as something of a luxury of peacetime that has to be suspended in order to face up to a common enemy. Dialogue, after all, connotes dissent and division, and warfare demands a single-voiced command structure if an army is to channel itself into a coherent force. The commander-in-chief must be a dictator – what he says is law by virtue of his saying it. But in peacetime, dissenters will not so easily accept dictation, yet neither will those who have exercised absolute power find it easy to tolerate dissent.

The dictator as refuser of dialogue finds his ultimate literary expression in Orwell's *Nineteen Eighty-Four* (1949). Big Brother, the head of the Party that rules Oceania (in effect, the English-speaking world) is not a person, but a symbol, and a symbol cannot engage in dialogue. In a sense, the dictator is always a symbolic, god-like personage whom it is not licit to contradict. A symbol exists merely to be perceived and interpreted. But interpretation is itself a problem for the Party, being too indeterminate. The Proles of Oceania, with their traditional language (termed 'Oldspeak'), can argue with Big Brother's dictates and question whether what the Party tells them is true. And so the Party has put together a large linguistic operation for the purpose of redesigning language in such a way that interpretation *is* determinate.

> Newspeak was the official language of Oceania and had been devised to meet the ideological needs of Ingsoc, or English Socialism ... The purpose of Newspeak was not only to provide a medium of expression for the world-view and mental habits proper to the devotees of Ingsoc, but to make all other modes of thought impossible. (Orwell 1989 [1949]: 312)

When we think of the language of dictatorial regimes, we tend to focus on their attempts to shape 'the world-view and mental habits' of the populace in their favour, to manipulate thought through propaganda and 'spin'. And although these are necessary characteristics of dictatorial language, they are not sufficient to define it, because they are used by every regime, dictatorial or otherwise, political or commercial or religious or educational or what have you. It is called rhetoric. I am not saying that there aren't degrees of intent to deceive within rhetoric – there are, and although the art of determining another person's intent is a utopian enterprise, it is also a necessary one. I am simply saying that we are subject to attempts to manipulate our way of thinking every day from all sorts of interests, and we wouldn't term all of them 'dictatorial'. If we did, we would simply bleach that word of any strong, distinctive meaning.

But because of our focus on active manipulation of thought, we overlook the last part of the quote from Orwell, about making 'all other modes of thought impossible'. Here is where enters the need to restrict interpretation – and that, I submit, is the defining characteristic of dictatorship. You must impose a single interpretation on your utterances. It is utopian to imagine you can do this, because the nature of the human mind is to consider various possible interpretations of any utterance and select from among them. What you can do is to prevent anyone from *uttering* an alternative interpretation, by threat or, failing that, by murder. But a true dictator, like a good practitioner of any art, will not be deterred by the utopian nature of the ultimate goal. The question is, how does one go about controlling the minds of those to whom one dictates? Based upon his long and intimate observation of imperialist, communist and fascist regimes, Orwell determined that the way to do this, at least for his satirical purposes in *Nineteen Eighty-Four*, was through a form of language standardisation.

> This was done partly by the invention of new words, but chiefly by eliminating undesirable words and by stripping such words as remained of unorthodox meanings, and so far as possible of all secondary meanings whatever. To give a single example. The word *free* still existed in Newspeak, but it could only be used in such statements as 'This dog is free from lice' or 'This field is free from weeds'. It could not be used in its old sense of 'politically free' or 'intellectually free', since political and intellectual freedom no longer existed even as concepts, and were therefore of necessity nameless ... Newspeak was designed not to extend but to *diminish* the range of thought, and this purpose was indirectly assisted by cutting the choice of words down to a minimum. (Orwell 1989 [1949]: 313)

Newspeak is the culmination of views Orwell had developed over the course of the preceding five years (see Orwell 1944, 1946, 1947) and is most directly a satire of Basic English. Orwell was initially attracted to Basic English and corresponded with Ogden about it. But he came to realise that it might actually have the opposite effect to the one intended. Propaganda can only be combated by rational analysis and argument. This entails rephrasing propagandistic statements in a different form. If such rephrasing were made impossible through the loss of alternative words in which the same idea might be given a different linguistic shape, then it might no longer be possible to question the truth of any statement.

The greatness of Orwell and *Nineteen Eighty-Four* lies in the fact that the butt of the satire is no particular political side, no particular government. Rather, it is the universal condition to which all government, all society, all language tends. The fact that this condition had recently been carried to unprecedented extremes only served to draw attention to the reality and depth of the problem, while also demonstrating that it affected the extreme left no less than the extreme right, and also the centre – for Orwell was extremely critical of the British imperial regime of which he was himself a child.

6.5 LINGUISTIC CREATIVITY AND MANUFACTURING CONSENT

According to Barsky (1998), the great intellectual passion of Chomsky's teenage years was Orwell, especially *Homage to Catalonia*, from which Chomsky claims to have derived

> the foundations of much of his later work on propaganda, the media, and the ways that groups such as the Spanish anarchists are discredited in Western society … 'Language in the Service of Propaganda' [is] one of his many later articles that draws upon George Orwell's writings and the reception of his work. (Barsky 1998: 31)

Chomsky (1986), one of the most successful and widely read of his attempts to synthesise his theory of language into an accessible form, concludes with a brief chapter entitled 'Notes on Orwell's problem' (1988: 276–87). Besides discussing Newspeak, Chomsky here quotes Harold Lasswell (1902–78), a leading American scholar of propaganda, to the effect that 'we must avoid "democratic dogmatisms", such as the belief that people are "the best judges of their own interests"' (Chomsky 1986: 286). In Chomsky's view, 'Propaganda is to democracy as violence is to totalitarianism' (ibid.). As a political critic, Chomsky has made it one of his central messages that governments and media conspire to 'manufacture consent' (the title of Herman and Chomsky 1988). He agrees to the use of titles such as 'Language in the service of propaganda' and 'Terrorism: the politics of language' to help sell a book (Chomsky 1992) in which he repeatedly asserts his reluctance to attribute too much importance to the connection between language and thought, in response to an interviewer (David Barsamian) who wants him to accept that they are deeply linked.

Chomsky is willing to go as far as the following where the relationship between politics and language is concerned:

> There is a tenuous relationship, in fact several different kinds. I think myself that they're exaggerated in importance. There is in the first place the question discussed, for example, by Orwell and by a number of others of how language is abused, tortured, distorted, in a way, to enforce ideological goals. A classic example would be the switch in the name of the Pentagon from the War Department to the Defense Department in 1947. As soon as that happened, any thoughtful person should have understood that the United States would no longer be engaged in defence. It would only be engaged in aggressive war. That was essentially the case, and it was part of the reason for the change in terminology, to disguise that fact. Terms like 'the free world' and 'the national interest' and so on are mere terms of propaganda. One shouldn't take them seriously for a moment. They are designed, often very consciously, in order to try to block thought and understanding. (Chomsky 1992: 1–3)

Barsamian understands, even if Chomsky doesn't, the power that these views take on by virtue of being articulated by the leading theoretician of language of the second half of the twentieth century, notwithstanding his initial disclaimers, which get forgotten in the rhetorical torrent that follows – especially since few people read these books who aren't already convinced that nefarious forces are conspiring to control minds.

How does all this connect with Chomsky's linguistics? His address to the 1962 International Congress of Linguists, the paper that made his international reputation in linguistics, states on its opening page that

> The central fact to which any significant linguistic theory must address itself is this: a mature speaker can produce a new sentence of his language on the appropriate occasion, and other speakers can understand it immediately, though it is equally new to them. Most of our linguistic experience, both as speakers and hearers, is with new sentences; once we have mastered a language, the class of sentences with which we can operate fluently and without difficulty or hesitation is so vast that for all practical purposes we may regard it as infinite. (Chomsky 1964c: 7)

Chomsky's 'infinite linguistic creativity' played brilliantly, not just to the 1962 ICL but to the whole *Zeitgeist* of the 1960s. It made every human being infinitely creative, starting from childhood, not just 'creative types'. Nobody liked creative types – the left associated them with bourgeois decadence, the right with socialism – but everybody liked the idea that all of us, especially children, are infinitely, and therefore equally, creative.

And yet, a curious asymmetry lurks beneath the surface of Chomskyan creativity. The passage quoted above appears to treat production by speakers and under-standing by hearers on an equal basis. Both have infinite creativity in the sense that speakers can produce an infinite number of sentences, and every one of these sentences can be understood by the hearers, provided that they share the same language. But a subtle and interesting trick is at work within the word 'creativity' as Chomsky uses it, such that it does not mean the same thing as applied to speakers and hearers. Speakers may have the freedom to 'create' new sentences at will, in something recognisable as the general meaning of the word 'create'. But when it comes to the hearers, they do nothing more than passively register what the speakers have created.

This becomes apparent when Chomsky (ibid.) points out that mastery of a language also involves 'the ability to identity deviant sentences', such as *Colorless green ideas sleep furiously*, and 'on occasion, to impose an interpretation on them', 'if a context can be constructed in which an interpretation can be imposed'. The poet John Hollander famously constructed such a context in 'Coiled Alizarine (for Noam Chomsky)' (from *The Night Mirror*, 1971):

> Curiously deep, the slumber of crimson thoughts:
> While breathless, in stodgy viridian,
> Colorless green ideas sleep furiously.

This is a clear case of 'imposing' an interpretation as Chomsky defines it. But no interpretation needs to be imposed on a sentence such as *Revolutionary new ideas appear infrequently* (Chomsky 1964c: 7–8, n. 2). The speaker's mental grammar assigns it a structural description which indicates that it is perfectly 'well-formed'. Interpretation then proceeds automatically out of the mental grammar.

We thus have two completely different mechanisms of interpretation, one for well-formed and the other for deviant sentences. The first is automatic and straightforward. The second is much more complex: the grammar assigns a structural description that indicates the manner of its deviation from perfect well-formedness, after which, 'an interpretation can often be imposed by virtue of formal relations to sentences of the generated language' (ibid.: 9). But the interpretation does not follow directly or automatically out of those 'formal relations' – if they did, the word *imposed* would not be applicable to them. The interpretation of the well-formed sentence is *generated* by the grammar, but that of the deviant sentence has to be imposed *by someone*, John Hollander for instance.

Now, of these two processes, which might one characterise as 'creative' in the ordinary sense of that word? Obviously the interpretation of the deviant sentence, the 'imposed' interpretation, is the creative one. And it is precisely on account of its creativity – the active role of a linguistic agent, namely the hearer – that it is marginalised as standing in direct opposition to the 'central fact to which any significant linguistic theory must address itself', namely that 'linguistic creativity' as defined by Chomsky in which the hearer's 'creative' role is to sit back and let his or her mental grammar assign an interpretation.

It puzzled me for a long time how Orwellian manufacture of consent could be reconcilable with 'infinite linguistic creativity' for Chomsky. Infinitely supple linguistic minds operating on innate principles should not be so immediately susceptible to verbal control, like rats in a Skinner box. The solution to the puzzle lies, I think, in another curious feature of Chomsky's history, his serial repudiation of his own terms and collocations. In the early stages of his work, it really is collocations he deals in – he does not invent terminology, but puts existing words together in a way that gives them new, specialised meanings in his particular context of use. A few years later, he gives them up, explaining that they have given rise to too many misunderstandings – 'deep structure' taken to mean a universal level of sentence structure that is the same across all human languages, which Chomsky insists is never what he meant. He had to replace 'deep structure' with D-structure, then with DS, then to stop talking about it altogether, lest his theories be distorted beyond all recognition.

This is the same man who believes in 'absolute freedom of speech' so strongly that he went to great lengths to become the world's most prominent advocate for Holocaust deniers, even though he himself is not one (see Joseph 1999). When it comes to his own collocations, it is quite another story – their meaning is not open for interpretation, the way something 'hypothetical' like Auschwitz is. But there is a consistency here: Chomsky has made clear that for him all interpretation is *political*, except when it is generated directly by grammar. This is precisely his position on the difference between *Revolutionary new ideas appear infrequently* and *Colorless green ideas sleep furiously*. For the latter, an interpretation must be 'imposed', and imposition is always potentially a political move. If people interpret that sentence differently, the one who argues most powerfully for his or her interpretation will impose it. Whereas, the 'perfectly well-formed' sentence is closed to political interpretation by the real interpretation generated physically by the grammar in the speaker's brain. Thus, the linguistic creativity Chomsky calls infinite is on the production side only. Interpretation is normally finite, and in the abnormal cases, where he might have called it creative, he instead castigates it as 'imposition'.

All those who were attracted to Chomsky's views on creativity because they understood him as meaning that everyone's linguistic utterances are 'creative' in any of the ordinary senses of that word – rather than the specialised sense it has in Chomsky's collocation – might have been disabused of this misinterpretation if they had paid closer attention to the actual example sentences he used. If you took him to mean that everyone is creative intellectually, his own linguistic example informs you that *Revolutionary new ideas appear infrequently*. And if you took him to mean that everyone is linguistically creative in a poetic way, along the lines of Carter's (1999: 207) assertion that 'All language is literary language', you ought to have taken note that *Colorless green ideas sleep furiously* does not in fact have a 'real' meaning.

Within the realm of rule-governed creativity, the authority to identify the rules which Chomsky claims in his capacity as a native speaker is absolute. The perceptive Archibald A. Hill (1902–92) was among the first to pick up on this, in a discussion he moderated in 1958 between Chomsky and the Romance philologist Anna Granville Hatcher (1905–78), where Chomsky denies that a collocation used by the Wisconsin-born Thorstein Veblen (1857–1929) in *The Theory of the Leisure Class* (1899) is really English.

Hatcher: ... I think the only way to study sentences is to study normal sentences, produced under no prejudicial theories, in ordinary language use. When a grammarian constructs sentences there are enormous distortions, and when we try to decide what we would or would not say, we are very likely to fool ourselves.

Chomsky: The trouble with using a corpus is that some authors do not write the English language. Veblen, for example, speaks of 'performing leisure', and the verb *perform* cannot take such an object.

Hatcher: I admit it sounds unusual. But I bet that if you studied the verb *perform* you would find other expressions not too far from this, pointing the way to this. He has gone farther perhaps along a certain road but I do not believe he has created something new.

Chomsky: No. He has broken a law. The verb *perform* cannot be used with mass-word objects: one can perform a *task*, but one cannot perform *labor*.

Hatcher: How do you know, if you don't use a corpus and have not studied the verb *perform*?

Chomsky: How do I know? Because I am a native speaker of the English Language.

Hill: I think at this point I would like to strike a blow for liberty ... (Hill (ed.) 1962: 28–9)

Hill goes on to argue for the liberty of linguists to use corpus, observational or intuitional data as they see fit. I think, though, that his comment can be interpreted as partly directed against Chomsky's blatant and militant prescriptivism – the clue Hill has left us, taking advantage of his editorial role, is the capital L in 'English Language' in Chomsky's last statement. This was not Hill's normal usage (cf. for instance Chomsky's first statement above), and there is of course a well-established tradition in Modern English of capitalising a common noun, *à l'allemande*, in order to deflate an overblown conception of it as an Institution.

Earlier in the same Symposium, Hill and Chomsky had engaged in an interesting exchange, where Hill refers to views of Sapir's:

Hill: I think on this matter of ungrammatical sequences that I should be more nearly in agreement with Sapir than with you. Sapir said, many years ago, that you could probably not present any written sequence of words to a native speaker without his trying to wring some kind of sense out of it ...

Chomsky: ... You are quite right in saying that people will read something into a sequence of nonsense syllables. But the point is that there is a very significant difference in how hard people have to work to read sense into different sequences, and it is precisely this difference which I think the linguist should investigate. (Hill (ed.) 1962: 19)

What Chomsky is calling 'hard work' in 1958 corresponds to the imposition of an interpretation in 1962. He certainly had a point in calling for the difference to be investigated; but by the 1962 ICL paper the difference is no longer to be investigated

– instead, the imposed type of interpretation is ruled out of consideration altogether. One can see why this had to happen by considering the exchange over Veblen's phrase 'performing leisure'. Neither Chomsky nor any English speaker has to 'work hard' to read sense into it. It is 'self-interpreting' *even though* Chomsky's mental grammar identifies it as deviant, to the point that he denies it is English.

Contemporary anxiety over linguistic mind control, with Chomsky as its patron saint, is the culmination of several trends. The idea of 'manufacturing consent' is the outcome of the loss of faith in the human will, in favour of a belief that a small oligarchy is exercising its will over the masses, who are like automata under the oligarchy's control. This belief has been developing since the late nineteenth century. For the American linguist William Dwight Whitney (1827–94), language itself was a democracy, an institution in the use of which speakers – *all* speakers – exercise their individual will (see Whitney 1867: 38). By the 1920s such a view already seemed dated, and by the 1950s, archaic. But the oligarchical position that underlies the modern Chomskyan anxiety poses huge problems. On one level, it is a form of middle-class loathing of the great unwashed. No one ever expresses anxiety that *they themselves* are having their minds controlled from without. Their awareness of the 'manufacture of consent' apparently immunises them from its effects. But they are certain that the vast majority of human beings are not so enlightened, and are therefore the pawns of the oligarchy.

Chomsky's decree that the great fact which linguistics must take as its point of departure is the infinite linguistic creativity of every speaker received wide attention for the political message it seemed to convey about the possibility, indeed the necessity of human freedom. Yet this was always a false impression, since the 'creativity' Chomsky proclaimed was limited to linguistic production, and was banned from the much more important matter of what that production *meant*, since semantics for Chomsky cannot be a matter of interpretation. That is precisely the model on which propaganda anxiety depends: the ordinary person processes whatever they are told automatically, without critical interpretation. It is the way Newspeak was designed to work – and that is because Orwell recognised that it is *not* how 'Oldspeak' works. The first and cleverest generation of Chomsky's students, the so-called 'generative semanticists', would attempt to rectify the error – only to have Chomsky impose the one true interpretation of his theory in a fashion that can only be described as dictatorial. More's the pity, because the theory he was left with cannot account for the fact that ordinary people do not simply accept what those in power tell them, but question it, are sceptical about it, resist it, appropriate it and tweak it in order to suit their own ends. *That* is infinite linguistic creativity, in the truest sense.

6.6 CRITICAL DISCOURSE ANALYSIS

In the 1970s a group of 'critical linguists', trained in Halliday's systemic–functional grammar, which aims at comprehending both the social and semiotic dimensions of texts (see e.g. Halliday 1978), emerged under the leadership of Roger Fowler (1938–99) (see Fowler 1987; Fowler *et al.* 1979). This in turn led to the 'critical discourse analysis' (CDA) of Norman Fairclough (1989, 1992), to which other important text analysts such as Teun A. van Dijk, Ruth Wodak and Paul Chilton, to name just three, have aligned their own work. CDA marries critical linguistics with the perspectives of Foucault and Bourdieu, and sees itself as capturing the 'dynamic' nature of both power relations and text production by uncovering the hegemonic structures within texts. This is in contrast with earlier analyses, including those of critical linguistics, which concerned themselves with static relations and how they are encoded.

While the discourse which Fairclough and other practitioners of CDA analyse is not limited by genre, they have shown the most intense interest in texts emanating from politicians and government agencies. Fairclough, for example, produced an entire monograph on the language of New Labour just three years after the Blair government's accession to power (Fairclough 2000). Van Dijk's output has included several books focusing on racism and its manifestations in official and unofficial discourse (his notion of 'elite racism' was mentioned in §5.4, p. 103) – and it is his analysis of racism in the discourse of European and American politicians in the early 1990s that I shall focus on here, first of all because it serves to demonstrate the methodology of CDA and to highlight its strengths and weaknesses, and second because it links with the race-related issues covered in previous chapters, allowing for greater depth to the discussion.

Van Dijk (1993) looks at official discourse concerning race as it manifested itself in half a dozen different national contexts in the period 1990–1, but the two most salient are France, where the *Front National* party headed by Jean-Marie Le Pen was entering the limelight, and the USA, where the Civil Rights Bill of 1990 was proposed, debated and passed by the Congress, then vetoed by President George H. W. Bush, after which another, compromise bill was passed and adopted in 1991. Van Dijk's method is to show how the same rhetorical strategies and devices are used across the nations and languages by the far right (such as the *Front National*) and conservative parties (such as the Republicans) to justify the perpetuation of racist policies while claiming not to be racist. Indeed, the parties in question actually maintain that the supposedly anti-racist policies of their liberal opponents are the ones that would perpetuate racism and ethnic tensions. I shall give a fairly full résumé of three of the seven rhetorical strategies which van Dijk uncovers, together with examples from the legislative record which he cites, before more briefly describing the rest.[10]

Positive self-presentation: nationalist rhetoric

Our country has for a long time been open to foreigners, a tradition of hospitality going back beyond the Revolution, to the *Ancien Régime*. (France, Mr Mazeaud, 9 July 1990, p. 3049)

This is a nation whose values and traditions now excite the world, as we all know. I think we all have a deep pride in American views, American ideals, American government, American principle, which excite hundreds of millions of people around the world who struggle for freedom. (United States, Mr Foley, 2 August 1990, H6768)

The very concept of 'foreigners', and of 'the world' beyond the nation, introduces the us–them dyad that is fundamental to racist thinking. The fact that it is introduced *sub reptice* in proclamations of openness to the foreign world is the key to how this rhetorical strategy operates – it misdirects the audience's attention, so that they do not even notice the dyad being slipped in. Van Dijk (1993: 74) points to the irony of the French representative's reference to the *Ancien Régime*, whose political opponents had to flee the country; and (ibid.: 75–6) to the particular importance the words *values* and *ideals* had taken on in Republican Party rhetoric in this period, as well as to the central place of *freedom* within American rhetoric generally.

Disclaimers and the denial of racism

The French are not racist. But, facing this continuous increase of the foreign population in France, one has witnessed the development, in certain cities and neighborhoods, of reactions that come close to xenophobia. (France, Mr Pascua, 9 July 1986, p. 3053)

Well, now can we also agree this afternoon that you can have different philosophies about how to achieve through law civil rights and equal opportunities for everybody without somehow being anti-civil-rights or being a racist or something like that. (United States, Mr Gunderson, 2 August 1990, H6781)

As Gertrude says to Hamlet, 'The lady doth protest too much, methinks'. Denials of racism nearly always accompany political arguments which favour one race or ethnicity over another. Interestingly, as van Dijk shows with other citations as well, it is acceptable within French political discourse to be 'xenophobic', but not to be racist – and politicians ritually place themselves within the pale of acceptability, even though the fact of the matter is that the 'foreigners' at whom the xenophobia is directed all happen to be people of colour. Moreover, references to 'the French' as being of a single character are themselves inherently racist. In the American context, 'how to achieve equal opportunities' is a linguistic subterfuge to avoid saying what the speaker is opposed to, namely, 'affirmative action' policies that give preference to members of racial minority groups in hiring, admissions and so on. Van Dijk comments: 'although [Mr Gunderson] explicitly affirms to be in favor of civil rights, he wants to realize them in a different way. This is a powerful argumentative move because it presupposes that the ultimate goal is the same and there is only a difference of means' (van Dijk 1993: 84).

Negative other-presentation

[T]he French … are worried in the face of an immigration out of control, in the face of a pure and hard Islam that might cross the Mediterranean. But the French stay tolerant. (France, Mr de Broissia, 28 June 1990, p. 3124 [translation amended])

[G]iven the huge litigation expenses that an employer would have to incur in order to vindicate his name, there is an encouragement to settle these cases, whether they have merit or not. And then we have turned this issue not into a civil rights bill but to a bill that legalizes extortion against employers who are subjected to claims of unlawful discrimination that are without merit. (United States, Sensenbrenner, 2 August 1990, H6773)

This strategy comes closest to 'racism' in the blatant, non-'elite' sense – but the actual negative comments made about the minority group in question are never the *real* views that underlie the fundamentally racist policies being defended. In the French example, van Dijk points to the mitigation effected by the use of the word 'worried' – it is acceptable for a 'tolerant' people to worry, but in fact this worry is indistinguishable from racism (van Dijk 1993: 88). Van Dijk describes 'pure and hard Islam' as a classic negative-other presentation, though 'pure' is not usually a negative term unless followed by something overtly negative (like 'pure evil'). His analysis of the American example here is undeniably incisive:

[T]his passage, and in particular 'vindicate', presupposes that accused employers are usually innocent, and that minorities often level unfounded accusations of discrimination. The use of 'extort' further implies that such accusations are ... acts of a serious criminal nature ... It even reverses the role in the sociopolitical drama of racism, following the Blaming the Victim move: Those who engage in criminal discrimination become victims, whereas the victims are turned into vindictive avengers. (ibid.: 89)

The other four rhetorical strategies described by van Dijk are as follows:

Firm, but fair. This phrase, or variants on it, appears frequently enough as part of positive self-presentations – e.g., in calls for 'firm but fair immigration controls' – for van Dijk to single it out as a distinct form of paternalistic window-dressing for racist policies.

For their own good. This is described as an 'Apparent Empathy or Apparent Altruism' move, again paternalistic in nature, whereby policies for limiting immigration, ending affirmative action, and so on, are characterised as being for the good of the minorities themselves, rather than in the interest of the majority.

Vox populi or white racism as a threat. Here the speaker, while denying having any racist motives himself or herself, warns that the *general public's* tolerance for policies supporting minority rights is wearing thin, and that the result of supporting these policies could be *increased* racial tension and discrimination, rather than the reduction that is being aimed at.

The numbers game. This refers to the 'rhetorical use of quasi-objective figures, convincingly suggesting how many 'come in' every day, week, month, or year', and is described by van Dijk as 'one of the most compelling scare tactics in the formation of public opinion' (ibid.: 107), even when the figures in question are not false or exaggerated. Not only does it create the impression that immigration, for example, is 'out of control', it also plays into fears and panic about high birth rates among immigrant groups, references to which are in turn 'a familiar disparaging qualification of "backward" peoples: Modern people have birth control' (ibid.: 108).

Van Dijk's catalogue of the rhetorical moves used in political discourse concerning immigration and civil rights is enlightening; the patterns it reveals are ones that emerge only after large-scale comparison of cross-linguistic texts. As with other CDA treatments of political discourse, it is a refreshing experience for those of us who are not political office-holders to see the often high-flown rhetoric of those who govern us brought down to earth. For these and other reasons I believe that CDA has a validity that transcends the methodological critiques that have been made of it from many quarters. At the heart of these critiques is a simple point: because CDA has its own strong political commitments, it does not provide any 'objective' analysis of texts, but a politically interested analysis.

Van Dijk, for example, is not presenting texts chosen at random from a corpus of speeches made within the context of immigration and civil rights debates, and analysing them to see which ones have racist content, how various political positions are put across rhetorically, etc. Instead, with only a handful of exceptions, he has selected texts produced by members of conservative or far-right parties, whose positions he has decided in advance are inherently racist, then sorted them according to which rhetorical devices they can be shown to manifest. For someone committed to CDA, there is unlikely to be a problem here: the whole point of the enterprise is to promote a better society by exposing the ways in which power is manifested and reproduced discursively, and in any legislation that aims at restricting immigration or cutting back on affirmative action, the majority is (re-)exercising its power over the minorities it has historically oppressed. Even to raise the question of whether this is the only possible way of conceiving things is to play into the hands of the anti-minority forces – which means to be party to racism. In a similar way, critics of Fairclough's single-minded focus on 'right-wing' discourse – which includes that of New Labour – risk having their calls for objectivity in methodology and interpretation dismissed as a smoke screen for conservative sympathies.

CDA thus shares a fundamental weakness with Phillipson and Skutnabb-Kangas's hegemony-based analysis of the spread of English (see §3.4). Any intellectual framework that requires a particular political commitment, and cannot open itself to application by people holding a variety of political views, has no place in the secular academic context. It is an ideology masquerading as a scholarly method. However, I don't believe that this is in fact what CDA is – despite the best efforts of some in the movement to make it such. The very fact that CDA wears its political commitments on its sleeve means that, in principle, they are detachable, and nothing prevents its methods being applied to discourse of any sort, representing any political persuasion or none (in which case it would be aiming to tease out the linguistic politics which I have asserted are there for every text). The analysis in §1.7 of the CIA report on Iraq's weapons of mass destruction, for example, is inspired by CDA categories and techniques, but I did not undertake it with the presupposition that it contained rhetorical structures purposely designed to camouflage secret political intentions. The fact that I nevertheless found structures that can cogently be interpreted in this way makes the analysis convincing for me in a way it would *not* be if that was what I had set out to find.

On the other hand, my views about language policy as expressed in §3.6 could be characterised as 'elite racist' by a CDA analyst based on the presence in my argument of van Dijk's 'Vox populi or white racism as a threat' move – for it has been my experience that minority language policies which fail to take account of majority reactions have often backfired on minority communities, setting back their just cause, where a more pragmatic policy might have advanced it. If a particular form of CDA makes it possible only to believe in an idealistic rather than a pragmatic approach to language policy in cases where idealism has proven historically to be counter-productive, then it is a form of CDA that needs revising.

Despite being so controversial, CDA is without question the most important mode of analysis of political discourse at the present time. The aim of this section has been simply to introduce it, within the context of a much broader conception of language and politics, to explain the methodological issues that have been raised concerning its political commitments and to suggest how those interested in applying it might deal with those issues.

6.7 THE FUNCTION OF LANGUAGE IN A DEMOCRACY

This chapter has reviewed a range of ideas about the nature of the relationship of language to thought, culture and society, and about whether and how the particular uses of language that constitute rhetoric and, in a more extreme form, propaganda, can be turned toward anti-democratic, even dictatorial ends. In some cases I have made clear what my own views are, notably about Chomsky's theory of interpretation, and about the pros and cons of CDA. On other matters I have preferred to expose readers to a range of options without expressing judgements that would tend to close any of the options off. But at this point I should make a few things clear.

Concerning realism, nominalism and conceptualism, I believe that the realist view is ontologically right, but epistemologically impossible – that is, there are ultimate truths, but as human beings we cannot know what they are. Perhaps after we die. Meanwhile, conceptualism is what we are left with; it is the closest we can hope to come to truth, and although it opens up space to indeterminacy, it is not a free-for-all where whatever anyone conceives has to be accepted by the rest of us as true for that person.

Concerning the Sapir–Whorf Hypothesis, I subscribe to the 'weak' version. In the process of acquiring our mother tongue (or tongues) – a long apprenticeship that occupies most of our waking moments for our first three or four years, and continues thereafter – we have transmitted to us the contents of our 'culture' along with it. The language is, in various ways, the primary *text* through which the culture is transmitted, and in the course of this early apprenticeship the knowledge involved becomes part not just of our memory but of our nervous system, our bodies, our *habitus.* It does not limit what we are able to think or do, but it does make it such that some things come more easily while others take an effort. It follows that I do not consider language a 'mere garment' of thought that exists independently of it; examining language really can open up important insights into another culture, or indeed into one's own, and there really are logical contradictions that the structures of languages tend to lead one towards, differing for every language and entirely surmountable; so there is something to both the magic key and metaphysical garbage outlooks, though one should avoid exaggerating how much.

It follows too that I believe we are susceptible to suggestion through language. An effective rhetorician knows how to exploit those potentialities of the language that the Sapir–Whorf hypothesis aims at describing and Basic English aims at eliminating, potentialities that have been used enough by governments, advertising agencies and other interested parties to give a rational basis to propaganda anxiety, in its milder forms. However, I also believe that *deep* propaganda anxiety, the sort that demands a major conspiracy theory, is misplaced, indeed that it is probably bound up with other fears that are less rational than the fear of propaganda itself. The fact is that we are surrounded by propaganda, are constantly barraged by it from all sides. The result *should* be, if the theory behind the linguistic mind control cultural discourse frame is right, that populations are becoming homogenised in their political views, and consistently in favour of the ruling parties; that for any particular product one single brand is driving all the rest off the market; and that we are heading towards one religion (or none), and one lifestyle that again is consistently the one that the political authorities would wish upon us all.

As a matter of empirical observation, I do not see these things happening. Are populations homogenising in their political views? Certainly not in the USA, where people's politics are at present more deeply divided than at any time since the Vietnam War. Certainly not in the European Union, which in 2005 had to abandon its long-standing attempts to ratify a constitution because of policy disagreements among and within member states. In the UK, one has the impression that New Labour has succeeded in taking over the traditional political turf of the Conservatives, leading to a unification of sorts; yet public opinion has moved anything but in the direction that the ruling party has struggled hard to push it in. Product brands are multiplying, not disappearing – one might point to Microsoft as a counter-example, but it was not through advertising, but business practices, that they attained their market supremacy, and even so, significant numbers of people across the world refuse absolutely to buy Microsoft products, as a reaction against the company's dominance. Religions continue a trend of fragmenting, with extraordinary growth for many novel sects in southeast Asia, Latin America, Africa and elsewhere. As for everyone adopting the lifestyle that our political masters would wish upon us – no smoking, no drugs, moderate drink, varied diet and regular exercise – if only propaganda *did* work as it is supposed to, we would all be better off. But for teenagers, for example, a large part of the appeal of smoking derives from the knowledge that it is highly risky and socially semi-taboo, something which the gruesome death warnings on the package and in the advertisements tend to support.

In out-and-out defiance of all government health ministries, of all national medical associations, and of Chomsky's theory of language, they impose their own un-authorised interpretations.

In the concluding chapter I shall elaborate more fully on these questions, broadening the context to include other issues of 'choice' that have run through this book, such as those having to do with the spread of English. Before doing so, however, I want to give some consideration to the role of language within a modern democracy, in the light of what we have seen so far. In its origins, democracy may not have been all that democratic – only a portion of the free adult male population was enfranchised – but it certainly was rhetorical. The processes of legislating and of conducting trials both depended squarely on the use of language to persuade a majority. Ideally this would be through the *content* of what one said, but unless one adheres to a strict mere garment view, content and linguistic form cannot be neatly separated. Ideally, too, the persuasive person would always be the most intelligent and morally upright person – but that would not be democracy at all, rather a version of Plato's Republic, with its philosopher–king. The point of democracy is that anyone can have the chance to persuade others, and that everyone has the chance to make up their own mind, just as they do when they go to the marketplace and decide from whom to buy.

Of course, when the democratic state reaches a critical size, representative democracy becomes inevitable. Now the value of rhetoric becomes even higher, as would-be representatives must persuade their fellows to elect them. Now everyone in the democratic assembly is not just a citizen, but a politician–rhetorican. Moreover, in the courts, anyone who can afford it will naturally prefer advocacy by a trained and experienced rhetorician over speaking for themselves. Access to the oppor-tunities and ability to persuade has narrowed dramatically. Still, though, every citizen has the chance to make up their own mind, whether as an elector or a member of a jury, just like in the marketplace.

What changed things significantly was another, later narrowing – that of the channels of communication, just around the time that semi-democratic modern nations were emerging in the Renaissance. With printing, news could spread further quicker, and in more detail – yet with the sense that one or a few people, in effect an oligarchy, was controlling it. As explained in §6.3, with the advent of broadcasting in the twentieth century, this sense intensified, helping to produce propaganda anxiety in its modern guise.

Yet the need within a democracy for information to guide the electorate, for communication from the government to the people, and for access to debate among people of different political views, has not changed. The media, limited though they may be, are the only available means for making these things happen. In a democratic society, the government has the responsibility to explain and justify its policies and actions, and it must use the media to do this. When does this constitute propaganda, and when does it not? That is the $64,000 question. There are easy cases – when a government does not permit any opposition voices to be heard, or when it tries single-mindedly to persuade people that policies it is implementing are for their own good, even when they patently are not. But what is 'patently'? In a democratic society there will always be a hard core of political opposition that considers *none* of the government's policies to be in the people's interests. Fringe parties will usually constitute this core, but even some practitioners of CDA, and certainly Chomsky in his political mode, come close to qualifying. For them, the government of the day, whatever its leanings, will *always* be engaging in propaganda.

This is not far from Orwell's position, and indeed it is useful to keep in mind that we are usually talking about differences of degree rather than kind when deciding whether a particular government or agency is propagandising or not. The essential thing, in my view, is not what is said, but the choices that are actually available to those in the population who *resist* the government's message. There will always be such resistance – it is fundamental to human nature. Forty years of propaganda by the Roman Catholic Church has not stopped the vast majority of faithful Catholics in the northern hemisphere from practising birth control. Seventy years of non-stop propaganda by the Soviet authorities could not stop citizens from eventually saying *nyet* to the system they had been raised from childhood to believe in with all their hearts. All it took was a little freeing up of the newspapers and the political discourse, and the government's propaganda went from provoking yawns to provoking laughter. The rest was inevitable.

SUGGESTED FURTHER READING

On Chomsky on propaganda: the best introduction is via Chomsky (2000), an audio recording; also Barsky (1998), Edgley (2000).

On propaganda: Pratkanis and Aronson (2001), Ramonet (1999, 2000).

On Critical Discourse Analysis: Chilton (2004), Chilton and Schäffner (eds) (2002), Fairclough (1995), Wodak and Meyer (eds) (2001).

On the Sapir–Whorf hypothesis: Lee (1995).

On the history of the language–thought–reality link: Joseph (2000a), Kretzmann (1967).

Analyses of political discourse from the CDA perspective feature regularly in the *Journal of Language and Politics* and *Discourse and Society*.

NOTES

1. As indicated above, the Sophists can be considered the predecessors of the Stoics as conceptualists, but it was Zeno and subsequent Stoic thinkers who formulated a coherent doctrine of conceptualism. A much fuller exposition of the medieval debates can be found in Kretzmann (1967).

2. Historians of linguistics often put the phrase 'Sapir–Whorf Hypothesis' in 'scare quotes' because neither Sapir nor Whorf ever articulated it as a hypothesis, and for each of them it represented a rather more complex set of ideas than either the normally encountered 'strong' view or its 'weak' counterpart comprises (see further Joseph 2002: 71–2). Having made this disclaimer I shall omit the scare quotes henceforth.

3. See Whorf (1956); Joseph, Love and Taylor (2001, Chapter 4); Lee (1995).

4. Whorf did not pursue the political implications of his view of language, but see Silverstein (2000) for an attempt to analyse national linguistic identity within the Whorfian framework, and Joseph (2004a: 123–5) for a critique of this attempt.

5. I.e., not as independent agents, but in interaction with one another. On the complex relationship between French structuralism and Marxism, see Joseph (2001).

6. See Joseph (2002, Chapter 9), for details of the dozens of publications about propaganda which began appearing in this period.

7. Matheson, one of the founders of BBC radio journalism, had been involved in the setting up of MI5 during WWI. At the start of WWII, she headed the Ministry of Information's Joint Broadcasting Committee, known informally as the 'anti-lie bureau', guiding its efforts to counteract the propaganda broadcasts of the pro-German 'Lord Haw-Haw'. It is also worth noting that the members of the BBC's Spoken Language committee in the mid-1930s included I. A. Richards.

8. Richards had written to his wife from Cambridge, Massachusetts, three years earlier that 'In fact, **at last**, I do have a clear lead to put in 12 hours a day on direct British Propaganda' (I. A. Richards to D. E. Richards, 15 July 1940; Constable 1990: 106, boldface in Constable).

9. This might well not have been possible with a work by a Japanese-American author after the bombing of Pearl Harbor on 7 December of that year. Hayakawa served as President of San Francisco State College from 1968 to 1973, attracting nationwide publicity for his hard-line stand against student protesters. He rode on the crest of this publicity to be elected for one term as a United States Senator (1977–83). In 1983 he founded US English, an organisation devoted to lobbying for English to be declared the 'official language' of the USA.

10. His discussion (van Dijk 1993: 72–113) ends with an eighth heading, 'Anti-racism and resistance', that does not in fact pick out a category on a par with the preceding seven. In the résumé of his categories I reproduce van Dijk's interpretations of the texts he is analysing even where I do not agree with them; the points of disagreement will be made clear later in the section.

Chapter 7

Conclusion: Power, hegemony and choices

7.1 AGENCY

This book has put forward a broad view of the range of topics that can be cogently and usefully grouped together under the rubric of 'language and politics' – cogently because, despite their surface diversity, they are linked by virtue of all being cases where language impacts directly upon the politics of identity, interpersonal relations, the relation of the individual to the community and the state, or all of these; usefully because of the light they shed upon one another, for example when an analogy from the use of familiar pronouns helps us to understand something about language change or the sort of bonding that occurs among people who swear profanely in each other's company.

Another thread has run through the chapters of this book, joining them rather loosely, and it is the job of this final chapter to pull it tighter. That thread is the issue of *agency* – the extent to which one's actions as an individual are freely chosen; or directed, either by invisible forces like 'society' and 'power' or by more tangible ones in the form of institutions, particularly those controlled by government; or even determined, by some power that can be imagined as a historical movement (evolution), a physical key (the genetic code) or as fate or Nature or God. We are emerging from a historical period, the second half of the twentieth century, in which language itself was widely taken to be the directing or determining master code – this was the impulse behind structuralism, and it largely endured in the post-structural ideas that followed in its wake.

Linguistics, the field that gave birth to structuralism, developed its own form of direction/determinism in the Sapir–Whorf Hypothesis, which the mainstream of the field then rejected; yet the leader of the mainstream in modern times, Chomsky, while denying any version of linguistic determinism in theory, simultaneously insists that all real interpretation of utterances is determined by the utterances themselves, and, which logically follows from this, that supposedly free peoples are in a false consciousness, being actually in the thrall of malevolent governmental and corporate forces that, through language, conspire to manufacture consent. Applied linguistics, meanwhile, is emerging from a period in which 'linguistic hegemony' was high on its list of concerns – in particular the belief that the current spread of English as a second language in many parts of the world is being forced imperialistically upon peoples who may think they are choosing to learn English or to have their children educated in English, but again are labouring under a false consciousness. But one of the key areas to have emerged within applied linguistics, Critical Discourse Analysis, takes a position very like Chomsky's described above; while certain other 'critical' applied linguistic movements continue to pursue a post-structuralist (and post-Nietzschean) view in which there is no reality outside discourse.

Little room appears to be left, then, for the belief that human beings *really are* agents who make choices that, while certainly bound up with the context in which they live, and no doubt conditioned by their personal histories, are nevertheless 'free' in the crucial sense that they are aware of more than one option being open to them, do not all select the same option (even if a large majority do) and can usually articulate why exactly they have made the choice they've made. To deny that this is so is not a 'liberating' move of any kind, for the denial of agency logically removes any possibility of people changing the situation they are perceived to be in. Yet, as 'critical realists' such as the sociologist Margaret Scotford Archer and the philosopher Roy Bhaskar point out, the fact is that those post-structuralists and others who deny agency – including Gramscian Marxists, with their theory of hegemony – almost without exception *do* see themselves as working in the cause of liberation, which means, implicitly, restoring an agency to people that others have taken away from them. For Archer (2001), this contradiction renders non-agentive theories absurd and means that some version of realism (and maybe just the critical realism she herself professes) is the only logically coherent view.

I think this is going too far. Once we recognise that a belief in the possibility of agency unites these warring theories, it becomes possible to reconcile them in such a way that the space restrictions on free choice are beaten back. Although I accept with the critical realists that agency is both a logical and a moral necessity – without it, for instance, it would be impossible to bring anyone to justice for any crime, up to and including genocide – what critical realism lacks is an account of the *limits* on the choices an individual can make and bring to fruition. I could choose to be rich; but really my choice is limited, initially at least, to *wanting* to be rich. Actually becoming rich is something else again. Many obstacles stand in my way, such as the armed guards at the bank, and the choices I made earlier in life to become an academic, not to marry into a wealthy family, etc. Then there are 'choices' which weren't up to me to make – not to come from a rich family myself, having an early education in which the importance of service to others rather than self-enrichment was incessantly hammered home. None of these things would make it impossible for me now to give up my academic career and start up a business that would have a chance of being lucrative, but my success would still depend on the choices made by others – potential customers who might or might not decide to buy my product or use my service.

To bring the discussion back to language: I could choose to become a speaker of Inuktitut. I could learn what I can about the language from books, seek out an Inuit or someone else who has studied the language to be my teacher, or better still (but more constrained by my family responsibilities), go to live for two years with an Inuit family in an Inuit community. If my circumstances permitted this, then I could be fairly confident that at the end of the stay I would understand most of what was said to me in Inuktitut, and could say most of what I wanted to say. My linguistic skills however would not be like those of a native, and I almost certainly wouldn't have developed even the simulacrum of a native *habitus* in my production of Inuktitut utterances. Many people would do better than me at this – that small minority of the population with a real gift for learning languages to native-like proficiency, even in adulthood; others wouldn't do as well as me, with all the previous experience of language learning and analysis I bring to the task. So – can I choose to learn to speak Inuktitut? The answer is yes – within the limits imposed by my *habitus* (mental and physical), my circumstances and the readiness of an Inuit community to accommodate me.

To comprehend this state of affairs requires a theory that will both allow me the choice and give a cogent account of the constraints that limit my ability to see what I've chosen through to completion. Since early in the twentieth century the balance has been weighted heavily in favour of constraints, and there are historical reasons for that: it was a period in which governments, largely through technological advances, were able to keep closer tabs on citizens than ever before, and consequently to exercise greater control over their lives. Innovations such as universal education, universal suffrage, universal male conscription, income tax, telephony and state pensions – not to mention advances in propaganda – brought about this control across the 'developed' world, with still further-reaching methods to follow in totalitarian states. What we think about language, and about agency generally, does not exist in a vacuum from the world in which we live and breathe.

Yet theories have been developed which offer a better balance between agency and constraint, particularly since the crumbling of the Soviet bloc starting in 1989, which ended (for all but a small number of ideologues) the Marxist illusion of the inevitable decline of individual agency. Two of the most promising such theories are those of Pierre Bourdieu and Talbot Taylor. Taylor (1997, 2000) has been developing a compelling account of how cultural conceptions of language – including, crucially, the notion of its uniformity – come to us through the meta-comments on our utterances that can be shown empirically to be part of everyone's daily experience from infancy onward. Bourdieu's theory is aimed at understanding constrained choices, in the aftermath of a structuralism that allowed for no real choices at all.

Still further along on this pendulum swing is Archer's Critical Realism, mentioned above, which is focused almost exclusively on the agency that makes the choice, and is still so busy fighting rear-guard actions against those who deny agency to ordinary individuals that her instinctive reaction at any hint of 'constraint' seems to be to reach for her tin of labels, where there is something to classify (and thus put aside) everyone who doesn't see things in just the critical realist way. (In Bourdieu's case, he gets classified as an example of 'centre conflation'.) Nevertheless, the robustness of Archer's demonstrations – showing that even those philosophical and methodological positions that most strongly deny the possibility of agency actually must assume that very possibility as their point of departure and *raison d'être* – pose a major problem for anyone who wants to continue with a non-agentive stance. My criticism of critical realists is that they want to throw the baby (constraints on choice) out with the deterministic bathwater; but it was an awfully filthy baby, so desperately in need of bathing that many could not even recognise it as human.

7.2 BROCCOLI THEORY

It is not at all noteworthy that a sentence such as the following can appear in print without any need of justification or any worry that readers will fail to nod in assent: 'The market has stripped us of our identities and consequently we have endlessly to refashion ourselves in accordance with the capitalist and the modernist imperatives to "make it new"' (Day 2005: 27). This follows a comment on 'our current pre-occupation with identity' – the implication being that we are so preoccupied on account of feeling our identities being stripped away. Strangely, that is not my perception at all. Rather, the growth of interest in identities in the social sciences and humanities in the last two decades has had to do with a *resurgence* of feelings of identity – national, cultural and personal – as the Cold War struggle between capitalism and Marxism ceased to be the master narrative for explaining history and our place in it. The temporary erasure of fears of a great threat from the East (before another such fear arose in September 2001) made it possible for a country such as the UK to contemplate the devolution of political power to its internal nations, which demanded it precisely on account of their feelings of identity, which 'the market' had not stripped away in the least. The break-up of the USSR was the same sort of event on a much grander scale – and here the resurgence of 'the market' after decades of repression was inseparable from the resurgence of identities. The fact that the consumer goods purchased were mostly of foreign manufacture in no way obliterated or diluted people's identities – it strengthened them, because the operative dyad in this case was [± Soviet], where a [+] represented the repression of their identity, and a [–] the freedom to claim and perform it.

One curious thing about Day's remark is that earlier in his article he has pointed to 'a range of thinkers, from Locke to Freud', and including Adam Smith, Schopenhauer and Marx, 'who all, in one way or another, see the rise of industry as a threat to work as a means of self-fulfilment'. It was mainly the division of labour they worried about, the relegation of people to mechanical tasks, denying them the fulfilment of producing a whole product. Day comments, 'Things are certainly different now. But our multi-tasking is not the same as being a fisherman in the morning and a philosopher in the evening'. All this suggests that the sapping of our identities by the market is a phenomenon that goes back at least to the late seventeenth century, when Locke was writing, and was certainly perceived as wide-spread by the early nineteenth. So what was left for 'modernism' to do? What was left for today's media and global corporations, routinely fingered as the culprits in the mass identity theft perpetrated upon the whole human race?

Most importantly, Day's example of when people really had identity and fulfilment in work is when one could be a fisherman (note the gender) in the morning and a philosopher in the evening. When was this time, exactly? I suppose it depends on how one defines 'philosopher'. If it includes evenings spent in the pub talking about life, or at home reading the Bible to the family, then yes, probably many fishermen had this kind of life between the seventeenth century and the 1950s, with their numbers decreasing (and working hours increasing) since then for various reasons. No, actually, already by the nineteenth century fishing was a very com- mercialised business in most places; fishermen didn't make their living with a pole, sitting by a stream, and didn't have the energy left for serious philosophical pursuits in the evening any more than the average worker does today. It is always a mythical time that Marxists, post-Marxists and *marxisants* imagine as their Paradise Lost, to which the present can never measure up. And whatever is the most convenient culprit of the moment will become the villain who has taken Paradise away and is blocking the path to its return.

Day is aware too of the fact that this Paradise really is for fisher*men*. Historically, access to work outside the home has meant liberation for many women, as have the products of manufacture and 'the market', including the washing machine. Who was washing and stitching Day's fisherman/philosopher's clothes, growing or buying food other than fish for his meals, fetching water, getting wood or coal for the fire, cleaning house, emptying chamber pots, tending the fire, hauling the ashes, taking care of the children, mending the roof, while he was off fishing or philosophising? Or is this how he spent his afternoons? If so, it has been elided – but more likely it was a woman doing all or most of this work in 'Paradise'. For her, work in the supposedly 'identity stripping' sense stood to free her and give her an identity she barely had before.

My experience of modern identities is not that the market strips us of them – as if the market were some kind of beast, distinct from us, rather than the activities and exchanges that all of us (except hermits) engage in. The market is us. Even the trans- national corporations accused of manipulating us are public corporations, owned by millions of shareholders, including probably Gary Day, you the reader, and me, if we have a pension fund (even an 'ethical' one), or a bank account or insurance policy, or are members of organisations with funds invested in stock portfolios, even if we don't hold such portfolios in our own names. The people who run these corporations work for us; their job is to ensure that there will be money to pay our salaries, to maintain us when we retire, and for our dependents when we die, and also to give individual investors a good return, while simultaneously bringing in the money that will pay their own corporate salaries and ensure employment for thousands of others who work for the corporation. In order to do this they have to *follow* consumer demand – also to *anticipate* it – but if they offer something to consumers that consumers don't want, it won't sell, and the corporation will flounder. The art here consists in knowing who the trend-setters are, spotting what they are doing that is likely to catch on more widely, and getting in on it just before it does catch on. The result is that it looks to the public as though the corporations are telling them what they want – but in fact this has never worked, unless what the corporation is telling them they want *really is* what they want, or are likely to want once they know about it.

Consider the broccoli of the field. This is a vegetable with a flavour that most children don't like and even many adults find mildly or wholly repellent, but once the taste for it is acquired, is enjoyable to eat as well as being decorative and healthy. If 'the market' really works the way people like Day suggest it does, why aren't Saturday morning children's television programmes saturated with commercials for broccoli? Both the Broccoli Growers' Association and the government have an interest in increasing its consumption, given its health value. Surely being barraged with commercials proclaiming that Broccoli Is Tasty! Broccoli Is Cool! Broccoli Makes You More Attractive! would quintuple consumption of the vegetable. Children would be demanding that their parents buy it, and would complain if it weren't part of their daily school lunch. Actually, I do not believe that these would be the results of a broccoli advertising campaign – if it were, the campaign would already have happened long since. It hasn't happened because it is obvious that it wouldn't work – increases in broccoli sales would not in fact pay the cost of the advertising.

Advertising can have dramatic effects on the sales of products that children spontaneously want, like over-sugared cereals with toys inside, or grease-burgers with fries, fizzy drinks and more free toys. No corporation has created the desire for such food; they discovered the desire, and their advertisements give children and their parents a sort of license to fulfil the desire. Desire for a particular brand, a particular variant on an already desired product, can be created through marketing – a form of rhetoric – that appeals to the emotions as well as reason (see my remark on p. 111 about how Aristotle might have reacted to the sort of advertisement that aims to 'set a mood'). But people are more intelligent and resistant to propaganda than the critics of the market and marketing give them credit for.

Ditto for political propaganda. The British and American governments' continued insistence on the need for a war against terrorism has not resulted in a majority of the public being convinced of the argument in either country (it did initially in the USA, but by three years after the invasion of Iraq, support for the war had plummeted). This is actually the worst possible result, because the threat of global terrorism is undoubtedly real – and now the populace simply dismisses the government's warnings as attempts at self-justification, and refuses to support much of what needs to be done to forestall the worst. This is the fault of the governments, to be sure; but at the same time it demonstrates the robustness of the average citizen's scepticism of, and resistance to, propaganda. My whole life experience of being with other people during political broadcasts, whether in someone's home, or in a café or pub, in every country I've ever been to, is that they *talk back* to the broadcast. Sometimes it is with outright disdain and derision. Other times – when people are frightened of some looming crisis – they are more sober, but still incapable of suppressing a certain dubiety about what is being said, with some of them questioning whether there is really a crisis at all and others worried that the government isn't dealing with the crisis firmly enough.

Something else is true without exception in my experience: I have known hundreds of people who were absolutely convinced that media propaganda was controlling the minds of their fellow citizens, but I have yet to meet anyone who thinks that he himself or she herself is acting under the influence of such manipulation. Oneself is always resistant to the perceived propaganda, but no one else is, or anyway very few, apart from the invisible string-pullers who are behind it all and whose interests are being served. It is, in other words, a classic conspiracy theory. But more than that, it is a form of class superiority – a fear not just of what those on top are up to but of the inability of the masses to see through it. They are not as intelligent or perceptive as we are, 'we' being the happy critical few of the educated middle-class elite, plus those running the conspiracy.

The fear of the masses has quite a good pedigree, going back at least to 1895 and Gustave Le Bon's *Psychologie des foules* (Crowd psychology), itself a reaction to fear of the 'yellow peril' as well as of the growing communist movement. Again this was a fear that belonged to the middle classes, those who had something to lose if and when the crowd rose up. Le Bon explained how, in a crowd, people lose their individual identity and become of one shared crowd mentality, which an adept leader can manipulate. The crowd reverts to a primitive form of humanity with a tribal mind, and demands a chieftain to tell them what to think and do. Hitler is said to have read Le Bon like a textbook, after the Bolshevik Revolution of 1917 seemed to have proved Le Bon right. The allied notion that the lower classes have only a group identity, with personal identity belonging only to members of the middle and upper classes, would die hard, being expressed as late as 1964 by Basil Bernstein (1924–2000; see Bernstein 1964: 63; Joseph 2004a: 68–70).

Yet George Orwell saw things precisely the other way round. In *Nineteen Eighty-Four* it is only the Proles who have retained the ability to think for themselves, in large part because they have hung on to Oldspeak, ordinary English, despite the government's massive efforts to replace it with Newspeak and limit and control their thought just as, in Orwell's view, Standard English limits and controls the thinking of the middle classes. The real language of working people, directly connected as it is to real, palpable things – classic British empiricism, this – makes it possible for them to see through the lies the government is trying to put over on them, though the educated middle classes cannot (apart from Old Etonian Blair/Orwell himself, naturally). I think Orwell is closer to being right than anyone, even if his faith in the 'language of the soil' was Romanticised, and has in any case become less relevant as class differences in English have lessened (anyone who doubts this need only listen to the English of the three current generations of the royal family). Hence my 'Orwellian' critique of the linguistic imperialism thesis, with its hegemony model. It is true that English is today connected with economic advantage in much of the world; however this is true not only of English, but of other 'world' languages as well, and even of 'medium'-sized languages of regional importance, like Berber in North Africa; and the individuals I talk to in and from countries like China, Malaysia, Lebanon, Latvia, Sri Lanka, the Sudan and elsewhere who have chosen to learn English or have their children educated in it, or who have not so chosen, are without exception capable of articulating precisely why they have made their choice. The fact that they do not all make the same choice is significant, as is the fact that they have specific goals for their children – university education overseas, for instance – that English or French is a requirement for. These are not 'passive objects' at the mercy of a hegemonic global power or market. They are active agents who are *aware* of the market and seeking to better their and their offspring's position within it. To a Marxist, of course, any such desire to play an active part in the market is reprehensible, whether or not the Marxist will admit that the desire can be realised. But try telling that to ordinary people in China or Malaysia or any other country where the average income is a fraction of what it is in the West. Their reaction will be one of disbelief and ridicule of such nonsense. The market is us, and pity the poor middle-class intellectual who imagines it as some great hairy beast coming to suck away our identities and our souls.

7.3 CONCLUSIONS

The range of linguistic topics considered in this book can all be usefully thought of in the framework of 'invitations' that may be accepted or refused. That is how we normally think of the use of an informal pronoun between people who have previously used the deferential one, and in §4.6 I have shown how this model can be extended to how language change takes place within a speech community. The enforcement of language standards is precisely the refusal of the invitation to change that has been issued from somewhere within the speech community; recognition of World Englishes is the acceptance of such an invitation. Language rights are a matter of change of linguistic habits at the community level, as are injunctions against swearing and hate speech, and even propaganda can be understood as an invitation to conceive of things in a particular way, which people have a more robust capacity for refusing than they're often given credit for. All these acceptances and refusals have political implications, starting at the interpersonal level and extending up to the national one. And the model has its own political dimension, centred on the question of whether people really choose to invite, accept or refuse, or are compelled to do so.

It is a complex question. Being human means being able to make choices. Bringing our choices to fruition depends on other people, whether they are supportive or standing in our way. Our relationships with them are negotiated through language, sometimes explicitly, always implicitly, including through that very peculiar form of language known as money. Our *identities* too are not something essential and permanent that stands aloof from our relations with others; their existence is manifested in those relations, including in their linguistic dimensions. In some cases the range of choices available to us for managing interpersonal relations is encoded into the grammar itself, as with deferential pronouns or highly con-ventionalised registers. In English other means are required, though there does operate a system of registers less conventionalised than that of Javanese. The way we manage conversation has a lot to do with how our interpersonal relations go, hence with where we stand in the social order. So too with our use or non-use of non-standard forms of speech, taboo words and anything else that is not socially sanctioned.

At the same time, we are constantly interpreting what others are doing when *they* talk or write. Are they being friendly? Are they trying to position themselves above us in some way? Is this someone who can be an ally to me, or a lover, or who might stand in my way, or just someone with whom I can have an enjoyable conversation? Are they trying to *persuade* me of something – in which case my evaluative mechanism will switch into high gear, whether it is a politician seeking my vote or support for a policy, or a salesperson trying to convince me to buy, or my children arguing that they're due a rise in their allowance. I interpret what they say in light of the fact that I know they're trying to persuade me of something that's to their advantage. This doesn't mean that the politician *isn't* necessarily the best person for the job, the policy the best for the moment, the vacuum cleaner the best available for the price, or that my children oughtn't to get more spending money. But before choosing what to do I am going to perform the best mental cost–benefit analysis I can in the circumstance, and base my choice on the outcome. If one of the politician's henchmen is holding a gun to my head, or I know that members of my family may disappear if I oppose his policy, then, no, I am not making a real choice. Too many millions of people in recent times have had to live under regimes that allowed them no real choice, mostly under Marxist regimes though of course they were far from alone. It is mistaken to maintain that people in a free society are in the same way incapable of making real choices because hegemonic market forces are directing them. Such an accusation is dehumanising, and represents, as explained earlier, a form of class hatred.

A final question: what is 'power'? When I wrote *Eloquence and Power* in 1987 the answer seemed obvious: the power was the elite who had the clout to make *their* choices about what were good and bad forms of a particular language into language standards. At certain stages in the development of some cultures it may have been the case that such choices could be imposed arbitrarily. But examining known historical cases, and particularly looking at contemporary ones, such arbitrary imposition appears exceptional. As with all language change, a vague process of acceptance or rejection has been the norm. Always many more attempts at 'imposing' particular variants took place than the actual standards that were established. As to why the victorious variants 'won', we are immensely adept at constructing stories after the fact; but just why, at a given point, a given form strikes a critical mass of influential people as being 'right' remains mysterious. Sapir described languages as an 'art' (see above §6.2, p. 113), and in at least this sense he was right – the creation and maintenance of a standard language is an art, and the power to shape it belongs to whoever is most adept at the art of foreseeing which forms are going to meet with acceptance, plus the second art of getting that form accepted and propagated by the publishers or dictionary writers or clerics or clerks or academicians or grammar-check programmers or whoever has authority in the public mind at the time. But the first art remains essential, because those holding authority will demit office at some point, and there is no guarantee that the next generation won't set out to reform the standard language according to their own ideas – unless whoever initially created the forms was artist enough to anticipate what would be acceptable, not just for their own time, but for ages to come. All of which is to say that 'power' is a complex and diffuse thing, a term in fact that misleadingly conflates a number of inter-related but ultimately quite different considerations and processes. As a concept, in other words, power is too powerful, and needs to be broken down.

7.4 IMPLICATIONS AND APPLICATIONS

I conclude with a series of implications which I believe this study has for the understanding of language generally, and for the practice of applied linguistics in particular.

1. Languages – not just standard languages – are historical constructs, with a political process at their centre. Since the 1960s a misunderstanding of Chomsky has led many linguists to treat languages as if they were natural objects, the details of whose form proceeds directly from the architecture of the human mind (something Chomsky has only claimed for 'Universal Grammar', the set of innate principles and parameters that underlie all languages, and for the linguistic knowledge of an individual, but has explicitly denied is true for languages). Where the teaching of language is concerned, this realisation frees us from the need to imagine that we are somehow bound to apply a native speaker model inflexibly. It gives us a principled basis for attending to the international cultural politics behind linguistic resistance and creating space for such resistance to flourish.

2. The opposing view – that the standard language is not a political product and that resistance to it, along with the new forms of the language which resistance engenders, are unacceptable – is likewise understandable in historical terms, and needs to be taken seriously. The histories of (standard) languages are closely bound up with forces of the greatest importance: nationalism, of course, but also religion and, as I've argued in Chapter 2, knowledge itself, with all the religious and social–hierarchical implications that knowledge has traditionally entailed. It would be naïve to promote an agenda based on (1) without anticipating a widespread negative reaction based on (2), and preparing arguments to counter such reaction.

3. 'World English(es)', those products of nationalism and resistance, can be conceived of as systems, just as any language or dialect can, but in the relatively early stages of their emergence it is more useful to think of them as an *attitude*, a willingness to accept variation in the 'Centre' norm. The linguist who rushes in to systematise a New English prematurely runs a serious risk of misrepresenting as fixed what is actually still quite fluid. If the speakers are in resistance mode, the key identity feature of their innovative linguistic forms is [– Centre], and a number of variants will fill the bill; but the linguist in search of a system always needs *one* form that is [+ Periphery]. This can take a long time to settle, and it is for the speakers of the New English to settle, as a community.

4. The fundamental fallacies underlying Phillipson's critique of 'linguistic imperialism' are by now well-known. Nevertheless, the critique strikes a nerve

because many people, particularly of the middle class, and more likely to be from a wealthy country than a poor one, perceive the spread of English language and American culture as a danger to their own language and culture. They generally underestimate the robustness of their own language and culture – it is worth remembering that for over 130 years now people have been predicting that the day when the whole world would speak English exclusively was just around the corner (see Joseph 2004c), and the ubiquitous statements about languages becoming extinct faster than ever before in human history are mere hype about something that cannot possibly be known. Yet the fact remains (and justifies these statements in the minds of those who make them) that too many 'small' languages are not being passed on to younger generations, which represents a great cultural loss. The fact also remains that this is not happening through force. Speakers of 'small' languages are choosing to learn 'big' languages and to have their children educated in them, because they perceive – quite rightly, in economic terms – that this is the route to a better life for them. I may not think that money matters more than cultural tradition, but then I have the luxury to think that way, and it would be callous, even brutal of me to pass judgement on someone who doesn't have the luxury I have, and desires it for themselves and their children. Phillipson & Co. argue that the fact that English is the ticket to a better life imposes a hegemonic situation in which free choices cannot in fact be made – but I have tried to show in this chapter that such an argument is invalid both logically and empirically. It dehumanises the very people it purports to help; it would remove choice for the people it purports to free from an imperialist yoke, and it plays only to an audience of those who already possess the advantages that English and other big languages confer, while incurring ridicule and resentment from those who do not.

5. 'Language rights' are actually claims for rights, claims which may or may not get established in law and then may or may not be retained over time (so the claiming must continue even after their legal enshrinement). They raise a number of difficult issues, especially where education is concerned. Minority language communities rarely if ever agree among themselves as to what the policy should be concerning teaching in their traditional language and in the national language of the place they inhabit, at the various levels of the education system. Governments must balance their responsibility towards such communities with their responsibility to individuals. 'Heritage' languages, those whose history in the country goes back farther than the national language, tend strongly to be privileged over immigrant languages when it comes to providing for language rights, but the moral basis for this is shaky at best (as is the pragmatic one). Philosophical models of language rights have helped bring the problem to wider and more serious attention, but only go so far in helping to set down basic principles, since the facts on the ground vary greatly from place to place, and it is those facts – what people actually want – that must feed 'bottom-up' into language legislation if it is to be successful (see further Stroud 2001). Moreover, the feelings of the linguistic *majority* must not be ignored, at the risk of creating a counter-reaction that ends up setting the rights of minority communities back rather than advancing them.

6. Regarding claims and performances, we need to work towards making distinctions between the full, original sense of wilful claims and intentional performances, and the extended, partly metaphorical sense which these terms normally have in the contemporary discourse of identity. Billig's insight about 'banal nationalism' has been so powerful because, in the past, we paid attention to deliberate claims exclusively, and ignored the forms of identity that involve most of the people most of the time. To remedy this it has been useful to fold the two types together, but ultimately we shall have to tease apart the differences.

7. Given the potent force of language in the creation of a unified national identity, it is not obvious how to perform a minority identity without having the majority interpret it as a threat to national unity. It is an empirical question, and the answer will come from studying cases of linguistic minorities who have achieved this successfully and those that have not, and determining what made the difference. Similarly, how the minority community negotiates its linguistic independence from its own motherland, if there is one, is an empirical question. The concept of 'third space', associated with cultural theorists like Bhabha (1994) and Hall (1995), has offered a conceptual way forward. But translating this into linguistic reality is a tricky business.

8. The process of 'legitimation' (to borrow Bourdieu's term) of a minority linguistic identity can create fragmentation and oppression within the minority community, as one particular form of the minority language is elevated to 'standard' status, eventually becoming identified as the language proper. By what path a language policy can avoid, or at least minimise, such an outcome, is a venerable problem, forming part of the history of every standard language. Probably there is no ultimate solution, and it would be utopian to hope for one. But we can look empirically for strategies that maximise a sense of 'ownership' of a standard dialect across a population, without imposing it doctrinally or through propaganda.

9. What is the most effective role of government policy in promoting the legitimation, retention and spread of minority languages? In every case I have examined or read about, government policy has worked best when it aligned with what the people on the ground already believed and felt. The 'top-down' approach, where authorities dictate and enforce what is right against the will of the population, can work only in an authoritarian state of the sort one does not find within the European Union, the Americas or Oceania. Policy needs to be formed in extensive consultation with representatives of both minority and majority groups, and they need to be given ownership of its ongoing enforcement as well.

10. Minority language identities thrive when they are repressed, and recede when they are tolerated. How to reconcile this fact with the claim/performance model? How to overcome the impasse which this fact suggests? The phenomenon in question has been described in §2.7 above, with particular regard to Catalan. It does not so much challenge the claim/performance model as underscore the importance of the *reception* of claims explicitly or implicitly made. If the out-group is rejecting the in-group's identity claims, potential members of the in-group who have not heretofore recognised themselves as such are all the more likely to accept the claims for their countrymen and for themselves. But on the political front, this really does make for a paradox. Catalan nationalists look back nostalgically to the era of repression under Franco, much as Scottish nationalists do to the Thatcher years, when the government in London poured scorn on any proposal to give power and responsibility back to Britain's historic nations and regions. The devolution of power to the Scottish Parliament and Welsh Assembly in 1999 has dealt a harsh blow to nationalists, whose arguments based on oppression from Westminster no longer get the public reception they formerly did. The answer to this paradox lies, in my view, in the need to disentangle linguistic identity from political aspirations. The two issues became inseparably bound up with one another in early nineteenth century Romantic thought, then were partially disentangled from 1880 onward (see Joseph 2006), but it is still all too easy to construct an argument for political separatism on the basis of linguistic difference – when in fact, as the case of the Valencians shows, one group's linguistic identity aspirations may be oppressing another's, and it cannot ultimately be in any people's interest to live in an oppressive regime, however fertile the ground there may be for linguistic identity.

11. How can education make space for the positive sort of 'resistance' in the teaching of the national language as L2 that will help minority communities to feel that the language belongs to them, and they to the nation, without at the same time threatening the minority languages and identities? Here the key lies in the attitudes of those of us who enforce the norms of the standard language. We create or refuse to create the space for 'world Englishes' or 'new French' or forms of German that mark immigrant origins. Refusing to create such space is the default setting, because the whole of our educational system and the career structures that fall out from it are set up on the basis of a uniform standard language, which we use as a substantial part of our measuring of people's scholastic ability. We have to shift from seeing any deviance, especially in written language, as a failure to measure up to standards, and instead to recognise certain deviations – not all – as positive performances of minority identity. Such shifts have happened over and over through history – we would not have distinct American and British English norms otherwise, nor would we have the modern European languages if a series of very large shifts of this nature had not changed the view that only Latin could serve as the norm. These are not shifts that happen overnight. But each of us, every time we mark papers by students writing our language as their second language, make choices that count toward determining just how fast or slow the change will be. The more accepting we are of deviations that appear to us to mark a minority identity, the more encouraging we are of their performance.

12. The nature of language and its role in human interactions is not something eternal and transcendent. It evolves as societies evolve. Key examples studied in this book include deferential address, gendered language, swearing and other forms of politically sensitive language. Recent efforts to control hate speech, to eliminate objectionable language from school textbooks, and to protect personal data, suggest that a new linguistic ethics is in the process of emerging. Under it, every individual has an implicit right of protection from verbal hurt, and the state is obliged to

prevent exposure to language that expresses any inherent difference among people, or connects to anything that a social-political consensus deems harmful. The study of earlier cases suggests that the policies currently being developed may not achieve their aims, and indeed that the aims themselves, although not misguided, are in an inherent tension with the right to free speech, and that the balance of rights will require an adjustment in due course.

13. Concern that political propaganda amounts to thought control by the government has been an enduring theme across the last ninety years. Since the 1960s it has enjoyed strong support from Chomsky, whose influential view of language and interpretation provides the theoretical model for such thought control, and whose political writings assert the existence of a governmental–corporate conspiracy to manufacture consent. More recently, Critical Discourse Analysis has pursued the agenda of uncovering propagandistic language in centre–right political discourse, including that of the Labour government in the UK. It is of course true that governmental agencies engage in 'spin' and in other discursive activities aimed at influencing the populace to accept the government's position on key issues. However, the populace's capacity for resisting such influence is much more robust than either Chomsky or CDA gives it credit for. Moreover, in a democratic society, the government has the responsibility to explain and justify its policies and actions, and it must use the media to do so. When does this amount to propaganda? Helping to elucidate the boundary is a signal service that applied linguistics can offer to society; but simply maintaining that *all* mainstream political discourse amounts to propaganda does not shed light where it is needed most.

14. Finally, linking most of the points made above is the fact that linguistics, theoretical as well as applied, has spent its recent history under the thrall of various views and models asserted by people who may have seen themselves as standing in direct opposition to one another, but who shared a belief that the mass of humanity do not actually make free choices on most of the occasions when they perceive that they are doing so. Rather, their perceptions, like their pseudo-choices, are held to be directed by language itself, or by the structure of the mind, or society, or the class struggle, or propaganda, or the genetic code – the list goes on. But strong assertions of real agency are now being made in many quarters and from many directions. If they are right, or at least come to define the mainstream of thought, there will be many blanks left to be filled in and new questions to be raised for our understanding of language generally and its political dimension in particular, as the questions focused on in the last century recede into the background.

References

Ager, Dennis E. (2001), *Motivation in Language Planning and Policy*, Clevedon: Multilingual Matters.

Alter, Stephen G. (2005), *William Dwight Whitney and the Science of Language*, Baltimore and London: Johns Hopkins University Press.

Ammon, Ulrich (1997), 'Language-spread policy', *Language Problems and Language Planning*, 21(1): 51–7.

Ammon, Ulrich, Klaus J. Mattheier and Peter H. Nelde (eds) (2002), *Sprachpolitik und kleine Sprachen/Language Policy and Small Languages/L'Aménagement linguistique et les langues modiques*, Tübingen: Niemeyer.

Ammon, Ulrich, Klaus J. Mattheier and Peter H. Nelde (eds) (2003), *Sprachstandards/ Language Standards/Standards linguistiques*, Tübingen: Niemeyer.

Anderson, Benedict (1991), *Imagined Communities: Reflections on the Origin and Spread of Nationalism*, 2nd edn, London and New York: Verso. (1st edn 1983.)

Andersson, Lars-Gunnar with Peter Trudgill (1990), *Bad Language*, Oxford: Blackwell, by arrangement with Penguin.

Androutsopoulos, Jannis K. and Evelyn Ziegler (eds) (2003), *'Standardfragen': Sozio-linguistische Perspektiven auf Sprachgeschichte, Sprachkontakt und Sprachvariation*, Frankfurt: Peter Lang.

Annamalai, E. (2003), 'Reflections on a language policy for multilingualism', *Language Policy*, 2(2): 113–32.

Anon. (1752), *A Discourse by a Soldier against Prophane Swearing, Blasphemy and Perjury* [s.l.: s.n.].

Archer, Margaret S. (2001), *Being Human: The Problem of Agency*, Cambridge: Cambridge University Press.

Aristotle (1885), *The Politics of Aristotle*, transl. by Benjamin Jowett, Oxford: Clarendon Press.

Aristotle (1924), *Rhetoric*, transl. by W. Rhys Roberts, in W. D. Ross (ed.), *The Works of Aristotle*, vol. 11, London: Oxford University Press.

Armour, William S. (2001), '"This guy is Japanese stuck in a white man's body": a discussion of meaning making, identity slippage, and cross-cultural adaptation', *Journal of Multilingual and Multicultural Development*, 22 (1): 1–18.

Augustine, St (1863), 'Sermo CCLXXXVIII (alias 23 inter Sirmondianos) in natali Joannis Baptistae', in *Sancti Aurelii Augustini, Hipponensis Episcopi, Opera omnia*, vol. 5, Paris: J.-P. Migne, pp. 1302–08. (*Patrologiae cursus completus, Series latina* , ed. by J.-P. Migne, vol. 38.)

Austin, J. L. (1960), *How to Do Things with Words*, Oxford: Oxford University Press.

Bakhtin, Mikhail (1981), *The Dialogic Imagination: Four Essays*, ed. by Michael Holquist, transl. by Caryl Emerson and Michael Holquist, Austin, TX: University of Texas Press.

Barclay, James, David H. Knox and George B. Ballantyne (1938), *A Study of Standard English*, Glasgow: Robert Gibson and Sons.
Bargiela-Chiappini, Francesca (2003), 'Face and politeness: new (insights) for old (concepts)', *Journal of Pragmatics*, 35 (10–11): 1453–69.
Barsky, Robert (1998), *Noam Chomsky: A Life of Dissent*, Cambridge, MA: MIT Press.
Bechhofer, Frank, David McCrone, Richard Kiely and Robert Stewart (1999), 'Constructing national identity: arts and landed elites in Scotland', *Sociology*, 22: 515–34.
Beeching, Kate (2002), *Gender, Politeness and Pragmatic Particles in French*, Amsterdam and Philadelphia: John Benjamins.
Bell, Allan (1984), 'Language style as audience design', *Language in Society*, 13: 145–204.
Bernstein, Basil (1964), 'Social class, speech systems and psycho-therapy', *British Journal of Sociology*, 15: 54–64.
Bhabha, Homi K. (1994), *The Location of Culture*, London and New York: Routledge.
Billig, Michael (1995), *Banal Nationalism*, London: Sage.
Bisong, Joseph (1995), 'Language choice and cultural imperialism: a Nigerian perspective', *ELT Journal*, 49: 122–32.
Blank, Paula (1996), *Broken English: Dialects and the Politics of Language in Renaissance Writings*, London and New York: Routledge.
Blommaert, Jan (1996), 'Language planning as a discourse on language and society: the linguistic ideology of a scholarly tradition', *Language Problems and Language Planning*, 20 (3): 199–222.
Blommaert, Jan (ed.) (1999), *Language Ideological Debates*, Berlin: Mouton de Gruyter.
Bolton, Kingsley (2003), *Chinese Englishes: A Sociolinguistic History*, Cambridge: Cambridge University Press.
Bolton, Kingsley (ed.) (2002), *Hong Kong English: Autonomy and Creativity*, Hong Kong: Hong Kong University Press.
Bonfiglio, Thomas Paul (2002), *Race and the Rise of Standard American*, Berlin: Mouton de Gruyter.
Bourdieu, Pierre (1986), 'The forms of capital', in John Richardson (ed.), *Handbook of Theory and Research for the Sociology of Education*, New York: Greenwood Press, pp. 241–58.
Bourdieu, Pierre (1991), *Language and Symbolic Power: The Economy of Linguistic Exchanges*, ed. by John B. Thompson, transl. by Gino Raymond and Matthew Adamson, Cambridge: Polity, in association with Basil Blackwell.
Bourdieu, Pierre and Jean-Claude Passeron (1977), *Reproduction in Education, Society and Culture*, transl. by Richard Nice, London and Beverly Hills: Sage.
Braun, Friederike (1988), *Terms of Address: Problems of Patterns and Usage in Various Languages and Cultures*, Berlin and New York: Mouton de Gruyter.
Breitborde, Lawrence B. (1998), *Speaking and Social Identity: English in the Lives of Urban Africans*, Berlin and New York: Mouton de Gruyter.
Brown, Adam (1999), *Singapore English in a Nutshell: An Alphabetic Description of its Features*, Singapore: Federal Publications.
Brown, Penelope and Stephen C. Levinson (1978), 'Universals in language use: politeness phenomena', in Esther N. Goody (ed.), *Questions and Politeness: Strategies in Social Interaction*, Cambridge: Cambridge University Press, pp. 56–311.
Brown, Penelope and Stephen C. Levinson (1987), *Politeness: Some Universals in Language Usage*, Cambridge: Cambridge University Press.
Brown, Roger and Albert C. Gilman (1960), 'The pronouns of power and solidarity', in Thomas A. Sebeok (ed.), *Style in Language*, Cambridge, MA: MIT Press, pp. 253–76. (Repr. in Giglioli [ed.] 1972: 252–82.)
Bruthiaux, Paul (2000), 'Supping with the dismal scientists: practical interdisciplinarity in language education and development economics', *Journal of Multilingual and Multicultural Development*, 21 (4): 269–91.

Brutt-Griffler, Janina (2002), *World English: A Study of its Development*, Clevedon: Multilingual Matters.

Burke, Peter (1993), *The Art of Conversation*, Cambridge: Polity.

Butler, Judith (1997), *Excitable Speech*, London and New York: Routledge.

Byram, Michael and Karen Risager (1999), *Language Teachers, Politics and Cultures*, Clevedon: Multilingual Matters.

Cameron, Deborah (1992), *Feminism and Linguistic Theory*, 2nd edn, Basingstoke: Macmillan.

Cameron, Deborah (1995), *Verbal Hygiene*, London and New York: Routledge.

Cameron, Deborah and Don Kulick (2003), *Language and Sexuality*, Cambridge: Cambridge University Press.

Canagarajah, A. Suresh (1999a), *Resisting Linguistic Imperialism in English Teaching*, Oxford: Oxford University Press.

Canagarajah, A. Suresh (1999b), 'On EFL teachers, awareness, and agency', *ELT Journal*, 53 (3): 207–14.

Carter, Ronald (1999), 'Common language: corpus, creativity and cognition', *Language and Literature*, 8: 195–216.

Chan, Elaine (2002), 'Beyond pedagogy: language and identity in post-colonial Hong Kong', *British Journal of Sociology of Education*, 23 (2): 271–85.

Chase, Stuart (1938), *The Tyranny of Words*, New York: Harcourt, Brace and Co.; London: Methuen.

Cheshire, Jenny and Dieter Stein (eds) (1997), *Taming the Vernacular: From Dialect to Written Standard Language*, London: Longman.

Chilton, Paul (2004), *Analysing Political Discourse: Theory and Practice*, London and New York: Routledge.

Chilton, Paul and Christina Schäffner (eds) (2002), *Politics as Text and Talk: Analytic Approaches to Political Discourse*, Amsterdam and Philadelphia: John Benjamins.

Chomsky, Noam (1962), 'The logical basis of linguistic theory', in H. Lunt (ed.), *Preprints of Papers from the 9th International Congress of Linguists, 27–31 August 1962, Cambridge, Mass.*, pp. 509–74. (Revised versions in H. Lunt (ed.), *Proceedings of the 9th International Congress of Linguists*, The Hague: Mouton, 1964[a], pp. 914–78; and in J. A. Fodor and J. J. Katz (eds), *The Structure of Language: Readings in the Philosophy of Language*, Englewood Cliffs, NJ: Prentice-Hall, 1964[b], pp. 211–45. Final revision: Chomsky 1964c.)

Chomsky, Noam (1964c), *Current Issues in Linguistic Theory*, The Hague: Mouton.

Chomsky, Noam (1986), *Knowledge of Language: Its Nature, Origin, and Use*, New York: Praeger.

Chomsky, Noam (1992), 'Language in the service of propaganda', in *Chronicles of Dissent*, Stirling, Scotland: AK Press, pp. 1–22.

Chomsky, Noam (2000), *Propaganda and Control of the Public Mind*, 2 CDs (recorded at Harvard Trade Union Program, Cambridge, MA, 7 Feb. 1997), Stirling, Scotland: AK Press.

Christie, Chris (ed.) (2004), *Tensions in Current Politeness Research*, special issue of *Multilingua*, 23 (1–2): 1–190.

Constable, John (ed.) (1990), *Selected Letters of I. A. Richards, CH*, Oxford: Clarendon Press.

Cooke, Michael (1995), 'Understood by all concerned? Anglo/Aboriginal legal translation', in Marshall Morris (ed.), *Translation and the Law*, Amsterdam and Philadelphia: John Benjamins, pp. 37–63.

Cooper, Robert L. (1989), *Language Planning and Social Change*, Cambridge: Cambridge University Press.

Coulmas, Florian (ed.) (1988), *With Forked Tongues: What are National Languages Good For?* Ann Arbor, MI: Karoma.

Courtine, Jean-Jacques (2004), 'La prohibition des mots: L'écriture des manuels scolaires en Amérique du Nord', in Patrick Sériot and Andrée Tabouret-Keller (eds), *Le discours sur la langue sous les régimes autoritaires*, Lausanne: Cahiers de l'Institut de linguistique et des sciences du langage de l'Université de Lausanne, no. 17, pp. 19–32.

Crawford, James (ed.) (1992), *Language Loyalties: A Source Book on the Official English Controversy*, Chicago: University of Chicago Press.

Crowley, Tony (1996), *Language in History: Theories and Texts*, London and New York: Routledge.

Crowley, Tony (2001), 'Bahktin and the history of the language', in Ken Hirschkop and David Shepherd (eds), *Bakhtin and Cultural Theory*, 2nd edn, Manchester and New York: Manchester University Press, pp. 177–200.

Crowley, Tony (2003), *Standard English and the Politics of Language*, 2nd edn, Houndsworth, Basingstoke and New York: Palgrave Macmillan.

Cummins, Jim (2000), *Language, Power and Pedagogy: Bilingual Children in the Crossfire*, Clevedon: Multilingual Matters.

Daftary, Farimah and François Grin (eds) (2003), *Nation-Building, Ethnicity and Language Politics in Transition Countries*, Budapest: Open Society Institute.

Dante Alighieri (1996), *De vulgari eloquentia*, ed. and transl. by Steven Botterill, Cambridge: Cambridge University Press.

Davies, Alan (1996), 'Ironising the myth of linguicism', *Journal of Multilingual and Multi-cultural Development*, 17 (6): 485–96.

Day, Gary (2005), 'Life's labour's cost', *Times Literary Supplement*, no. 5347, 25 Sept., p. 27.

Defoe, Daniel (1697), *An Essay upon Projects*, London: Printed by R[obert] R[oberts] for Tho. Cockerill, at the Three Legs in the Poultrey.

DeFrancis, John (1984), *The Chinese Language: Fact and Fantasy*, Honolulu, HI: University of Hawaii Press.

Dessalles, Jean-Louis (2000), *Aux origines du langage: Une histoire naturelle de la parole*, Paris: Hermès.

Deumert, Ana and Wim Vandenbussche (eds.) (2003), *Germanic Standardizations: Past to Present*, Amsterdam and Philadelphia: John Benjamins.

Disney, John (1729), *A View of Ancient Laws, against Immorality and Profaneness: under the following Heads; Lewdness; profane Swearing; Cursing and Blasphemy; Perjury; Profanation of Days devoted to Religion; Contempt or Neglect of divine Service; Drunkenness; Gaming; Idleness, Vagrancy, and Begging; Stage-Plays and Players; and Duelling; Collected from the Jewish, Roman, Greek, Gothic, Lombard, and other Laws, down to the Middle of the Eleventh Century*, Cambridge: Printed for Corn. Crownfield; and John Crownfield, at the Rising-Sun, in St. Pauls Church-Yard; and are also sold by J. and J. Knapton.

Dua, Hans R. (ed.) (1996), *Language Planning and Political Theory*, special issue of *International Journal of the Sociology of Language*, no. 118, Berlin: Mouton de Gruyter.

Dunbar, Robin (1996), *Grooming. Gossip and the Evolution of Language*, London and Boston, MA: Faber and Faber.

Edgley, Alison (2000), *The Social and Political Thought of Noam Chomsky*, London and New York: Routledge.

Eelen, Gino (2001), *A Critique of Politeness Theories*, Manchester: St Jerome Press.

Eggington, William, and Helen Wren (eds) (1997), *Language Policy: Dominant English, Pluralist Challenges*, Amsterdam and Philadelphia: John Benjamins; Canberra: Language Australia.

Eisenstein, Elizabeth L. (1993), *The Printing Revolution in Early Modern Europe*, 2nd edn, Cambridge: Cambridge University Press.

Erling, Elizabeth J. (2005), 'The many names of English', *English Today*, 21 (1): 40–4.

Evans, Stephen John (2003), *The Introduction and Spread of English-Language Education in Hong Kong (1842–1913): A Study of Language Policies and Practices in British Colonial*

Education. PhD thesis, University of Edinburgh.

Fairclough, Norman (1989), *Language and Power*, London: Longman.

Fairclough, Norman (1992), *Discourse and Social Change*, London: Polity.

Fairclough, Norman (1995), *Critical Discourse Analysis: The Critical Study of Language*, London: Longman.

Fairclough, Norman (2000), *New Labour, New Language*, London and New York: Routledge.

Ferguson, Charles A. (1959), 'Diglossia'. *Word*, 15: 325–40. (Repr. in Giglioli [ed.] 1972: 232–51).

Fisher, John H. (1996), *The Emergence of Standard English*, Lexington, KY: University Press of Kentucky.

Fishman, Joshua A. (1967), 'Bilingualism with and without diglossia; diglossia with and without bilingualism', *Journal of Social Issues*, 32: 29–38.

Fishman, Joshua A. (ed.) (1999), *Handbook of Language and Ethnic Identity*, Oxford: Oxford University Press.

Fishman, Joshua A. (ed.) (2001), *Can Threatened Languages Be Saved? Reversing Language Shift, Revisited: A 21st Century Perspective*, Clevedon: Multilingual Matters.

Foucault, Michel (1977), *Discipline and Punish: The Birth of the Prison*, transl. by Alan Sheridan, Harmondsworth: Penguin.

Foucault, Michel (1980), *Power/Knowledge: Selected Interviews and Other Writings, 1972–1977*, ed. and transl. by Colin Gordon, Brighton: Harvester; New York: Pantheon.

Fowler, Edward (1692), *A Vindication of an Undertaking of Certain Gentlemen: in order to the Suppressing of Debauchery and Profaneness*, London [s.n.].

Fowler, Roger (1987), 'Notes on critical linguistics', in Ross Steele and Terry Threadgold (eds), *Language Topics: Essays in Honour of Michael Halliday*, vol. 2, Amsterdam and Philadelphia: John Benjamins.

Fowler, Roger, Robert Hodge, Gunther Kress and Tony Trew (1979), *Language and Control*, London: Routledge and Kegan Paul.

Freire, Paolo (1970), *Pedagogy of the Oppressed*, transl. by Myra Bergman Ramos, Harmondsworth: Penguin; New York: Herder and Herder.

Galtung, Johan (1979), 'A structural theory of imperialism', in George Modelski (ed.), *Transnational Corporations and World Order: Readings in International Political Economy*, San Francisco: W. H. Freeman and Co., pp. 155–71.

Gardt, Andreas (ed.) (2000), *Nation und Sprache: Die Diskussion ihres Verhältnisses in Geschichte und Gegenwart*, Berlin: Walter de Gruyter.

Geertz, Hildred (1968), 'Latah in Java: a theoretical paradox', *Indonesia*, 5: 93–104.

Gelber, Katharine (2002), *Speaking Back: The Free Speech versus Hate Speech Debate*, Amsterdam and Philadelphia: John Benjamins.

Gibson, Edmund, The Right Rev., Lord Bishop of London (1760), *Admonition against Profane and Common Swearing: in a Letter from a Minister to his Parishoners; to be put privately into the Hands of Persons who are addicted to Swearing*, 20th edn, London: printed by E. Owen in Warwick-Lane, and sold by W. Johnston in Ludgate-Street.

Giglioli, Pier Paolo, ed. (1972), *Language and Social Context*, Harmondsworth: Penguin.

Gillies, William (ed.) (1989), *Gaelic and Scotland*, Edinburgh: Edinburgh University Press.

Goffman, Erving (1955), 'On face-work: an analysis of ritual elements in social interaction', *Psychiatry*, 18 (3): 213–31. (Repr. in Goffman [1972], pp. 5–45.)

Goffman, Erving (1972), *Interaction Ritual: Essays on Face-to-Face Behaviour*, Harmondsworth: Penguin.

Gorham, Maurice (1952), *Broadcasting and Television since 1900*, London: Dakers.

Grant, Sir Francis, Lord Cullen [attrib. to] (1700), *Discourse, concerning the Execution of the Laws, made against Prophaneness, &c: which contains some Account of the Reasons and Tendency of these Laws … and the spiritual and temporal Happiness, that will ensue on setting about it, without further Delay in the same*, Edinburgh: printed by George Mosman.

Graves, Robert (1927), *Lars Porsena, or The Future of Swearing and Improper Language*, London: Kegan Paul, Trench, Trubner and Co.; New York: E. P. Dutton.

Gray, Douglas (1983), 'Captain Cook and the English vocabulary', in E. G. Stanley and Douglas Gray (eds), *Five Hundred Years of Words and Sounds: A Festschrift for Eric Dobson*, Cambridge: Brewer, pp. 49–62.

Grillo, Ralph D. (1989), *Dominant Languages: Language and Hierarchy in Britain and France*, Cambridge: Cambridge University Press.

Grob, Lindsey M., Renee A. Meyers and Renee Schuh (1997), 'Powerful/powerless language use in group interactions: sex differences or similarities?', *Communication Quarterly*, 45 (3): 282–303.

Habermas, Jürgen (1984), *The Theory of Communicative Action, Vol. 1: Reason and the Rationalization of Society*, London: Heinemann.

Habermas, Jürgen (1999), *On the Pragmatics of Communication*, ed. by Maeve Cooke, Cambridge: Polity.

Hall, Stuart (1995), 'New cultures for old', in Doreen Massey and Pat Jess (eds), *A Place in the World? Places, Cultures, and Globalization*, Oxford and New York: Oxford University Press, pp. 175–213.

Halliday, M. A. K. (1978), *Language as Social Semiotic: The Social Interpretation of Language and Meaning*, London: Edward Arnold.

Harris, Sandra (1997), 'Strategic discourse: power, cooperation and conflict', in Marc Maufort and Jean-Pierre van Noppen (eds), *Voices of Power: Co-Operation and Conflict in English Language and Literatures*, Liège, Belgium: L3-Liège Language and Literature, for Belgian Association of Anglists in Higher Education, pp. 57–73.

Harris, Sandra (2001), 'Being politically impolite: extending politeness theory to adversarial political discourse', *Discourse and Society*, 12 (4): 451–72.

Hayakawa, S. I. (1941), *Language in Action*, New York: Harcourt, Brace. (Later edns entitled *Language in Thought and Action*.)

Head, Brian F. (1978) 'Respect degrees in pronominal reference', in Joseph H. Greenberg (ed.), *Universals of Human Language*, vol. 3: *Word Structure*, Stanford, CA: Stanford University Press, pp. 151–211.

Herman, Edward S. and Noam Chomsky (1988), *Manufacturing Consent: The Political Economy of the Mass Media*, New York: Pantheon.

Hickey, Leo and Miranda Stewart (eds) (2005), *Politeness in Europe*, Clevedon: Multilingual Matters.

Hill, Archibald A. (ed.) (1962), *Third Texas Conference on Problems of Linguistic Analysis in English, May 9–12, 1958*, Austin, TX: University of Texas.

Hiraga, Masako (1991), 'Metaphors Japanese women live by', *Working Papers on Language, Gender and Sexism*, 1 (1): 38–57.

Hobsbawm, E. J. (1990), *Nations and Nationalism since 1780: Programmes, Myth, Reality*, Cambridge: Cambridge University Press.

Hogan-Brun, Gabrielle (2005), 'The Baltic republics and language ideological debates surrounding European Union accession', *Journal of Multilingual and Multicultural Development*, 26 (5): 367–77.

Holborow, Marnie (1999), *The Politics of English: A Marxist View of Language*, London, Thousand Oaks, CA and New Delhi: Sage.

Holmes, Janet (2001), *An Introduction to Sociolinguistics*, 2nd edn, Harlow, London and New York: Longman.

Holmes, Janet and Miriam Meyerhoff (eds) (2003), *The Handbook of Language and Gender*, Malden, MA and Oxford: Blackwell.

Honey, John (1997), *Language Is Power: The Story of Standard English*, London: Faber and Faber.

Hughes, Geoffrey (1991), *Swearing: A Social History of Foul Language, Oaths and Profanity in*

English, Oxford: Blackwell.

Hutton, Christopher M. (1999), *Linguistics and the Third Reich: Mother-Tongue Fascism, Race and the Science of Language*, London and New York: Routledge.

Jakobson, Roman (1959), 'On linguistic aspects of translation', in Reuben A. Brower (ed.), *On Translation* , Cambridge, MA: Harvard University Press, pp. 232–9.

Järve, Priit (2003), 'Language battles in the Baltic states: 1989 to 2002', in Daftary and Grin (eds), pp. 75–105.

Jarvis, Simon (1999), 'The Frankfurt School and critical theory: introduction', in Simon Glendinning (ed.), *Edinburgh Encyclopedia of Continental Philosophy*, Edinburgh: Edinburgh University Press, pp. 429–37.

Jespersen, Otto (1922), *Language: Its Nature, Development and Origin*, London: George Allen and Unwin; New York, Henry Holt.

Joseph, John E. (1987a), *Eloquence and Power: The Rise of Language Standards and Standard Languages*, London: Pinter; New York: Blackwell.

Joseph, John E. (1987b), 'Subject relevance and deferential address in the Indo-European languages', *Lingua*, 73: 259–77.

Joseph, John E. (1999), review of *Chomsky no Brasil/Chomsky in Brazil (Revista de Documentação de Estudos em Lingüística Teórica e Aplicada* 13, no. especial, 1997), *Historiographia Linguistica*, 26: 421–8.

Joseph, John E. (2000a), *Limiting the Arbitrary: Linguistic Naturalism and its Opposites in Plato's* Cratylus *and Modern Theories of Language*, Amsterdam and Philadelphia: John Benjamins.

Joseph, John E. (2000b), 'Language as fiction: writing the text of linguistic identity in Scotland', in Heinz Antor and Klaus Stierstorfer (eds), *English Literatures in International Contexts*, Heidelberg: C. Winter, pp. 77–84.

Joseph, John E. (2000c), 'Language and "psychological race": Léopold de Saussure on French in Indochina', *Language and Communication*, 20 (1): 29–53.

Joseph, John E. (2000d), 'Changing English, linguistic identity and ELT', *PASAA: A Journal of Language Teaching and Learning in Thailand*, 30: 30–8.

Joseph, John E. (2001), 'The exportation of structuralist ideas from linguistics to other fields: an overview', in Sylvain Auroux, E. F. K. Koerner, Hans-Josef Niederehe and Kees Versteegh (eds), *History of the Language Sciences: An International Handbook on the Evolution of the Study of Language from the Beginnings to the Present*, vol. 2, Berlin and New York: Walter de Gruyter, pp. 1880–1908.

Joseph, John E. (2002), *From Whitney to Chomsky: Essays in the History of American Linguistics*, Amsterdam and Philadelphia: John Benjamins.

Joseph, John E. (2004a), *Language and Identity: National, Ethnic, Religious*, Houndmills, Basingstoke and New York: Palgrave Macmillan.

Joseph, John E. (2004b), 'The linguistic sign', in Carol Sanders (ed.), *The Cambridge Companion to Saussure*, Cambridge: Cambridge University Press, pp. 59–75.

Joseph, John E. (2004c), 'Linguistic identity and the limits of Global English', in Anna Duszak and Urszula Okulska (eds), *Globalization: English and Language Change in Europe*, Frankfurt, Berlin, Bern, Brussels, New York and Oxford: Peter Lang, pp. 17–33.

Joseph, John E. (2005), 'The tongues of men and of angels: knowledge, inner speech and diglossia in medieval linguistic thought', in Andrew R. Linn and Nicola McLelland (eds), *Flores grammaticae: Essays in Memory of Vivien Law*, Münster: Nodus, pp. 119–39.

Joseph, John E. (2006), 'Language and nationalism, 1880–1945', in Guntram H. Herb and David H. Kaplan (eds), *Nations and Nationalisms in Global Perspective: An Encyclopedia of Origins, Development, and Contemporary Transitions*, 4 vols, Santa Barbara, Denver and Oxford: ABC-CLIO.

Joseph, John E., Nigel Love and Talbot J. Taylor (2001), *Landmarks in Linguistic Thought II: The Western Tradition in the Twentieth Century*, London and New York: Routledge.

Kaplan, Robert B. and Richard B. Baldauf (1997), *Language Planning from Practice to Theory*, Clevedon: Multilingual Matters.

Kibbee, Douglas A. (ed.) (1998), *Language Legislation and Linguistic Rights: Selected Proceedings of the Language Legislation and Linguistic Rights Conference, the University of Illinois at Urbana-Champaign, March, 1996*, Amsterdam and Philadelphia: John Benjamins.

Kienpointner, Manfred (ed.) (1999), *Ideologies of Politeness*, special issue of *Pragmatics*, 9 (1).

Klemperer, Victor (1949), *LTI: Notizbuch eines Philologen*, Berlin: Aufbau-Verlag. Engl. transl. by Martin Brady, *Language Of The Third Reich: LTI, Lingua Tertii Imperii: A Philologist's Notebook*, New York and London: Continuum, 2002.

Kloss, Heinz (1967), '"Abstand" languages and "Ausbau" languages', *Anthropological Linguistics*, 9 (7): 29–41.

Kloss, Heinz (1978), *Der Entwicklung neuer germanischer Kultursprachen seit 1800*, 2nd edn, Düsseldorf: Schwann. (1st edn 1952.)

Korzybski, Alfred (1921), *Manhood of Humanity*, New York: E. P. Dutton and Co.

Korzybski, Alfred (1933), *Science and Sanity: An Introduction to Non-aristotelian Systems and General Semantics*, Lakeville, CT: International Non-artistotelian Library Publishing Co., distributed by the Institute of General Semantics.

Kretzmann, Norman (1967), 'History of semantics', in Paul Edwards (ed.), *The Encyclopedia of Philosophy*, vol. 7, New York: Macmillan and The Free Press, pp. 358–406.

Kroskrity, Paul V. (ed.) (2000), *Regimes of Language: Ideologies, Polities, and Identities*, Santa Fe, NM: School of American Research Press.

Kymlicka, Will (2001), *Politics in the Vernacular: Nationalism,Multiculturalism, and Citizenship*, Oxford: Oxford University Press.

Kymlicka, Will and François Grin (2003), 'Assessing the politics of diversity in transition countries', in Daftary and Grin (eds), pp. 5–27.

Kymlicka, Will and Alan Patten (eds) (2003), *Language Rights and Political Theory*, Oxford: Oxford University Press.

Laforge, Lorne and Grant D. McConnell (eds) (1990), *Language Spread and Social Change: Dynamics and Measurement*, Québec: International Centre for Research on Bilingualism.

Lakoff, Robin (1973), 'Language and woman's place', *Language in Society*, 2: 45–80.

Lakoff, Robin (1975), *Language and Woman's Place*, New York: Harper and Row.

Lakoff, Robin Tolmach (1990), *Talking Power: The Politics of Language*, New York: Basic Books.

Lakoff, Robin Tolmach (2000), *The Language War*, Berkeley, Los Angeles and London: University of California Press.

Lakoff, Robin Tolmach (2004), *Language and Woman's Place: Text and Commentaries*, ed. by Mary Bucholz, Oxford and New York: Oxford University Press.

Landau, Jacob M. (ed.) (1999), *Language and Politics: Theory and Cases*, special issue of *International Journal of the Sociology of Language*, no. 137, Berlin: Mouton de Gruyter.

Langton, Rae (1993), 'Speech acts and unspeakable acts', *Philosophy and Public Affairs*, 22 (4): 293–330.

Lapesa, Rafael (1968), *Historia de la lengua española*, 7th edn, Madrid: Escelicer.

Le Bon, Gustave (1895), *Psychologie des foules*, Paris: Félix Alcan.

Lee, Penny (1995), *The Whorf Theory Complex: A Critical Reconstruction*, Amsterdam and Philadelphia: John Benjamins.

Leets, Laura, Howard Giles and Kimberly Noels (1999), 'Attributing harm to racist speech', *Journal of Multilingual and Multicultural Development*, 20 (3): 209–15.

Lester, Paul Mark (1996), 'On the n- and f-words: quantifying the taboo', paper presented at annual convention of Association for Education in Journalism and Mass Communication, Anaheim, CA, Aug. 1996. Currently available on <http://commfaculty.fullerton.edu/lester/writings/taboo.html>.

Linn, Andrew R. and Nicola McLelland (eds) (2002), *Standardization: Studies from the Germanic Languages*, Amsterdam and Philadelphia: John Benjamins.

Locher, Miriam A. (2004), *Power and Politeness in Action: Disagreements in Oral Communication*, Berlin: Mouton de Gruyter.

Locke, John (1690), *An Essay upon Humane Understanding*, London: Printed for Tho. Basset, and sold by Edw. Mory.

Makoni, Sinfree (1995), 'Linguistic imperialism: old wine in new bottles', *British Association of Applied Linguistics Newsletter*, no. 50: 28–30.

Maley, Catherine A. (1974), *The Pronouns of Address in Modern Standard French*, University, MS: Romance Monographs.

Mansour, Gerda (1993), *Multilingualism and Nation Building*, Clevedon: Multilingual Matters.

Mar-Molinero, Clare (2000), *The Politics of Language in the Spanish-Speaking World: From Colonisation to Globalisation*, London and New York: Routledge.

Martín Rojo, Luisa and Angel Gabilondo Pujol (2002), 'Michel Foucault', in Jef Verschueren, Jan-Ola Östman, Jan Blommaert and Chris Bulcaen (eds), *Handbook of Pragmatics: 2000 Installment*, Amsterdam and Philadelphia: John Benjamins.

Matheson, Hilda (1933), *Broadcasting*, London: Thornton Butterworth.

Matsuda, Mari (1993), 'Public response to racist speech: considering the victim's story', in Mari Matsuda, Charles Lawrence, Richard Delgado and Kimberle Williams Crenshaw (eds), *Words that Wound: Critical Race Theory, Assaultive Speech, and the First Amendment*, Boulder, CO: Westview Press, pp. 17–52.

May, Stephen (2001), *Language and Minority Rights: Ethnicity, Nationalism and the Politics of Language*, Harlow: Longman.

Minnini, Giuseppe (1994), 'Marxist theories of language', in R. E. Asher (ed.), *Encyclopedia of Language and Linguistics*, Oxford: Pergamon, 2390–93.

Montagu, Ashley (1967), *The Anatomy of Swearing*, New York: Macmillan.

Mühlhäusler, Peter, Rom Harré, Anthony Holiday and Michael Freyne (1990), *Pronouns and People: The Linguistic Construction of Social and Personal Identity*, Oxford: Blackwell.

Murray, Denise E. (1999), 'Whose "standard"? What the Ebonics debate tells us about language, power, and pedagogy', in James E. Alatis and Ai-Hui Tan (eds), *Language in Our Time: Bilingual Education and Official English, Ebonics and Standard English, Immigration and the Unz Initiative* (Georgetown University Round Table on Language and Linguistics, 1999), Washington, DC: Georgetown University Press, pp. 281–91.

Murray, Lindley (1795), *English Grammar*, York: Printed by Wilson, Spence and Mawman. (Repr. Menston: Scolar Press, 1968.)

Myhill, John (2004), *Language in Jewish Society: Towards a New Understanding*, Clevedon: Multilingual Matters.

Ng, Bee Chin, and Kate Burridge (1993), 'The female radical: portrayal of women in Chinese script', *Australian Review of Applied Linguistics* (Series S), 10: 54–85.

O'Barr, William M. (1982), *Linguistic Evidence: Language, Power, and Strategy in the Courtroom*, San Diego, CA: Academic Press.

O'Barr, William M. (2001), 'Language, law and power', in Robinson and Giles (eds), pp. 531–40.

O'Barr, William M. and Jean F. O'Barr (eds) (1976), *Language and Politics*, The Hague: Mouton.

O'Connor, James (2000), *Cuss Control: The Complete Book on How to Curb Your Cursing*, New York: Three Rivers Press.

Ogden, C. K. (1944), *The System of Basic English*, 3rd edn, New York: Harcourt, Brace and Co. (1st edn 1934.)

Ogden, C. K. and I. A. Richards (1923), *The Meaning of Meaning: A Study of the Influence of Language upon Thought and of the Science of Symbolism*, London: Kegan Paul, Trench,

Trubner and Co.; New York: Harcourt, Brace and Co.

Orwell, George (1944), 'Propaganda and demotic speech', *Persuasion*, 2 (2, Summer). (Repr. in *The Complete Works of George Orwell*, vol. 16: *I Have Tried to Tell the Truth: 1943–1944*, ed. by Peter Davison, London: Secker and Warburg, 1998, pp. 310–16.)

Orwell, George (1946), 'Politics and the English language', *Horizon*, 13, no. 76 (Apr.), 252–65. (Repr. in *The Complete Works of George Orwell*, vol. 17: *I Belong to the Left: 1945*, ed. by Peter Davison, London: Secker and Warburg, 1998, pp. 421–32.)

Orwell, George (1947), *The English People*, London, Collins. (Written 1944. Repr. in Sonia Orwell and Ian Angus (eds), *The Collected Essays, Journalism and Letters of George Orwell*, vol. 3, London, Secker and Warburg, 1968, pp. 1–38.)

Orwell, George (1949), *Nineteen Eighty-Four*, London: Martin Secker and Warburg. (New edn 1987; repr. Harmondsworth: Penguin Twentieth Century Classics, in association with Martin Secker and Warburg, 1989.)

Patten, Alan (2003), 'Liberal neutrality and language policy', *Philosophy and Public Affairs*, 31 (4): 356–86.

Pauwels, Anne (1998), *Women Changing Language*, London and New York: Longman.

Pêcheux, Michel (1982), *Language, Semantics and Ideology*, London: Macmillan.

Pei, Mario (1949), *The Story of Language*, Philadelphia: J. B. Lippincott.

Pennycook, Alastair (2001), *Critical Applied Linguistics: A Critical Introduction*, Mahwah, NJ: Lawrence Erlbaum.

Perta, Carmela (2004), *Language Decline and Death in Three Arbëresh Communities in Italy: A Sociolinguistic Study*, Alessandria, Italy: Edizioni dell'Orso.

Phillipson, Robert (1992), *Linguistic Imperialism*, Oxford: Oxford University Press.

Poedjosoedarmo: see under Soepomo Poedjosoedarmo.

Pratkanis, Anthony and Elliot Aronson (2001), *Age of Propaganda: The Everyday Use and Abuse of Persuasion*, 2nd edn, New York: W. H. Freeman.

Priedīte, Aija (2005), 'Surveying language practices and attitudes in Latvia', *Journal of Multilingual and Multicultural Development*, 26 (5): 409–24.

Rajagopalan, Kanavillil (1999a), 'Of EFL teachers, conscience, and cowardice', *ELT Journal*, 53 (3): 200–6.

Rajagopalan, Kanavillil (1999b), 'Reply to Canagarajah', *ELT Journal*, 53 (3): 215–16.

Ramonet, Ignacio (1999), *La tyrannie de la communication*, Paris: Galilée.

Ramonet, Ignacio (2000), *Propagandes silencieuses: Masses, télévision, cinéma*, Paris: Galilée.

Rampton, Ben (1995), *Crossing: Language and Ethnicity among Adolescents*, London: Longman.

Rauch, Jonathan (1993), *Kindly Inquisitors: The New Attacks on Free Thought*, Chicago and London: University of Chicago Press.

Ravitch, Diane (2003), *The Language Police: How Pressure Groups Restrict What Students Learn*, New York: Alfred A. Knopf.

Rawls, John (1971), *A Theory of Justice*, Cambridge, MA: Belknap Press of Harvard University Press. (Rev. edn 1999.)

Reid, Thomas (1788), *Essays on the Active Powers of Man*, Edinburgh: Printed for John Bell, and G. G. J. and J. Robinson, London.

Ricento, Thomas (ed.) (2000), *Ideology, Politics and Language Policies: Focus on English*, Amsterdam and Philadelphia: John Benjamins.

Richards, I. A. (1943), *Basic English and Its Uses*, London: Kegan Paul, Trench, Trubner and Co.

Robinson, W. Peter and Howard Giles (eds) (2001), *The New Handbook of Language and Social Psychology*, Chichester and New York: John Wiley and Sons.

Rojo: see under Martín Rojo.

Ross, H. E. (1960), 'Patterns of swearing', *Discovery* (Nov. 1960), pp. 479–81.

Rossi-Landi, Ferruccio (1975), *Linguistics and Economics*, The Hague: Mouton.

Rossi-Landi, Ferruccio (1983), *Language as Work and Trade*, South Hadley, MA: Bergin and Garvey.

Sacks, Harvey (1992), *Lectures on Conversation*, ed. by Gail Jefferson, 2 vols, Oxford and Cambridge, MA: Blackwell.

Sacks, Harvey, Emanuel A. Schegloff and Gail Jefferson (1974), 'A simplest systematics for the organization of turn-taking for conversation', *Language*, 50: 696–735.

Sapir, Edward (1921), *Language: An Introduction to the Study of Speech*, New York: Harcourt, Brace and Co.

Sapir, Edward (1924), 'The grammarian and his language', *American Mercury*, 1: 149–55. (Repr. in Sapir 1949: 150–9.)

Sapir, Edward (1949), *Selected Writings in Language, Culture, and Personality*, ed. by David G. Mandelbaum, Berkeley and Los Angeles: University of California Press.

Saussure, Ferdinand de (1922), *Cours de linguistique générale*, ed. by Charles Bally and Albert Sechehaye with the collaboration of Albert Riedlinger, 2nd edn, Paris and Lausanne: Payot. (1st edn 1916. Engl. transl., *Course in General Linguistics*, by Wade Baskin, New York: Philosophical Library, 1959; another by Roy Harris, London: Duckworth; La Salle, IL: Open Court, 1983.)

Schieffelin, Bambi B., Kathryn A. Woolard, and Paul V. Kroskrity (eds) (1998), *Language Ideologies: Practice and Theory*, New York and Oxford: Oxford University Press.

Schiffman, Harold F. (1996), *Linguistic Culture and Language Policy*, London and New York: Routledge.

Schneider, Edgar W. (2003) 'The dynamics of new Englishes: from identity construction to dialect birth', *Language* 79 (2): 233–81.

Searle, John (1968), 'Austin on locutionary and illocutionary acts', *Philosophical Review*, 77 (4): 405–24.

Sélincourt, Basil de (1926), *Pomona, or the Future of English*, London: Kegan Paul, Trench, Trubner and Co.

Shapiro, Michael J. (ed.) (1984), *Language and Politics*, Oxford: Basil Blackwell.

Shepard, Carolyn A., Howard Giles and Beth A. LePoire (2001), 'Communication Accommodation Theory', in Robinson and Giles (eds), pp. 33–56.

Siegel, James T. (1986), *Solo in the New Order: Language and Hierarchy in an Indonesian City*, Princeton, NJ and Chicester: Princeton University Press.

Silverstein, Michael (2000), 'Whorfianism and the linguistic imagination of nationality', in Kroskrity (ed.), pp. 85–138.

Skutnabb-Kangas, Tove (2000), *Linguistic Genocide in Education – or Worldwide Diversity and Human Rights?*, Mahwah, NJ and London: Lawrence Erlbaum.

Smith, Anthony. 1973. *The Shadow in the Cave: A Study of the Relationship between the Broadcaster, his Audience and the State*, London: George Allen and Unwin.

Soepomo Poedjosoedarmo (1968), 'Javanese speech levels', *Indonesia*, 6: 54–81.

Spender, Dale (1980), *Man Made Language*, London: Routledge and Kegan Paul.

Spolsky, Bernard (2004), *Language Policy*, Cambridge: Cambridge University Press.

Stephens, Edward (1695), *Phinehas: or, The common Duty of all Men: and the special Duty of Magistrates, to be zealous and active in the Execution of Laws against scandalous Sins and Debauchery; and of that in particular, against prophane Cursing and Swearing*, London: printed for Richard Smith …, to be sold by Richard Baldwin.

Stroud, Christopher (2001), 'African mother-tongue programmes and the politics of language: linguistic citizenship versus linguistic human rights', *Journal of Multilingual and Multicultural Development*, 22 (4): 339–55.

Suleiman, Yasir (2003), *The Arabic Language and National Identity: A Study in Ideology*, Edinburgh: Edinburgh University Press.

Suleiman, Yasir (2004), *A War of Words: Language and Conflict in the Middle East*, Cambridge: Cambridge University Press.

Swaen, A. E. H. (1898), 'Figures of imprecation', *Englische Studien*, 24: 16–71, 195–231.

Swift, Jonathan (1720), *The Swearer's-Bank, or, Parliamentary security for establishing a new bank in Ireland: wherein the medicinal use of oaths is considered …*, Dublin: printed by Thomas Hume …; reprinted at London by J. Roberts in Warwick-Lane.

Tajfel, Henri (1978), 'Social categorization, social identity and social comparison', in Henri Tajfel (ed.), *Differentiation between Social Groups: Studies in the Social Psychology of Intergroup Relations*, London: Academic Press, pp. 61–76.

Tannen, Deborah (1990), *You Just Don't Understand: Women and Men in Conversation*, New York: Morrow.

Tannen, Deborah (ed.) (1993), *Gender and Conversational Interaction*, New York: Oxford University Press.

Tannen, Deborah (1994), *Gender and Discourse*, New York: Oxford University Press.

Taylor, Charles (1994), *Multiculturalism: Examining the Politics of Recognition*, Princeton, NJ: Princeton University Press.

Taylor, Talbot J. (1997), *Theorizing Language: Analysis, Normativity, Rhetoric, History*, Oxford: Pergamon.

Taylor, Talbot J. (2000), 'Language constructing language: the implications of reflexivity for linguistic theory', *Language Sciences*, 22: 483–99.

Thomason, Sarah G. (1999), 'Speakers' choices in language change', *Studies in the Linguistic Sciences*, 29 (2): 19–43.

Thorne, Barrie, and Nancy Henley (eds) (1975), *Language and Sex: Difference and Dominance*, Rowley, MA: Newbury House.

Thornborrow, Joanna (2002), *Power Talk: Language and Interaction in Institutional Discourse*, Harlow: Pearson Education.

Todorov, Tzvetan (1984), *Mikhail Bakhtin: The Dialogical Principle*, transl. by Wlad Godzich, Minneapolis, MN: University of Minnesota Press.

Tollefson, James W. (1991), *Planning Language, Planning Inequality: Language Policy in the Community*, London and New York: Longman.

Tollefson, James W. (ed.) (1995), *Power and Inequality in Language Education*, Cambridge: Cambridge University Press.

Tollefson, James W. (ed.) (2002), *Language Policies in Education: Critical Issues*, Mahwah, NJ: Lawrence Erlbaum.

Tongue, R. K. (1979), *The English of Singapore and Malaysia*, 2nd edn, Singapore: Eastern Universities Press.

Trappes-Lomax, Hugh (2005), 'Language and discourse descriptions', paper given at workshop on Applied Linguistics and the Teaching of English and Modern Languages, sponsored by the UK Subject Centre for Linguistics, Languages and Area Studies, Edinburgh, 19 Jan. 2005.

Tsui, Amy B. M., and Stephen Andrew (eds) (2002), *Maintaining and Setting Standards and Language Variation: A Dilemma for Language Education in the Asia Pacific Region*, special issue of *Journal of Asian Pacific Communication*, 12 (1).

Twomey, Anne (1994), 'Laws against incitement to racial hatred in the United Kingdom', *Australian Journal of Human Rights*, 1 (1): 235–47.

Ullmann, Stephen (1957), *The Principles of Semantics*, 2nd edn, Oxford: Blackwell.

van Dijk, Teun A. (1993), *Elite Discourse and Racism*, Newbury Park, CA: Sage.

van Dijk, Teun A. (1995), 'Elite discourse and the reproduction of racism', in Rita Kirk Whillock and David Slayden (eds), *Hate Speech*, Thousand Oaks, CA: Sage, 1–27.

Voloshinov, V. N. (1973), *Marxism and the Philosophy of Language*, transl. by Ladislav Matejka and I. R. Titunik, Cambridge, MA and London: Harvard University Press.

Weinstein, Brian (1983), *The Civic Tongue: Political Consequences of Language Choices*, New York and London: Longman.

Weinstein, Brian (ed.) (1990), *Language Policy and Political Development*, Norwood, NJ:

Ablex.

Whitney, William Dwight (1867), *Language and the Study of Language: Twelve Lectures on the Principles of Linguistic Science*, New York: C. Scribner and Co.; London: Trübner.

Whorf, Benjamin Lee (1940), 'Science and Linguistics', *Technology Review*, 42 (6) (April, 1940): 229–31, 247–8. (Repr. in Hayakawa 1941: 302–21; Whorf 1956: 207–19.)

Whorf, Benjamin Lee (1956), *Language, Thought, and Reality: Selected Writings of Benjamin Lee Whorf*, ed. by John B. Carroll, Cambridge, MA: MIT Press.

Wiley, Terrence G. (2002), 'Heinz Kloss revisited: National Socialist ideologue or champion of language-minority rights?', *International Journal of the Sociology of Language*, no. 154, 83–97.

Wodak, Ruth, Rudolf de Cillia, Martin Reisigl and Karin Liebhart (1999), *The Discursive Construction of National Identity*, transl. by Angelika Hirsch and Richard Mitten, Edinburgh: Edinburgh University Press.

Wodak, Ruth and David Corson (eds) (1997), *Encyclopedia of Language and Education*, vol. 1: *Language Policy and Political Issues in Education*, Dordrecht, Boston and London: Kluwer.

Wodak, Ruth and Michael Meyer (eds) (2001), *Methods of Critical Discourse Analysis*, London, Thousand Oaks, CA, and New Delhi: Sage.

Wright, Laura (ed.) (2000), *The Development of Standard English, 1300–1800: Theories, Descriptions, Conflicts*, Cambridge: Cambridge University Press.

Wright, Sue (2004), *Language Policy and Language Planning: From Nationalism to Globalisation*, Houndmills, Basingstoke and New York: Palgrave Macmillan.

Index

LIBRARY, UNIVERSITY OF CHESTER